I Shall Not Fail

Between Two Worlds

Maria Bandol

Suite 300 - 990 Fort St
Victoria, BC, V8V 3K2
Canada

www.friesenpress.com

Copyright © 2021 by Maria Bandol
First Edition — 2021

Front Cover Design by Codrut Miron

All rights reserved.

No part of this publication may be reproduced in any form, or by any means, electronic or mechanical, including photocopying, recording, or any information browsing, storage, or retrieval system, without permission in writing from FriesenPress.

ISBN
978-1-03-910880-6 (Hardcover)
978-1-03-910879-0 (Paperback)
978-1-03-910881-3 (eBook)

1. Biography & Autobiography, Personal Memoirs

Distributed to the trade by The Ingram Book Company

TABLE OF CONTENTS

Acknowledgements i
Foreword iii
1: Gino 1
2: Buon Giorno, Roma! 10
3: How Did We Get Here? 18
4: In Search of a Shelter! 28
5: Is Santa Coming This Year? 34
6: Merry Christmas! 41
7: We're Going to School! 52
8: "Mamma, Ho Fame!" 57
9: Never Again! 64
10: It's Magic! 71
11: Thank You, Mom! 78
12: La Vita È Bella! 86
13: The Canadian Dream Is Over! 91
14: Madre Teresa 101
15: Happy Easter! 106

16: School Is Over...114

17: First Peaceful Night 125

18: Communism Is Falling Apart.................................131

19: Life Goes On...136

20: European History in the Making.............................142

21: Routine 148

22: Just Hopes...154

23: Happy New Year!..160

24: Spring Is in the Air!......................................168

25: Where Is Evelyn?!..174

26: On the Move Again..179

27: Bad News...184

28: Good News 192

29: Ferragosto 196

30: Halt!..201

31: We Hate You, Mom!!...207

32: My Danube Is Blue!! 213

33: Canada, Here We Come!......................................222

34: Carabinieri..227

35: Welcome to Canada! 231

Afterword 237

In loving memory of my parents and my husband.
You will always be in my heart.

ACKNOWLEDGEMENTS

As the saying goes, it takes a village to raise a child, but it also takes a village to create a book! Writing this memoir has been on my agenda for a long time, but publishing it would not have been possible without all the support I received throughout the past years.

I would like to start by thanking my grandchildren, especially Amni and Eli, for showing genuine interest in the story and asking me to read a part of my book to them, for suggesting names for my characters (thank you, Amni), to Eli for his suggestions and encouragements, for actively listening and getting engaged in valuable conversations.

I wish to acknowledge the efficiency and professionalism of the entire team from FriesenPress; special thanks to my publishing specialist, Kayla Lang, who has always offered me extensive time to go over the different details regarding the publishing process, to my editor, Sharon Chisvin, for her valuable advice and objective comments, as well as to the entire FriesenPress design team.

My special thanks are extended to Daniela Cupse Apostoaei, a published author and a special friend, for our valuable discussions, for her sensitivity in writing the Foreword, for her treasured suggestions regarding the publishing process, as well as for recommending me to publish my book with FriesenPress.

I would like to offer many thanks to my friends: Sofia Laceanu, for lending me an ear, for allowing me to share my emotions with her and for offering me a shoulder to cry on; to Donna Farrow for listening to my tales, as well as to Carol Spradlin for taking my stories to heart and for her suggestions regarding a title for my book; to my many friends who have occasionally listened to fragments of my stories and have always encouraged me, one way or another, to write a book one day…

Last but not least, I am particularly grateful to my friend, Jimmy DeSousa. I owe you an enormous debt of gratitude for your constant support and advice to "just put my thoughts in writing and get that book done." Thank you for being my "unofficial" proof-reader, my mentor and advisor, for giving me detailed and constructive comments on my early drafts, for discussing with me nuances of the text and pushing me to clarify concepts, for having been my unrelenting source of inspiration, and especially for assisting me with finding the right title for my book that needed to be both suggestive and relevant. Thank you.

Maria Bandol

FOREWORD

In this volume of memoirs entitled: "I Shall Not Fail - Between Two Worlds", the Romanian-Canadian writer Maria Bandol is reaching an inner and temporal stature of full maturity, while revealing herself to the readers and to all those who know how to appreciate the art of the word and the deep feelings.

As the author's debut book, this volume is also a literary picture of the period of the totalitarian communist regime in her native country and the first years following its fall after the 1989 Revolution. The image of that time will be reflected in the writer's life and it will cause her to make the decision to leave her country of origin to go into exile with her two children.

Lucid observer of those times, Maria Bandol invites her readers in an incursion of life and morals. She unravels the thin thread of fine memories, of the candid joys of childhood and youth, while she is, at times, caught in the hard knots of the troubles she went through between the two worlds -- one left behind, another only glimpsing ahead.

Even though tears of despair and sadness sometimes drip from the chalice of her female soul, the author has always found the strength, faith and resources to put the disguise of a brave fighter, sometimes alone in the struggle with the hardships of life, and sometimes having her husband and her children by her side.

Maria Bandol is an innate storyteller. The full description of events and places envelop you as the reader in an inherent curiosity and aesthetic pleasure of the fascinating journey in which you walk with her. Many hectic events will test your patience, eager to know what will happen next.

Going through Maria Bandol's book "I Shall Not Fail -- Between Two Worlds", you stop to think, and even reread certain paragraphs for the beauty of writing and the depth of teaching.

The disturbing reminiscences, still alive in the author's memory, compose the pages of this book, which is undoubtedly also a literary portrait of the writer.

It can be at the same time a promise that touches our hearts, as we browse page by page the memories of Maria Bandol and experience the joy of reaching that "harbour" that we call "Home."

Certainly, reading this book will be an encouragement to those who have left memories in one world to be able to write memoirs in another.

Daniela Cupșe Apostoaei
Writer / Member of the Writers' Guild of Alberta

1
GINO

"Buon giorno, Signora!"

The deep, guttural voice coming from behind startles me. Who is this man? All I can make of him is a resemblance to a Mafia hitman: dark skin, sleek grayish hair, and also quite a rotund shape, if I can express myself that way…But what do I actually know about the Mafia? From all the movies I've seen back home, he looks like one of them, but why would he be after me? I hesitate, not knowing how to go about this.

"Buon giorno. I heard you speak Romanian…" Here he goes again.

Did I hear that right? Did he eavesdrop into my conversation with my daughters? Or did he just accidentally overhear our chatting? Then if he's not belonging to the Mafia, who is he? My mind goes right away to the Romanian secret police, the so-called "Securitate", who has haunted us for years and years during the communist regime. Things don't add up. I don't know what to make of this.

"Buon giorno. Yes, we speak Romanian. Who are you, sir?" I am trying to camouflage my suspicions, making my voice sound confident.

"My name is Gino." Right on. His name is Italian, he speaks Romanian, albeit with a strong Italian accent, but who is he? What is he doing here, in Rome? As if he could read my mind, he goes on: "I was born in Romania many, many years ago, but Italy has become my country of choice back in the 40's. Looks like you need help. Is there anything I can do for you?"

That's a weird question. He has just approached us, introduced himself, and now he's asking <u>us</u> if we need help. And if we do, what's the chance I would ask <u>him</u> for help? How can I tell him that I don't trust anybody?

That I am afraid that the Mafia may kill my children? Or Carabinieri… or…I don't know. I am afraid, but I am lost, too, and I do need help. The least I can do is to introduce myself. After all, he is not going to kill us in plain sight, in the middle of such a crowd.

"What is your name? Do you need any help?" He keeps pressing, and I finally break down and answer his questions.

"My name is Maria, and these are my daughters, Amanda and Evelyn. And in fact, we are in Italy just in transit because we are supposed to join my husband in Canada." There, I need to say it. I have no idea when I'm going to join Greg in Canada, but I want Gino to know that I do have a husband somewhere in the world, just to eliminate any thoughts or possibilities…Still, I don't understand what he's doing here. If we need help? Hell we do! We have just arrived in Rome, it's 7:30 in the morning, and this whole place called Stazione Termini—the main railway station of the Italian capital—is a total zoo. However, I am not sure if I want him to help us. I don't know who he is. I choose to decline.

"I'm sorry, but we have just arrived, and we would like to explore the surroundings a little, if you don't mind."

"No, not at all. If you need any help, you will find me in that corner", and he points out to one of the side entrances to the station. He takes off, shuffling his feet away.

* * *

Well, here we are, back to square one! Or square…zero!!!

Roma! Stazione Termini—the main railway station. This is truly the terminus point of our trip, for now…Our final destination, for a while.… Three nights and two days on the road, on trains and in railway stations. And now what? I am counting all my "possessions": two kids and six pieces of luggage. If Bucharest was a zoo, if Belgrade looked like chaos, Rome cannot be described. It is a Tower of Babel in all respects. According to an old Roman saying, all roads lead to Rome. Indeed. The *binari*—platforms—in this main station alone are 35, assuming I counted well; and there are trains operating at each of them. I am speechless and so seem my daughters. Besides all this, we cannot even talk properly. We have to yell so we can hear one another, such is the level of noise. All we can do is get out of here and find a spot where we can sit and discuss the plan for the day.

"Amanda, Evelyn, I want you both to stay put in this corner. You can sit on the floor, stand, lean against the glass window, but you do not move from here! Understand? Keep your back to the corner, do not let anybody get behind you. I am going to leave the luggage here with you so I can move freely. We need to know how to get to Latina or how to find Dina's *Pensione*. I'll be back shortly. Deal?"

* * *

Thirty minutes later I am rejoining my daughters. Before we left Romania my understanding was that we should go to Latina, which is a refugee camp, but when I asked at the information booth how to get to Latina, I was told that I would have to take the train. A train? Another train? No way! I'm not getting on any other train!

"I don't have very good news. Latina is one hour away from Rome by train. No, we are not leaving this place! No more trains!!"

"What about Dina's *Pensione*?" the girls seem to have had enough of this trip, too.

"I asked about that, as well. They have no idea where such a *pensione* is. The guy at the information booth says that there are a lot of hotels and *pensioni* around the station. I checked a few of them, left and right of the station, but they are all very expensive. We can't afford them. I'm afraid we have to accept Gino's offer to help us."

* * *

Gino is standing right in the spot that he showed us earlier.

"So, Signor' Gino, you said you would be willing to help us…" I'm still hesitant. Concern. Mistrust. However, we are still in need of a roof over our heads.

"I can take you to an *albergo* in the vicinity of the station, clean and very affordable. Would you like to follow me?"

Do we have a choice? He says it is at walking distance, and it's daylight, so worse come to worst, we can scream, we can drop the luggage and run…

We are following Gino. We exit the station and go down Marsala Street schlepping our luggage, the same luggage that we've been carrying around for the past few nights and days. I'm reading the names of the streets so I know where we are going, not that it makes any sense. I've never been in Rome and I have no idea what to expect. Take a left turn and here's a little *albergo* on Via Milazzo. It looks quite dilapidated, but I like to assume that accommodation would be reasonable.

"This is Hotel Galli. I will make sure they won't charge you too much for a room." Gino says something to the receptionist. I have no idea what arrangements they have. I guess he brings people down here and he gets a commission. I don't care. We can afford to pay $40 per night and, for the first time in three nights, we will get to sleep on real beds.

"Thank you, Signor' Gino."

"Make yourselves comfortable, ladies, have a rest, and come back to see me around 11. You will need some information about how to get around Rome."

"Thank you, Signor' Gino." I can take a deep breath now. We are set for a while.

"Mommy, why is Gino helping us?"

"I have no idea, Amanda, but we can take a chance. In fact, as long as it is daylight and there are people around, we don't have much to fear. We don't have choices."

Our room is on the second floor. The staircase is quite narrow, and it keeps spiralling. We are maneuvering our luggage, one step at a time. At least the room is decent. Two beds, one queen bed for the girls and one twin bed for me. Toilets and shower are in the hallway and we are supposed to share them with other guests. That's fine with me. There is also a sink in the room, a table and a chair, and we also have a large window, but no view. Just a backyard that looks more like a storage place or a dump…It doesn't matter. We have a roof over our heads!!!

How long are we going to stay in this hotel? I don't know. I have no idea. At this point we are very tired. I am trying to collect myself.

"Mom, I am hungry," Evelyn's little whining voice brings me back from my short reverie. Of course, the girls are hungry. Thank goodness I have provisions in the suitcases. I pull out the hot plate and a little pot. A hot chocolate and a sandwich will do it for now. It feels good. A shower and a bite later we are ready to go see Gino. On our way back to the railway station I am trying to make sense of everything I see around us, reading names of the streets, small food stores on street corners, everything. I am trying to absorb it all. After all, this is the Eternal City—Rome!! The City of Seven Hills. The "Caput Mundi"—the end of the world according to the Latin poets Marco Anneo Lucano in 61 CE, or Publio Ovidio Nasone before him.

Stazione Termini…It is ironic that the main railway station is called "Termini"…Almost like a terminus point. This is the end of everything, of "all roads that lead to Rome"? For us it is a beginning, not an end.

* * *

"Buon giorno, Signor' Gino!"

"Good, so you are back. *Va bene*. Here is the plan for the day: first, here is a map of Rome. This is Stazione Termini, and this area is the *centro storico*, the so-called historic part of the downtown," Gino is giving us a 101 course in getting around Rome. "I will give you a few public transit tickets, but I suggest you walk so you get used to the surroundings. In Via Matteo Boiardo, 10 minutes from here, you will have hot *minestrone* for free. In this cold weather you need some hot soup."

"For free? We don't have to pay?"

"No, Signora, there are lots of places where one can eat for free in Italy. Italians have big hearts, they give a lot of donations and we don't let people starve. When you come back, I will have more instructions for you. How is your hotel room?"

"Very decent, thank you."

"It shouldn't cost you too much and you will pay at the end of your stay. When are you planning on seeing or joining your husband?"

Gino's questions are becoming a bit too personal and they make me uncomfortable, but I have to play the game, and I can't lie. He seems to be honest and willing to help.

"I don't know, but right now he is in Canada, and we hope to join him soon."

"How come he is in Canada and you and the girls are here?"

5

This is a bit too intruding, and I am not going to tell him the whole story. He doesn't need to know about how Greg managed to get a visitor's visa. I don't think it is necessary to tell him about our year-long struggle to leave for Canada as a family, on temporary visas, and then "forget" to come back. All that matters is that we will have to join Greg—sooner rather than later.

"Well, he has some distant relatives in Canada and the only way we could exit our home country was to go to different directions for a while, and hopefully, we'll reunite with him soon."

"So, you are not planning to stay in Italy."

"No, not for ever. We want to join my husband in Canada!"

"But you will still need some papers to make your stay here in Italy legal. Go have your hot *minestrone* and we'll talk when you come back. Take your time and if you have questions you can find me here most of the time. *Capisci*?"

"Si, grazie. Thank you, Signor' Gino." I still don't understand why this man is helping us. I would like to ask him right now, but I'm not comfortable enough. I have other things to be concerned about.

* * *

Here we are, playing the "Tourist card"?! Walking around, map in hand, oblivious of any possible wrong-going or wrongdoing, presumably worry-free, a roof over our heads and free hot meals for unfortunate people like us, mostly in transit through Italy, and maybe some just trying to settle down and make a living in this country. We go left and right, discovering new streets, most of them cobbled and old, reading their names on the map and trying to figure out where we are and struggling to not get lost. It's extremely easy to get lost in Rome! Streets run in all directions, no logic to them!! Life is good, or so we want to think. Being positive helps, especially when the first hot soup we can have in three days nourishes us completely on the inside, body and spirit, mind and soul altogether. The winter is no longer cold and humid, my back no longer hurts, we are no longer tired, and Rome presents itself to us like a big, unexpected Christmas present coming from above. Being able to walk on the 2000-year-old pavement, to see and touch constructions that have been erected two millennia ago, is dreamlike. All the movies and movie characters, all the pictures we have seen throughout the years, all the slides and picture postcards are here, at arm length, descended on earth, just for us. Our most beautiful Christmas gift ever!

We come across a flea market, Piazza "Vittorio Emanuele," lots of fruits and vegetables and actually a lot of everything, absolutely everything. It's a food lover's paradise. Local produce abound; it's a real treat to our eyes and noses, but our taste buds would also like to taste them, provided that we can afford to buy anything…Local vendors invite us to have a little piece of mozzarella or pecorino cheese. Never tried before. Everything looks so fresh. There is a huge variety of locally grown vegetables and fruits, as well as—what it appears to be—some of the finest freshly caught fish and sea food and meat produce, all on small but tempting displays.

"Look Mom! Fuzzy potatoes!" Evelyn has her own way of making associations. She has a vivid imagination. Frankly, I would not know what that fruit is had it not be for the sign: "Kiwis." So, that's what a kiwi looks like. A fuzzy potato!

"Evelyn, when you write to Dad, make sure you tell him about the 'fuzzy potatoes.' He will surely need a good laugh."

In fact, the kiwis are not the only fruit displayed outside, in front of the food stores. It's almost mid-December and we have never seen such a variety of fruit: bananas, oranges, grapefruit, mandarins, tangerines, even cherries and watermelons! Coconut slices being sold off interesting small, mounted fountains where the water is continuously running, keeping them constantly wet, chestnuts roasted on the spot and sold hot in tiny paper cones. Aromas of fresh roasts, fragrances of fine pastries pouring down the streets…We may be hungry, but such abundance we have never seen in our lives. All my kids know is the few oranges they have been lucky to eat around each Christmas and the two kilos of green bananas that, in order to be able to buy them, we were supposed to stand in line for hours, always before Christmas. This is all that the communist regime was "spoiling" us with for the winter holidays, year in, year out, the 80's being the worst. Dark ages, by all means!

I wish I could buy a couple of kiwis for the girls, but I have no Italian lira. I do have Canadian dollars, but I have to find a way to exchange them into Italian money.

"Mom, look at this fruit. They look like pinkish eggs with spikes…What are they?" It's Amanda's turn to get a lesson in Botanical sciences!! She has never seen a fruit like that. Actually, I have never seen them in reality either. All I know is that they are tropical fruits and they are called rambutans. We are all on a steep learning curve!

Around 5 pm we are back to the hotel. Our first day in Rome was short, but we have seen a lot, and we also had our first real lunch: hot soup, our first minestrone, the first real Italian minestrone that we've ever had. And how yummy it was! Considering that we haven't had a hot cooked meal in a few days, it tasted divinely delicious! We have to stop by the station. What is that? I see a kind of a booth, with a sort of an "entrance" made out of a small curtain. Oh, it's a photo booth. Some other time! No money today…

* * *

"How was the *minestrone*?" Gino seems to be on duty at his usual spot in the station.

"Good, very good, grazie."

"We have business to do. Open the map I gave you earlier, and I'll show you and explain to you what you need to do tomorrow. First thing in the morning, not later than 8 am, you will be in Via Nazionale, at the *Questura*—the Police Department. You will need a *Permesso di soggiorno*—a permit to stay in Italy, but listen to me carefully! You will have to declare your passport stolen or lost."

"But I haven't lost it…Why…"

"Signora, tomorrow you do as I say. Just don't ask questions. You will understand later on. Do you speak some Italian?"

"I do."

"Good, you'll be fine. You will have to fill out forms, so you need to understand what is written. Once you submit all those applications, you are free to go. Then come back to me here and I will give you more directions for the next step which is going to be the Canadian Embassy. *Capisci*?"

It's dark already. I'm going to make a sandwich for the girls, and we will go to bed early tonight. It's a new day tomorrow and right now I have no idea what our life is going to bring next, what we're going to do in Rome, how long we will be staying here. The girls have been amazing. Not only today, but for the past three days. We have all been on an eye-opening adventure! Where is this "adventure" taking us? For now, this is all my brain can contend with. Good night!

2
BUON GIORNO, ROMA!

"Number 163." It's our turn. We have been at the police station (*Questura*) since 7:30 this morning. Gino advised us to be here before 8 am, but when we got here there was a huge group already waiting outside. When the doors opened, everybody rushed inside, far from being civilized!!! Obviously, everybody is here in need to apply for a permit of stay. I am applying for refugee status. After all, we endured enough in Romania during the communist years and things have not improved much after the 1989 Revolution. We continued to be dissidents, in spite of the "new" regime, a pseudo-communist one which was not capable of accepting a true opposition. My intention is to seek international protection in Italy, and I understand that there is a whole procedure to follow. I am glad that I am able to communicate in Italian. (My mother was right when she suggested I get a university degree in languages. Thank you, Mom!).

Today we are taking the first step which consists of an identification and registration process, fingerprinting and photographs included. I am told that this procedure is called "*fotosegnalamento*."

I filled out the form, to the best of my knowledge.

"Signora Bandol?"

"Yes", we stand up and we approach the main desk.

"These are your daughters?"

"Yes."

"So, you are applying for political asylum, correct?"

"Yes."

"You are supposed to be scheduled for an interview after the registration process."

"Yes, I understand."

"Signora, you have declared your passport as being lost."

"Yes, sir. Lost or stolen. I don't know when and how it happened, but I found out that it was gone upon our arrival in Rome. I assumed it was stolen while we were travelling by train." I am lying through my teeth and I am truly ashamed of myself, but this is what Gino adamantly advised us, to declare my passport stolen or lost. I still don't understand why, but I guess he knows better than I do. I have to play this card. The officer has a look of disbelief on his face. He gives the impression of doubting me and he stares at me for a few seconds. I manage to stand the glare in his eyes. I have to stay true to my lies! He checks all the other details, and we are scheduled for an interview on February 28th, almost three months from now. Long wait…

Anyways, this was the so called *fotosegnalamento*, and we have just received an invitation (*invito*) to reappear before the *Questura* in order to lodge the asylum application.

The officer is giving me all the details, so I know what the next steps are:

"So, today's *"fotosegnalamento"* will be followed by a second step, consisting of the formal registration of the asylum application, which is carried out exclusively at the *Questura*, here in Rome. The second phase deals with lodging the application (*verbalizzazione*). You have all the information here." He is giving me a piece of paper with all the details.

I will have to submit a second form, complete with more information regarding our personal history, our journey from our home country that we have undertaken to reach Italy, as well as the reasons for fleeing our homeland. I will have to sign this form and then have it sent to the Territorial Commission, before the interview. As an asylum seeker I shall receive a copy of this form and copies of all other documents submitted to the police authorities.

I understand that there will be a delay until I reach the final stage, and we will not have access to the national health system in the meantime, with the exception of emergency health care. I trust that there will be no emergencies!!!

I say 'thank you', I take the paper he gave me and my little ticket showing the date of our appointment in two and a half months when we will have to come back to get our permit of stay (*permesso di soggiorno*) that will allow us to obtain a temporary Italian document of identity. It sounds so complicated.

Well, the five-hour wait at the *Questura* was well worth it.

"Mom, we have to call Dad today. Grandparents, too." Amanda keeps track of everything: a true walking and talking agenda!

"I know, sweetie. We need to change some money first. Let's go back to the railway station and get some Italian lira from a money exchange." I have to admit that I've never done this. No idea what I am supposed to do, but we will find out. You certainly learn a lot when you have to.

"Can we go back to that spot where we had the hot soup yesterday? That minestrone was so good…"

"Sure." The girls are hungry, but they have behaved amazingly well. Of course, it was to be expected, but still…It's true that they had been exposed to travelling from the diaper age and they had never raised the 'are-we-there-yet' inquiry. They didn't even know that such a question existed in the first place. Going on trips around the country, by car, by bus or by train, had been the normality of their winter and summer vacations. Yet, they have not complained or whined for a single moment during the past few days. Amazing kids. Yes, they know that we have embarked on an adventure and the unknown is the rule of the day. We have travelled extensively in Romania during our summer vacations, all across the country, but the only foreign country where we have taken them with us was in Hungary, Budapest, just for one day last summer. However, they have never made comments about time spent on the bus, or on a train or in a car. Never asked, "Are we there yet"? This was not a concept in our home country. Yes, we did travel before, but this time it's different. Not only have we never visited Italy, but we have no idea what every day is going to bring to us.

"Buon giorno, Signor' Gino."

We are back at the station, so Gino can give us more details about what we need to do next.

"Ciao, ladies! So, how was your stop at the *Questura*?"

"Good. No issues."

"Now you know where to get your daily lunch, but you'll need to have dinner, as well. Here on the map is Via Dandolo. It is not at walking distance, so bus 173 from Stazione Termini will take you close enough. Then you can walk. Tonight they will give you a free meal without asking too many questions, but tomorrow you will need to make some passes for you and the young ladies, so you may have access to other caritas services. So, you said that your husband is in Canada, right?"

"Yes."

"Good. Tomorrow you will have to go to the Canadian Consulate to apply for immigration to Canada. Now you will understand why I told you to declare the passport lost…I will tell you more tomorrow about your next steps."

"Grazie, Signor' Gino."

So much to do and absorb in just a couple of days. I feel overwhelmed.

* * *

"Hi, Dad! How are you?" We managed to exchange some money so we can make phone calls to Canada from a public phone, using coins.

"Evelyn, how nice to hear from you! I'm ok, I miss you. How are you doing? Where are you?"

"We are in Rome. We arrived yesterday and we already did a lot of things. Mom will tell you more. Dad, you know what? Yesterday we went to a huge local market and I saw fuzzy potatoes!!!"

"You saw…what?" Greg was probably assuming he didn't hear well.

"Fuzzy potatoes. Mom says that those are kiwis…We haven't bought any yet, so we don't know what they taste like. I'll pass Amanda to you. Bye, Dad. Love you." Evelyn is glowing. She is definitely missing her father.

"Hi, Dad!" It's Amanda's turn. "How are you? Did you apply for political asylum? Any chance we'll get to come to Canada any time soon? How is Regina in winter?"

So many questions. The girls are missing their father, and apparently, they are concerned, too.

"Hi, Greg. I'm afraid we won't be able to talk for too long. This phone is eating up our coins at incredible speed. I'll write you a letter soon. For now, we are fine. We are staying at a hotel in Rome. No reason to be worried. How are you? Any progress with the application for political asylum?"

"No progress at all." There is a mix of sadness and excitement in Greg's voice, which is understandable. "Nothing is moving here. Everybody is in festive mood, Christmas is coming, and nobody seems to care much about me…"

"I'm sorry to hear this. I'll send you a letter tomorrow and give you more details about our arrival here, and you can write back to us to the address of the hotel. I'm sorry, we have to cut the conversation short. We have to make ends meet with the money your aunt left us. Say 'hi' to her and everybody else. Love you."

I don't know what to make of Greg's comments. Unfortunately, we cannot talk for too long. Phone conversations are expensive. I will write him a letter.

"Mom, now that we have money, can we get some instant pictures in that photo booth? We can send some to Dad. He misses us."

"Good idea. We can stop briefly at the station on our way to dinner. Let's give it a try!"

Five thousand lira later ($5), four smiles in less than two minutes, and the girls have cute pictures. Four of them!

"We can send two to Dad and two to grandparents!"

"Sounds great!"

Our first pictures in Rome. We look kind of dishevelled but who cares?!

* * *

Dinner in Via Dandolo was fabulous! There was a little wait, but the hot meal—pasta and turkey with mashed potatoes, as well as three mandarins for dessert—was fantastic. Students volunteering, apparently some teachers, too, and a few nuns, as well. All of them serving people like us, all refugees or immigrants, judging by the different languages they were speaking as well as by their looks.

This was another long day. Our second day in Rome. What's awaiting us tomorrow? The girls are tired. It's bedtime for them, but I promised Greg a letter and I also have to write to my parents. I can't afford to go to bed…

Dear Greg,

This is the first letter I am writing to you from Italy, besides the postcard I sent from Venice. By the time you'll receive this letter everything will be "history" as they say. The events are rolling down at such a speed that I can hardly keep up with them. We have met a nice older gentleman in the station and he is giving us directions almost every day. I don't know why he's doing this, but for now everything has been all right. He has helped us get a two-bed room in a decent yet inexpensive hotel and find some food banks where we can eat for free every day, he sent us to the police station to apply for a permit of stay in Italy and ask for political asylum, he's also going to send us to the Canadian Consulate to apply for immigration so we can come to Canada shortly—and all these in only two days. There is so much more to do. I will have to start looking for a place to stay because the hotel costs us 40,000 lira per day (the equivalent of $40 Canadian dollars); it's not much but I cannot spend the money your aunt has given us without replenishing the "bank," so I'll have to find a job, as well. The refugees here do not have camps like I hear they have in Germany or Austria. Everybody has to make his or her own arrangements, each of us on our own. It's very tough. There are lots of unfortunate people everywhere in the streets, sleeping in sleeping bags on the sidewalk, on pieces of cardboard, or warming up around improvised fire pits lit up here and there, in the open. It is a grim world, extremely unfriendly, very challenging. The toughest people can only survive. We are in good spirits—pretending we are tourists and enjoying all we can see during our daily walks, long walks everywhere. We jump on a bus or a tram once in a while, but most of the time we walk.

Earlier today, we went to eat at a charity food bank, and we passed by the Colosseum, the Roman Forum, the

Vittorio Emanuele Monument and so many other historic sites. We have walked quite a bit and we have seen a lot. I am still in amazement, but I am getting used to all this as it becomes part of our daily life. The girls can't contain their surprise at how many beautiful things we see every day when we do our window shopping: clothes and undergarments of the finest, jewelry of the most exquisite, shoes of the most expensive, and the list is endless. Besides, there is an abundance of fruit of all sorts: exotic or seasonal, pastries and so many other goodies that make us salivate every day, a few times a day. But I can't afford to buy anything yet, not yet...The day I will find a job, things will change. Tomorrow I am planning to buy a newspaper and start looking for work.

How are you? Have you made any progress with your request for political asylum? You can write back to the address of the hotel as indicated on the envelope. I don't know how long it will take until you get my letter. I will try to write you every day or every other day. Unfortunately, I cannot call because it's too expensive. I hope you will hear soon from the Canadian authorities in regard to your application.

I will have to stop here because I want to write to my parents and to your Mom, and I am so exhausted. The girls are sleeping already. They are happy because they have their own bed. Tomorrow they will write you letters, too.

Love you.
Maria

My dearest parents,

I would like to write you a letter every day, but we have so many things to do on a daily basis that at night I am so tired that I can hardly feel my legs and keep my eyes open.

I SHALL NOT FAIL

We have been looking for a place to stay since we came, and we are getting to know Rome pretty well, sometimes we don't even need the map. The fact that we have to eat each day for lunch and dinner at different locations takes a lot of time to get there, but the food is so good, it's incredible. For example, the food bank in Via Dandolo is really exquisite, both service and food quality. Tonight we ate the usual pasta sprinkled with lots of 'parmiggiano' on top for the first dish, and the second consisted of turkey breast and potatoes. As for dessert, we all received three mandarins each. We feel spoiled. We never had mandarins every day! You remember when the one single time we could buy oranges, in limited quantities, was only around Christmas? And even those were never enough so we, as parents, had always to save them for the kids and we were happy to have only a slice or two. As for mandarins, that was a rare fruit indeed!

Today we have walked around, and we've seen some rental apartments, but the rent is impossible. I will never have enough money to afford to pay rent. We've knocked on the door at some monasteries and convents, but to no avail. Tomorrow we have a few more convents to go to and try our luck. Don't worry, Mom. I trust that Somebody-up-there loves us. I am positive we will find something pretty soon.

Please do not be sad for us. I know it is hard for you, too. You are so alone, and we are so far away. One day, we will get together, and we will share all the stories that are left untold. Just trust that all is going to be well, Mommy. We love you both. Give a hug to John [my stepfather] and tell him to stay positive.

Love you,
Maria, Amanda and Evelyn

3
HOW DID WE GET HERE?

Time goes by quite fast. It's been only a week since we left our home country, but a lot has happened in the meantime. Romania seems so far away, both in space and time; especially in time. It feels almost unreal to think that only seven days ago we were embarking on the train, in the main station—the North Railway Station—of the capital city, Bucharest. Our destination: Italy! Where exactly? No idea! Just Rome. Rome was supposed to be the end of our journey; also a beginning…

* * *

The trip was far from easy. Travelling with two young girls—one pre-teen and the other one who had just turned thirteen—was a huge task. The travel part was not a problem, but this time everything was different. The fact that we were leaving our country for good added a dramatic aspect to this trip. I was turning my back to my hometown, to my country, leaving behind parents, memories, an entire life…Heading out to a future which had no shape, which hadn't even been planned out…Just like a boat, *à la dérive,* in the beat of the waves, suspended between two worlds, between a past that was now gone and an uncertain and frightening future that I had no control over. Less than a year had gone by since the so-called "Revolution" threw the country in disarray.

Here we are, a year later. December 1990. We went from hope to resignation in just a few months. The euphoria of the political unrest followed by the anticipation of a people who would roll up their sleeves to start building a new country, based on decency and trust, on honesty and civility, vanished in the months to come. There was just one solution: escape. Romania's future was going to be a sombre one from all points of view: political, social, economical. We didn't want to become sacrificial lambs. We couldn't accept the possibility that our own daughters might become guinea pigs in a society that seemed to have no compass. We knew that corruption was going to be the rule of the day, but for us that was not an option. We did NOT want to live in a country that would be ruled by corrupt governments in the years to come…

By a twist of fate, a remote relative of Greg—a great-grandaunt—who had been born in Canada from Romanian parents but had never visited the country, decided to come to Romania for a visit. On her way back home to Canada, because she was old and needed some assistance, she got my husband a visitor's visa. This was a great opportunity for us. We hoped that once Greg was in Canada, we would eventually join him there, sooner rather than later. However, a week later I decided that I would take a chance! I bought train tickets for myself and the girls, destination Rome. We had already received visitors' visas for Italy, so on December 9th, 1990 we took off! Left behind heart-broken parents who were trying to hide their tears as the train was picking up speed, getting farther and farther away from them, until we disappeared… Sadness. Sorrow. Tremendous grief.

Travelling by train was the first challenge. That first night on the train, I had nowhere to sit. I was exhausted, physically and mentally, and I was trying to close my eyes while standing, leaning against the window of the train and the hallway. The train was packed, people standing everywhere. Occasionally, my legs were giving in and sitting on the train floor was the only choice…my eyelids were getting heavier and heavier…I was glad that at least the girls had decent seats, albeit in two different compartments.

***

Around 6 am, on December 10th, 1990, I see a sign saying Vršac. We probably just crossed the border into Yugoslavia while I was dozing off. The last Romanian city I remember seeing was Timisoara. I don't know what to make of this place. Customs guards are getting on the train and start pushing people off the train, gesturing at us to get off and take our entire luggage with us. I don't understand what is going on. We walk across the rails and make it to a huge warehouse, carrying the heavy suitcases, one in each hand, obviously no wheels of any sort. ("Spinners" had not been invented at that time!) I have everything in these suitcases to help us survive for a couple of weeks. From food to clothes for the girls and myself, schoolbooks for grades five and seven respectively, even a hot plate, some plastic plates, a couple of metal cups, and a little pot in case I need to make some food, to cook something somewhere.

Why are these guys being so brutal? Where are they pushing us? I understand from the different gestures they make and from what people around me are saying that we need to make it to that huge warehouse and open all our luggage. The whole area looks like a huge flea market. People seem to be engaged in some sort of illegal commerce: buy merchandise in one country and sell it in the other. Smuggling. Now I understand why the guards want us all off the train, so they can check our luggage.

The customs guards are wandering around with whips in their hands, pointing to suitcases and ruffling people's belongings or merely throwing everything on the floor. It is a horror scene. I don't know what is going to happen next. We have tickets to go to Rome. I am not selling anything, no smuggling, not trafficking any merchandise. All we need is to keep going, across the border and continue our trip.

About an hour later we survive the "inspection" and some of us are redirected back onto the train. We finally have seats. For a while. I am taking a deep breath. We can continue our journey.

Surprise! The nine carriages of the train have been reduced to four! What happened to the other five carriages? After all, why should I care? We are safe for now and we can keep going.

A couple of hours later we are in Belgrade, the capital city of Yugoslavia. I don't understand the Serbian language, but I can read the Cyrillic letters. (When I was about seven years old my Mom—who had not been able to finish her last year of high school because of World War II—was studying Russian for her last examination. Russian language was compulsory at that time. Inquisitive as I was, trying to figure out what those symbols in Mom's books were, I was continuously bugging her, so eventually my mother decided to teach me the Cyrillic letters—maybe in an attempt to get rid of me! Who knew that it would come in handy one day?)

Anyways here we are in a small railway station. Too small for the capital of a country. Something is not right. From people around me who speak my language I understand that we have to get to the main railway station so we can continue our trip. I have no idea how to go about this. How do we get to the main station? Where is it? We are in Belgrade, a city that I have never visited in my life, with two kids in tow and a lot of luggage to schlep around.

Looks like everybody is trying to get on a bus that apparently goes to the main station. I'm desperate. We have to make it! I push my girls on the bus, each of them carrying her piece of luggage, and myself the rest. There are so many people on this bus. We are all squished. It's 9:00 in the morning, and it's so cold. The doors of the bus cannot close because there are people literally hanging onto the doors. The bus is so heavy on the right side that it's tilting dangerously that way. Nevertheless, the bus leaves the station slowly, and I have no idea where the main station is. We have no choice but to keep going. Following the crowd. I'm losing track of time. Eventually we arrive at the main train station in Belgrade. I manage to find my way around and see when the next train is leaving and from which platform. I am somewhat relieved; it's almost 10:00 in the morning, we still have some time until about noon when we need to board the next train. We are exhausted.

"Mom, I need to go to the bathroom." Well, call of nature, obviously. How am I supposed to know where the bathroom is? This is another busy railway station, definitely just as big as the one in Bucharest. And the fact that it looks like a zoo doesn't help with finding our way around. I send the girls together to find a bathroom so I can keep an eye on our luggage.

"Mom, Evelyn is begging!" What? What is this?! I sent both girls to the bathroom and Amanda is coming back claiming that her sister is begging for money. For money?

"And where is Evelyn? Why is she begging for money?"

"She's at the other end of the railway station. She needs money to go to the bathroom."

"And you left her alone???"

"Yeah...I just thought I should come and tell you what she's doing..."

"So you left your sister alone and you came here to tell me that she's begging? Go back, find your sister, find a solution, and do not leave each other, please. Run!"

I don't know whether to be angry or appalled. Angry because Amanda left her eleven-year-old sister all by herself in a huge and unknown railway station in a strange city and in a foreign country, or shocked because Evelyn was begging for money. Besides, I cannot move; I am stuck with the suitcases and the girls' backpacks and the bags. However, the immediacy of having both girls back by my side, begging or not, but safe and sound, is critical. I don't even know what is worse: Evelyn begging for money or each of them being alone. Oh, Lord, give me patience!!

"Mom, here's the change!" Before I have the chance to figure out how to go about this entire situation, the girls are back and Evelyn is gloriously showing me a banknote.

"What change?"

"I'm sorry...I needed money to pay for the washroom, so I got 1,000 *dinars* [Serbian currency, equivalent of $1.00], and it cost me half of this to use the restroom...So, here is the rest." She is handing me a banknote of 500 *dinars* [$0.50]. Evelyn's innocent smile is disarming. This is called doing business! Not quite orthodox, but when the law of nature is calling, what can you do?

"I'm glad you are both back. Make sure you never separate from each other again. I don't even want to think that one of you may disappear... Anyways, we have to move all this stuff to platform 21. That's where the train for Venice will arrive and depart. It's the Balkan Express, it's supposed to be in Belgrade at 5:30 pm and leave at 6:15 pm."

"Mommy, do we have seats?"

"Well, Amanda, I guess we just got used to not having seats! We'll have to find a way. What can I say? We will survive. You need to put on some warmer clothes because we are getting more tired and you will really feel the cold. It's damp, too."

"So, we have at least eight hours to kill until the train is coming."

"That's right, Amanda. We'll eat later on; maybe we'll have a combination of lunch and dinner, all cold, and a couple of snacks in the evening, so we can last until tomorrow morning. So, we'll have to kill the time somehow. Maybe we can write letters to Dad and to your grandparents. You can write letters to them about our adventurous trip. They will be really happy to receive news from you, and we will mail the letters from Italy because I am not going to exchange the few dollars we have into *dinars* for just a one-time stop in this country. You can also draw, you can read, sit, doze off, rest, what else can you do?"

* * *

"Girls, get ready to get on the train. The train is late and the stop is advertised for 15 minutes only." It arrives at 8:20 pm! It was supposed to be here about three hours ago. And it is so packed. Greeks, Bulgarians, Turks, you name it, and no seats.

"Evelyn, there is one seat in this compartment. Please excuse yourself and sit. Amanda, one more for you in the next one. Do the same. I'll take care of the luggage and I'll see where I can squeeze it. At least it's warm inside. You'll sleep well tonight, you'll have to!"

"Mom, where are you sitting?"

"No sitting for me. I just got used to sleeping in the stand-up position, right? I'll become a horse…"

* * *

Ljubljana. Last city in Yugoslavia curving around a beautiful meandering river, before entering Italy. The physical exhaustion is taking over. Eight long hours of torture. Between standing and leaning against any solid surface or sitting on the train floor, I don't know how my body is still holding up. It's good to know that some people will get off in Ljubljana so maybe I can get a couple of hours of sleep in a sitting position.

* * *

"Buon giorno, signori!"

Buon giorno? Where are we? What time is it? The Italian border police. Passport checking. It's awful dark, though…The border patrol officer has not turned the cabin lights on. He's using his flashlight. How nice…My eyes are still sleeping. He's said "Buon giorno?" I guess you can say "Buon giorno" at 5 am, of course.

"Where are you going, ma'am?" Same question, different language, but what a difference! This man is very polite and the Italian sounds so musical.

"To Rome." Short answer. No details. If he wants to know more, he'll ask more questions. We have to pretend we are tourists. In fact, we are, but we won't come back, so we only travel one way…

"What are you planning to do in Rome, ma'am?"

"Visit places, sight-seeing, getting to know the Italian history, culture and civilization first-hand."

"The girls are your daughters?"

"Yes." He didn't even wake them up. How nice…

"Grazie, signora. Buon viaggio!"

This is all? Have a nice trip?! Welcome to Italy, girls! We are free now, really free! So, this is Trieste. Maybe I can sleep a bit more. Or maybe not… The sun will rise soon. The Adriatic coast is a must-see. We are tourists after all, so we might as well take advantage of this trip. Who knows when we'll ever be back to see all this beauty?

* * *

"Good morning, sunshine!"

"Where are we, Mom?"

"Adriatic coast, Amanda. Look at the blue sky and the sun's reflection on the sea waters…" Amanda's blue eyes are absorbing the azure colours of the Adriatic sky and sea, and I don't know if the waters have taken the shade of Amanda's eyes or it's the other way around. Italy is welcoming us with the most magnificent view. Navy blue and aqua-marine, cerulean and turquoise shades of blue, white vessels spread about the small lagoons and gulfs, white sand shores, and high promontories. It's like living on a cloud. The train is meandering along the coast of the Trieste Gulf. We'll soon leave it behind; Venice is not far away.

"Mom, where will we be staying in Rome?"

"Sweetheart, we haven't even arrived in Venice and you're asking me about Rome…Don't break the spell, please."

"When will we arrive in Venice, though?"

"By noon or so. No arrival or departure has been on time so far, so this is my rough estimate. Are you tired?"

"Yeah…I'd like a warm bath…"

"So would I, but we don't know what other surprises are awaiting us. If all goes well, we should be in Rome tomorrow morning, and then we'll have to find the *Pensione* of Signora Dina."

"Where is that?"

"Apparently in a place called Latina, in Rome. My understanding is that this Signora Dina is somehow hosting some lost people like us…We'll see tomorrow."

"Hi…" Evelyn's sleepy head is popping out from under her coat.

"Ciao, bella! We are in Italy."

"We are?"

"Si, amore…Now that you are up, too, we'll have to eat something before we get off the train so we can simplify our lives especially after we have had the luxury for the past few hours to be alone in this compartment. I hope you two had a good sleep because we'll have another day of unexpected adventures ahead of us. Make sure you go to the washroom before we arrive in Venice because I am not planning to exchange any money yet, and begging is not an option!"

* * *

Oh, Venezia…Gloriously *romantic,* triumphant and equally seductive. Its scenic beauty and its charming vistas over the water make one forget about all his or her sorrows and hurting. Venezia was known to us from the history books, from movies and slides, from picture postcards and from TV documentaries, but Venezia is to be experienced through all senses. Take in the unique beauty of the canals, the gallery of colours, light and texture, the singing of the Venetian *gondolieri* strolling along the Canal Grande, serenading away to the pairs of dreaming lovers. If the canals were streets, all these gondolas would be taxis.

We have six hours to spend in Venice, so this is the time to pretend we are tourists. Neither Evelyn nor Amanda seem to have complaints, so we head out to the *centro storico* with the Piazza San Marco as one of our main objectives. We can't afford to take the *vaporetto* on the Grand Canal, which is waiting for tourists at the main railway station. Walking is the only option and, after all, how can we absorb this civilization other than walking so we can get immersed into everything Venezia has to offer in a few hours? Ponte di Scalzi and Ponte Rialto offer us the view of the constant stream of *vaporetti*, barges, water taxis, police boats, ambulances, gondolas, and other boats populating the Grand Canal. Piazza San Marco…Absolutely surreal.

"Mom, look, pigeons!" Yes, lots of them and so friendly, landing fearlessly on people's arms, used to being photographed from all angles at all times. I can't miss this opportunity. The girls are oblivious of the fact that these flying creatures may leave some droppings as their unique signature or a sign of…good luck!

Piazza San Marco is flooded with people. It's Tuesday noon, but sidewalk cafés are inviting with their tempting aromas to a fresh espresso or cappuccino. One day we will come back for sure and we will sit at one of these tables, sipping from a glass of wine or a tiny, small cup of coffee… One day…

"Mom, what are these stacked tables for? What does *acqua alta* mean?" The girls seem to take advantage of our tourist status and are taking their role seriously, or maybe it's just their innate curiosity. I explain to them that once in a while Venice is affected by flooding and the tables serve as…pathways or…sidewalks, all lined up above the high waters, connecting different parts of the flooded area while keeping the people's feet dry when walking!

Venice is an interesting place to see and visit. It's our first port of entry in this country, the first time we get to meet real Italians, although they are passersby, rushing to go to work or going home after a day's work. Most of these people are tourists, but one can hear the Italian merchants chanting as they hang around their boutiques, inviting you in a singing tone to walk into their tiny store and buy some souvenirs, or sit at a sidewalk table and indulge in a slice of homemade pizza or sit on a highchair at a bar and sip your fifth espresso of the day. It's equally eye-catching to see cloth lines hanging over the canals. Maybe this is the most striking of everything we can see around us. It's the last thing one would expect to see displayed outside, in everybody's sight, left and right, as we cross the bridges. Clothes of all kinds, all colours and all lengths, underwear included, exhibited outside as part of the décor, pinned with cloth pins on a retractable cloth line that is reeled back and forth using a pulley system. This is so Italian! Or should I say Venetian?!

It's getting dark already. We are ten days away from the winter solstice and in Italy it seems to get dark earlier. The night lights are inundating the streets now. Neon lit shop windows, multicoloured Christmas lights hanging in front of the bars, restaurants, cafés and stores, draped around windows and doors, glittering garlands dangling everywhere, this seems to be such a happy world!

It's almost mid-December, and with Christmas approaching, this appears to be a truly dazzling time. The festive ambiance, the mist-shrouded canals twinkling with holiday sparkle, creating an utterly enchanting effect—everything around us reveals the vibrant soul of this eternal city. I feel enveloped in the magic of plenitude and serenity.

* * *

The six hours of waiting in Venice have become…almost ten. The girls are exhausted. Sleeping on benches, eating cold food from jars and cans, drinking tap water. Half an hour before midnight, our train is finally leaving Venice for Rome. Another cold night on a cold train. The snowsuits are proving to be useful. I don't care that my kids look funny. Nobody is wearing snowsuits around here, but I can't afford to see them getting sick. I do have provisions of medication for all sorts of illnesses, but I'd rather keep them healthy. 10:35 pm…The train was supposed to leave four hours ago. I wonder whether these trains are ever on time…It doesn't matter anymore. It's the last night on the train and this time we have seats, too. Bonus!

4
IN SEARCH OF A SHELTER!

The days are getting shorter and shorter. Around 5 pm it's quite dark and that's the time when we go for our evening meal at the soup kitchen in Via Dandolo. Most of the time we take the tramway, but sometimes we walk. It's about a four km distance—one-hour walk back to the hotel. I'm very mindful of the money we have. It has to last as long as possible. I keep looking for a job, but I don't seem to have any luck. I would like to find something in cleaning or babysitting, but I do not have a work permit. Anyways, I hope something will happen one of these days. However, the most important thing right now is to find a place to stay. It's been a week since we came to this hotel and we have to leave soon. But where?

A few days ago Gino introduced me to a fellow who was supposed to take me to a rental place. It was quite an experience! I met this guy around 5 pm. It was dark already. He was built short, skinny, not talkative at all. A conversation with him seemed to be impossible. He only told me that the apartment was located at a "considerable distance" so we had to take a bus, then a tram and then walk, too. It took about 90 minutes until we got there. I had no idea where he was taking me. I was definitely uncomfortable, but I didn't want to show any sign of weakness. Short as he was, I could have punched him hard and knocked him out if needed be, but he seemed very quiet and calm. So, I was following him. Eventually, we arrived in front of a four-story building. It looked quite dilapidated.

We walk in. No elevator. The apartment is on the third floor. Wait a second! What is this? The door has a hole in it! My goodness! What am I doing here? Nobody with a safe mind would want to live here! Definitely not a woman with two young daughters. I cannot leave though. The door opens.

"Buona sera." A tall guy wearing a type of a "wife-beater" sleeveless shirt shows up at the door.

"Buona sera." My voice is stern.

"Come on in. We have a large room that is available right now."

Large or not, I don't care. Two more men are in the kitchen, obviously all sharing this apartment. Who could think that a woman with two girls would want to live in such a place? Yet, I'm not going to say anything that might upset any of these men! I'm alone here with four of them around.

"I'll think about it." I pretend to have a look at the room. I have no idea how many bathrooms are there. I don't care. I want to get out of here as soon as possible.

Going back to the hotel is just as long. Over three hours have gone by. I'm sure the girls are worried. They know that they are not supposed to open the door to anybody. We do have an agreement though. Once arrived at the door, I would use my fingernails to gently knock according to a certain beat that only we know. I am also singing a kids' tune while my nails tenderly complement the little song. As they open the door to our room I feel thankful for seeing them again, feeling safe.

"Hi Mom! What happened? What took you so long?"

I told them the whole story, and the night that followed brought us the calm we so desperately needed.

* * *

Today is another day, though. A new day, new hopes. We have another shot at the chance! Through the grapevines I've heard about a certain convent that occasionally has some space open for poor or homeless people. We fit into the category! We're definitely homeless! The convent is under the umbrella of Mother Teresa of Calcutta, the well-known missionary of the Indian charity. We have to give it a try.

"Hi, Mommy…"

"Hi, sleepy-head! How are you? You want to give Mommy a hug?"

"I had a dream. Amanda and I were riding on two beautiful white horses, and we crossed a stream of water…and then I forgot…"

"That's a good dream, Evelyn. Definitely a good omen. Maybe we'll have some success today and get accepted in that convent. Go have a shower before Amanda wakes up. Who knows if we still have the chance to shower every day?"

"Mom, do we still have to meet with Gino? He gives me the creeps…"

"No, we don't. He seems pretty weird to me, too. Well, it's not nice to talk like this about him, but we've learned a lot of things from him, and we did pretty much all he told us to, so we are now on our own, more or less. One thing is for sure: he won't find me a job, and even if he does, I am not too sure I can trust him. We'll see. One step at a time. First, we need to secure a safe roof over our heads. Go have a shower!"

"Good morning, blue-eyes!"

"Hi…Mom, when can we go to school again?"

"Amanda, did you sleep well? Or are your dreams telling me that you are missing school? Schools are closed. It's Christmas break. We'll talk about school in January."

"But Mom, do you think we'll be accepted in the same grades as in our home country?"

"Yes, honey. We will do our best and try our hardest. Today though we have a test to pass: get into a convent or not. It is our last chance. When Evelyn comes back from the shower, you go next. OK? We have another challenging day coming up, and we need to hurry because we have to be at the convent door around 8 o'clock. Apparently the nuns go to the mass before noon and we have to talk to a certain nun."

* * *

"Bonjour. J'aimerais parler avec Sœur Jeanine."

"C'est moi Sœur Jeanine. Comment est-ce que je pourrais vous aider?"

The icebreaker is working fine. How can I impress this young yet very educated nun other than approaching her in French? San Gregorio seems to be a convent where women are not easily accepted, although it is run by Madre Teresa di Calcutta. And here goes my story in brief: two young daughters, no money, no roof over our heads, no beds to sleep on, no food, my husband is in Canada and we are in transition through Italy, for just a couple of months until we can join my husband. My humble tone, my use of French (this is how I had been instructed) seem to make the right impression on Sœur Jeanine. She is promising she'll talk to Madre Superior right away, and we will have an answer shortly. And the heavy door of the convent closes on us.

"So, what do you think, girls? Any luck?"

Before the girls have the chance to say anything, the door opens again, and Madre Superior shows up at the entrance and invites us in. And here my story goes again, this time in English. The horses in Evelyn's dream have surely been a sign of good news coming up. Madre Superior is suggesting we bring our luggage to the convent this very morning. In exchange, we will have to participate to the life in the convent and help around with different chores. No problem! I can't expect anything for free!

Yes! On growing wings we fly to the hotel to pay the bills and bring our luggage to the convent.

Dear Daddy,

It is time we write you a letter, as well. I will write mine first, and Evelyn will write hers later. How are you? It must be very cold in Canada at this time, but it's definitely not warm here either. For the past week we slept comfortably in our hotel room, but I wonder if the Italian people heat up their homes. For all this past week we had no heat and there was no indication that heating was a possibility. Plus, the tile floors are not helping either. At least, it was a decent room.

This morning we said good-bye to the hotel, and we just moved into the convent. If the hotel room was cold, the convent is a shock! At the end of an endless flight of stairs, the main entrance opens into a huge hallway. An opening on the left is the "refectorium": a combination of kitchen and bathroom, two-in-one! Some women were washing dishes in some sort of a kitchen sink, and behind there was a toilet and a shower, also two-in-one, or maybe three-in-one if we consider the bidet, as well! And this seems to be the only washroom for about 40 - 50 people!

Down the hallway are the two…bedrooms. I don't know if "bedroom" is the right word. They look more like huge hospital salons. The first room where we and Mom have been given three beds, counts in fact 15 beds altogether, all disposed in all directions: by the two huge windows, by the door, in the middle of the room, by the walls. No closets, just a small cupboard by Mom's bedside. I understand that our suitcases and luggage and all go under the beds. In this room, besides the three of us, there are 12 more women, most of them coming from other countries: Albania, Ethiopia, Somalia, Yugoslavia, and a few older ones are Italian, too.

The room next door is shared by about 25 younger women with lots of small kids of younger ages (a few months to 7-years-old). Some of those kids sleep with their mothers, some others have cribs. I guess there are about 35 people in that room, plus 15 in ours…and, as I already said, only one washroom for all these people…

Anyways, Christmas is coming, and everybody is in good mood. After we settled in, we have been offered a cup of hot chocolate and panettone. Daddy, you have no idea how good the panettone is! There are chunks of chocolate and raisins inside, and it's so yellow and so soft…Yummy!

Today Mom is planning to take us around and wander about to get to know this part of Rome, as well. It's very close to Colosseum so we get to see it every day. Can you imagine? Walking by this huge monument which we got to see only in our history books…It's like magic! The first time we saw it was at night. It was lit from below by thousands of colourful sparkling lights and it looked eerie. There are tall pine trees like we have never seen before. They say this is a type of Mediterranean pine trees. Very pretty. They look like big, green parasols. What I like the most is the Christmas lights at night, lots of them, very colourful. And of course, all the goodies in the shop windows…I guess Santa Claus is not coming this year. Have you been a good boy? Is Santa coming to you?

I miss you, Daddy. I can't wait until school starts so I go to school and see what it is like here. I'll write again soon.

Love you, Daddy.
Hope to see you before long.
Amanda

5
IS SANTA COMING THIS YEAR?

"Mom, I need to go to the bathroom, really badly!"

The everyday stress and the chaotic daily schedule, the lack of a bathroom in our own room at the hotel as well as being constantly outside, exploring Rome in all directions took a toll on Evelyn's system. We run to the bathroom and although it's 6 am, there is a line up already. About four or five women ahead of me. Somebody is in there already.

"Mom, I need to go NOW"!

The bathroom door opens and I leave all the courtesy behind. I push past the women in front of me, I grab Evelyn's hand and we thrust our way into the bathroom, locking the door behind us. It's brutal. It's survival. Manners do not seem to have a place in this convent. At least not today, not this morning. I have no time to scrutinize my feelings. There is definitely no guilt. As a mother in a survival mode, I do what I need to do.

Welcome to *Missionarie della carità*! It will take a few days until we understand how things are going and what we need to do to survive. For how long? I have no idea. One day at a time. For now, we are here, we have beds and food. "Free" as all this is, we still need to contribute somehow, to pay by doing some work for the people in the convent.

The first floor is occupied by women, but on the second floor there are men, all of them old or with some disabilities. The kitchen where the food is being prepared is on the second floor. Amanda helped in the kitchen for the past couple of days, and she was appalled at the lack of hygiene! What can I say? I pray that we don't get sick.

My help consists in doing laundry. No washing machine, but just some huge bathtubs, where the bed sheets are supposed to be washed by hand. After two days of heavy washing, tens of sheets and pillowcases, most of them soiled, I have had enough! I realize that if we stay in the convent, we have to help with all these chores. Evelyn managed to get a…free pass! She seems to be considered a child! Too young to work on anything… Instead, Evelyn found another occupation! She discovered that in the basement of the convent there are lots and lots of bags of donated clothes and toys. Every day she brings to our room all the Barbie dolls she never had and different other toys that she has never seen. Besides, her eyes are also attracted to different outfits, some of them really elegant. She puts on several skirts, blouses, dresses, and she basically steals them; then she comes upstairs, dressed up with all those layers on!!!

"Mom, look what I've found! A pretty skirt for you." I have to admit it is quite pretty. Nice fabric too.

"Amanda, I got you a pair of pants. Leggings. Very fancy!"

However, if Evelyn can go by and manages to charm the nuns, the same doesn't apply to me and Amanda. So, if we leave the convent all day, we can skip our "duties"! It's worth trying. After all, Evelyn is safe in the convent so we don't have to take her with us, and I don't have to be worried. She has free lunch at noon and then, besides enjoying browsing through the basement "fashion boutique," when she is not stealing toys, she seems to like baby-sitting a couple of babies next door, cooing and holding them, and playing with them.

Unfortunately, the convent is not open all day. We cannot go in and out whenever we want. Obviously, it's not a hotel!!! Pietro, the doorman, a morose old man, opens the door only three times in the morning: at 7, at 8 and at 9 am. If anybody wants to leave the convent at any of these times, they are allowed to come back only at noon when Pietro would open the door for 15 minutes. However, if we are back by noon, we still have time to do different chores in the convent, so the last option is to come back between 6 - 7 pm. No problem. Now that we have a shelter, we can focus on finding a school for the girls.

Rome unveils itself to us day by day. Amanda is a wonderful travel companion. Not only does she have an instinctive curiosity, but she has enough knowledge from her history classes about Rome to help her place Rome on the world map. Although Rome is unknown to us, walking around, taking in everything we see, all the sites we come across—everything is a true enjoyment. We are tired, but we keep going. Once in a while we go into a church and sit in a pew, just to rest our legs for a little bit. The Vatican, the Colosseum; the Spanish Steps and the Trinità dei Monti Renaissance church next to it; Keats and Shelley's house where the English Romantic poet died of tuberculosis at the beginning of the 19th century, and where Percy Bysshe Shelley had also lived, a museum today, commemorating both poets; Piazza Navona, Trastevere, the Pantheon, Fontana di Trevi, Foro Romano in Piazza Argentina—they all seem to "come" to us, amazing treasures of the Roman times. The *Centro Storico* is an area that has been inhabited, almost without a break, for over 2000 years. Buildings and sites are generally dated between 2000 and 300 years old.

On our way to eat our evening meal in Via Dandolo, we cross the Trastevere River several times, sometimes on Ponte Garibaldi, and some other times on Ponte Palatino, walking past the famous Bocca della Verità. (Is it true that this "Mouth of Truth" will eat your arm if you tell a lie? At least this is what the legend says…!) Between these two bridges we can see the Isola Tiberina (Tiberian Island) right in the middle of the river. Trastevere. It doesn't do justice to call it by the English name, the Tiber, although we know that its name comes from the Latin trans Tiberim, meaning literally "beyond the Tiber." Trastevere is the right word.

We do have a "mission," though. My main focus is finding a school for the girls. I learn that Evelyn being in the fifth grade will go to an elementary school. However, Amanda will be in the seventh grade. Not far from the Colosseum, walking through Colle Oppio Park (on one of the legendary Seven Hills of Rome) we find a school, Ruggiero Bonghi. It says "Primary and Secondary School." It's Christmas time and everybody is on vacation, but I'll be back soon.

* * *

The days go by, mostly slowly…We managed to go to the Canadian Consulate, but all I could do was fill out an application asking for immigration to Canada. Based on what? I tried to fill in the blanks the best I could.

Address? Just the address of the convent. Will we ever get a response? We did the same once we found the American Consulate and the Australian Embassy. I'm sure this is not leading anywhere, but we had to try. I understand now why Gino suggested I declare my passport "lost." This is where we needed it. All the authorities of these foreign consulates asked me to show proof that we had a passport. Obviously, I may have not been allowed to submit an application if I did not have this document. Strangely enough, according to Romanian—still—communist rules, I only have ONE passport with the girls being included—photos and all—in my passport. So, it's triple-valuable!

Today it's Christmas Eve. It is going to be the first time our family won't be together to celebrate, to gather around the tree, to welcome Santa, to open gifts and sing, and eat…Greg is in Canada, our parents are in Romania, and we are here in Italy…No celebration. I miss Greg's dressing in Santa's clothes and showing up with his bag full of presents for our kids, for our parents, tricking the girls into believing he was a real Santa. Amanda knew that behind those clothes and mask it was her Dad hiding, but Evelyn, in spite of her 11 years, still believes in Santa. I remember last year, while sitting on Santa's knees and telling him poems and stories, Evelyn was trying to pull him by his fake beard and moustache, poking her little fingers into Santa's mask…until, all of a sudden she said: "Mom, Santa is wearing Dad's aftershave! He smells like Dad!" Well, then "Santa" had to explain to Evelyn that lots of people use the same fragrances.

Sure…so, for the last Christmas we spent in Romania last year we planned to have a friend of our family dress up like Santa. We wanted to keep the spell, the magic…also because Evelyn asked one year: "Mom, how come every single time Santa is coming Dad is not home? Why does he have to work that very night? Too bad Dad doesn't get to see Santa…" But Evelyn still believes that Santa truly exists. Before we left our home country, Evelyn wrote a cute letter to Santa and left it on the windowsill for…Santa to pick up that night so he could make her wishes come true. Evelyn's last letter to Santa:

Dear Santa Claus,

Do you know what I want this year? I want lots of things… I would like a pair of skates and a pair of new skis, a pair of ballet shoes and a couple of oranges, and I have one more wish, a special one, for me and my family: we want to immigrate to Canada…I don't know if you can make all my wishes come true. I just hope so…Thank you so much, Santa!

Evelyn

Yes, indeed, Evelyn had lots of wishes, put on paper less than a month ago. Skis, skates? Not this year, for sure. Oranges? Two oranges…How sad to want just two oranges in a country that was once one of the most developed countries in Europe. A country where the "imported" communism ruined everything, killed people's hopes and expectations. We will surely have plenty of oranges this Christmas, but immigrating to Canada? Not this year. Maybe by next Christmas, Santa will make Evelyn's wish come true.

It's been about a week since we moved to the convent. The routine is, to say the least, interesting! Fifteen women, including us, in just one single room, all of us coming from at least six different countries, from totally different backgrounds, and with entirely diverse attitudes and approaches.

The four Albanian women, aged 22—48, seem to be complacent of their situation. The youngest one, Enida, dreams of being sponsored by some rich American or get married to one and hopes to leave Italy soon. She "disappears" almost every day. After all, she's young, but she is not working anywhere.

Elena was a teacher in her home country. Her husband worked for a radio station and her son was a student in an Albanian university. The two men sleep outside, under some sort of improvised tents made out of bed sheets and blankets, all soiled, while Elena is lucky enough to be accepted inside the convent. She seems to be lollygagging all day long. She speaks English quite well, so we have some communication.

Then there is Arjeta, an Albanian woman in her 40's, and another senior lady, also Albanian; they speak no language other than Albanese, so no communication is possible. All day long, these two ones in particular do nothing, but lie on their beds, or sit up, or talk between themselves and pretend they are ill, so the nuns don't ask them to do any chores around the convent.

One Somali woman, Marianna, who speaks Italian amazingly well, seems to be a "resident" of this convent. She basically runs our room and everybody tacitly recognizes the "leader" in her. Not for any particular character traits, but just because she is extremely moody. Rumours go that she is drugged most of the time which explains her behaviour. I don't know what a person using drugs acts like, but Marianna surely has some issues! She arrives at the convent a little before the doors close, around 6:45 pm every evening, and she walks as if she's drunk. She puts up a show almost every night: swearing, yelling, screaming, picking up fights with anyone, and by 7:30 pm, she turns off the lights. God forbid we wake her up! Everybody is tiptoeing…In the morning, she wakes up at 5 am and wakes everybody up—sometimes swearing, sometimes laughing…depending on which side of the bed she slept on! And the circus goes on, day in, day out.

Eleonora, a woman in her early 60's, is Italian, apparently abandoned by her family. She sleeps next to my bed. She drinks quite often and quite a bit!! When she is sober, which it doesn't happen very often, she talks to me, but she appears miserable and bitter. She has a nice vocabulary and sometimes she gives me sound advice. One night though, I saw Eleonora literally been dragged by the nuns who had found her on the streets, drunk and dirty, as if she had rolled in mud. She was so drunk that she had no control over her legs. The nuns had to haul her up the stairs, to the upper floor of the convent, to wash her and then they tried to put her to sleep, of course in her bed, next to mine…

Then there is Nina. She's also in her, probably, late 60's and she speaks to herself most of the time, when she's around. She has a lot of oddly shaped religious statuettes on a shelf above her bed, all representing Jesus or Virgin Mary, most of them elongated, measuring about 20 cm in height and about 5—6 cm in diameter…She seems to play with them at night…Not quite sure what she's doing, but she's weird.

However, Anna is the most "interesting" character. She is also Italian, about 70 or less, heavy set. She has no teeth or very few, rotten anyways, and she seems to have a speech impairment. Nobody makes much sense of what she says, so we don't know anything about her biography. Anna drinks, too, sometimes, but not heavily. Instead, she has a particular "lifestyle." During the day she spends time in the kitchen with the nuns, helping with preparing food, but knowing that she hardly ever touches the water, makes me wonder what goes in that food. It's a good thing it's being cooked. At night, Anna goes to the washroom very often; maybe bladder issues…That's not in fact a problem, not MY problem, anyways. The trouble comes with the way she comes back from the washroom. Short and heavy as she is, suffering also from some asthma by the way she breathes, Anna doesn't have any body flexibility at all. She cannot bend, she cannot use toilet paper, she probably misses the toilet when she is trying to use it, and then she steps in her own body fluids…Wearing socks all the time, soaked in everything she steps into, she comes back to our room, shuffling her feet on the mosaic floors, stinky and wet with urine and feces, and she slips back into her bed next to Eleonora. It doesn't matter how far or how close her bed is to any of us, because the stench fills up the entire room and takes over the hallway too. It's like living in a pigsty.

The other women are pale figures in comparison to these three ones. At least, our room is somewhat quieter, most of the times, especially when Marianna is not around. The other room, next to ours, is like a zoo, with young kids of all ages crawling, jumping, bouncing, running, screaming, crying. We are…lucky!

Besides the human presence that makes our lives…vibrant, at times, and constantly full of unexpected, we have "pets" too! Lots of mice all over the place. Under the beds, on the beds, and basically everywhere. Infestation? For sure…I suggested to the nuns that they may want to bring a cat if they didn't feel like…killing the mice or do something drastic about this issue. No one seems to consider my suggestion. Maybe they believe that a cat chasing or eating mice is a sin! Oh, we also have ants. At least these ones are only annoying.

Well, life goes on.

6

MERRY CHRISTMAS!

Christmas has come and, just as fast, it was gone. Santa had a different present for us this year. A very special gift in its own way. On Christmas Eve a group of teenagers, mostly high school students, came to the convent to sing carols with us, to keep us company for the special evening and bring some joy to our solitary lives. It was absolute joy! True celebration through singing Christmas songs, so melodious, in such a harmony that I had never heard before, spreading a feeling of joy, and bringing us all together. Luckily, these young people had lyrics on paper that they handed out to us, so we could sing along. And just like that, the convent with its own ad-hoc choir turned into a mini-concert hall for that night. The Christmas songs were mainly related to the theme of the birth of Jesus Christ, of course. We were in a convent and it was right to sing religious songs, mostly in Italian, but a few songs were in Latin, too, *Adeste Fideles* being one of them. Simply beautiful. A truly solemn way to celebrate Christmas.

At some point, one of the girls takes a step away from her friends, emerging like a flickering light, and approaches us, speaking English.

"Hi, my name is Maria." Maria! Maria? Same name as mine!

"My name is Maria, too! Nice to meet you."

She is a lovely girl of about 15, dark hair, dark eyes, and a beautiful, genuine smile, enchanting and delightful. Her appearance is emanating a feeling of love and care, sincere interest and a true desire to help.

"Where are you from?" As I am trying to make my story as succinct as possible, I can read trustworthiness in her eyes; she seems to be such a good listener, encouraging me to give her more details about our journey and our adventures for the past couple of weeks.

"So, you have been here only for the past few days. Do you have an idea for how long you will be here?" The girl is trying to get more information from us.

"I don't know. We take it day by day, doing our best to adjust, trying to find our way around." Truly, I have no idea. For now it's just that: one day at a time. My main focus right now is to enroll the girls in school and find a job. We have some money but not much and I don't know what the girls will need once they go to school. Maria's eyes seem to absorb every single detail. The girls join us.

"Maria, these are my daughters, Amanda and Evelyn."

"Hi, Amanda. Do you, girls, speak English, too?"

"I do. I'm also learning Italian." Amanda is starting her conversation with Maria, excited to speak with a girl of almost her age, mainly in English but using some Italian phrases as well.

"Me, too," Evelyn pitches in.

"So, are you looking forward to going to school?"

"Yes. I think we just found two schools not far from here." Amanda's voice has a tone of excitement.

"Two schools?"

"Yes, I am in grade seven, so hopefully I'll be admitted in a secondary school at the same level."

Evelyn doesn't want to feel left out. "I'll be in grade five. I can hardly wait!"

The evening ended on a happy note. We continued to sing more Christmas carols, and we had a conversation in English with an Italian girl called Maria. For an unexplained reason a feeling of plenitude, of meaningfulness envelops me. A feeling of belonging somewhere. A feeling of miracles happening, coming our way.

"*Ave Maria, piena di grazia, il Signor' è con te…*", the daily Rosary we all get to say in the evening brings the day to an end.

Buon Natale! Merry Christmas!

* * *

"Get up, girls! We need to get ready, have breakfast and get out of here as soon as Pietro opens the door."

"How are we getting to the Vatican City, Mom?" I guess Amanda has had enough of walking for the past few days, crisscrossing Rome in all directions.

"We'll take the bus today." It's about five km one way and it should take us over an hour to walk, but we need to be there earlier to beat the crowds, if we also want to secure a spot inside St. Peter's Basilica. We have already been in Vatican City a couple of times, but today it's Christmas day and we get to see the Pope.

About an hour later we are in Vatican. It is very crowded indeed. Two hours before the mass starts and it's packed already. Step-by-step, excusing ourselves, gently elbowing our way in, inch by inch, we manage to secure a spot, obviously a standing one, but from where we can see the Pope. From this spot we get a glimpse of the *Pietà, the* famous marble sculpture of Mary holding the dead body of Jesus, completely protected by a bullet-proof acrylic glass panel.

Michelangelo carved this statue in genuine Carrara marble, bringing life to this unique piece of art. Virgin Mary looks so young considering that she was presumably older at that moment in her life. Her face has a solemn disguise, displaying rather the abandonment of a loved one instead of the pain of a loss one would normally see on a depressed and sorrowed face. The lively features give a unique beauty to Mary's face.

I remember vaguely a news article that made the headlines about 20 years ago. A presumably mentally deranged geologist walked into the chapel with a hammer in hand and, while screaming off the top of his lungs, "I am Jesus Christ", he started to break the statue. Fifteen blows later, Mary's arm was removed at the elbow, a chunk of her nose was gone, one of her eyelids was chipped, and the veil covering her hair was shattered. Onlookers were witnessing this sacrilege in complete dismay. Apparently, the statue was saved from being further damaged by an American sculptor from Missouri who happened to be around. The statue was eventually restored, but some pieces had been stolen by onlookers. Thankfully, they were later returned. However, Mary's nose had to be reconstructed using a piece of marble out of her back. As we are admiring this unique beauty, an invisible aura of sanctity, of piety is enfolding me.

San Pietro Basilica is truly magnificent. The largest church in the world is built on Vatican Hill, across the Tiber River (Trastevere) from the historic center of Rome. The location is highly symbolic: this was the site where Saint Peter died a martyr and where he was buried in 64 AD. St. Peter is considered the first Pope, so the papacy built the principal shrine of the Catholic Church here.

On our way to San Pietro Basilica, we passed Piazza San Pietro, a grandiose elliptical esplanade created by Gian Lorenzo Bernini in the 17th century. Massive colonnades symbolizing outstretched arms surround the square, and atop of each of them there are 140 statues of saints also built by Bernini and his assistants. From what I remember reading back in my home country, it took eleven years to build (1656-1667) using 44,000 cubic metres of travertine stone and hundreds of workers. The stone was transported from Tivoli (about 30 km east of Rome) by land or dragged along the banks of the Trastevere River by horses and buffaloes. As a curiosity, the colonnade marks the border between Italy and the Vatican, the smallest fully independent nation-state in the world. A strip of travertine on the ground joins the two ends of the colonnade.

The Mass along with the festive celebration give this place a wonderful aura of holiness. The Mass in Saint Peter's is hugely impressive. People gathering here seem to be coming from different places—visitors, locals, tourists, all of them ready to enjoy and celebrate the birth of Christ. I have my camera ready, and as the Pope is on his way out, I manage to snap a couple of photos, over the heads of the onlookers standing in front of me (I'm glad I am quite tall, so stretching my arms up helps me with taking unobstructed pictures of the Pope). Once the mass is finished, the Pope makes his way towards the upper balcony. People are going outside; we are, too. The Pope's voice is being projected all over the square through huge speakers. It is amazing! We are really in Vatican City. We can see and hear the Pope saying "Merry Christmas" in over 30 languages. It is a glorious moment; it truly feels so holy. We receive his *benedizione* and we leave Vatican City in a state of elation. Unparalleled to anything.

Buon Natale! Merry Christmas!

I SHALL NOT FAIL

* * *

December 25, 1990

Dear Daddy,

It's my turn to write you a letter. Merry Christmas from all the three of us! Maybe Santa has received my last letter and he will make my special wish come true. So, hopefully, by spring we'll be together again, and maybe we'll celebrate Easter together.

Last night we had guests. A group of teenagers came to help us decorate a Christmas tree, and we all sang carols in different languages, but none in Romanian. Mom met one of the girls, also called Maria, and they talked in English a lot.

This morning Mom took us to the Vatican Square and to San Pietro Basilica. In fact, we woke up at 6 am (actually, Marianna woke us up), but it was a good thing because we went to the Vatican to participate to the Christmas Mass officiated by the Holy Pope himself. There were thousands and thousands of people in the Vatican Square, but because we got there very early, we managed to find good spots just by the entrance, so we got to see the Pope from very, very close: just one metre distance. Then the Pope went to his balcony and he gave the people gathered in the square the "benedizione." And then he did something very cool: he wished us all Merry Christmas in 30 languages. Mom took pictures of him from our own spot. It was so neat, Dad. Vatican is so beautiful and so big…

For the rest, the convent is certainly not a hotel, but I usually have fun. Sometimes I help the nuns, but Amanda helps in the kitchen or with laundry, just like Mom, and one of these days I also discovered the basement of the convent. Dad, there are so many toys, and clothes, and shoes that people who don't need them just donate them to the church. I received a Barbie, too. She's so pretty… My first Barbie doll ever! Maybe Santa IS listening to my wishes. One of them came true: I got oranges, lots of them, and I eat oranges every day.

I miss you, Daddy. Write back please.

*Love,
Evelyn*

* * *

"Signora, you have visitors." Visitors? Who can visit us here? We don't know anybody. This is strange. The nun tells me to meet our visitors in the refectory. We walk out of our room. Surprise!

Maria is back. There's a lady with her.

"Ciao, Maria. I'd like to introduce you to my mother. Mom, this is Maria, and these are her daughters, Amanda and Evelyn."

"It's a pleasure to meet you." I am humbled as this encounter surprises me almost to speechlessness. Giovanna speaks some English but not much. We communicate in both languages, alternating between English and Italian. It doesn't take long until I found the actual reason of their visit.

"Signora Maria, we would like to invite you and your daughters to our place to spend New Year's Eve with our family, unless you have other plans." Plans? We have none. Our life in the convent is dull, to say the least. Spending New Year's Eve with an Italian family? This is really special.

"Yes, I'm honoured. Thank you so much." Feelings of gratitude, of plenitude and astonishment are engulfing me.

"We will come to pick you up in the evening of the 31st, if that's okay with you." "Absolutely…Grazie, grazie mille." The girls are ecstatic. Their smiles stretch from one ear to the other!

"Also, if you don't mind, we have a little present for you. I hope you won't feel offended, but we would like to give you $200,000 lira (equivalent to $200 Canadian dollars). It is our pleasure to offer you this present from our entire family for Christmas."

I'm really amazed. Truly astounded. This is something I honestly did not expect. There seems to be a continuation of our Christmas present. Maria's visit and now Maria with her Mom…I say thank you again and again, thank you thousand times…We say goodbye. 'Somebody' up there loves us…

New Year's Eve brings back memories from our native land. Christmas has never been a public celebration, not an open one and not during my life in Romania. Rather a family gathering, since going to the church was not encouraged. Sometimes it was even prohibited. In fact, 14 years ago when Greg and I got married, we had to have our religious ceremony in a different city for fear of persecutions …However, New Year was always a celebratory moment. Ballroom parties were the norm and, given Greg's being an officer, we were always celebrating New Year's in a festive way. Nice meals, elegant outfits—always dressed up to the nines—and a lot of dancing. Waltzing around the dance floor of the Military Centre was the highlight of the night. For a whole night I was indeed on cloud 9! The Viennese waltz has always been my favourite and every single time we were on the dance floor, other couples were making room to give us the space we needed to enjoy all the swirling and twirling and spinning. It seems like a long time ago. Who knows if I ever get to have the occasion to dance a Viennese waltz again?

I'm glad Evelyn has modernized my wardrobe with all the fashionable garments she has brought from the basement of the convent. I have two pairs of high winter boots on high stiletto heels that I brought with me from Romania. A nice long skirt and a sparkling top will match the rest. The girls have chosen some pretty clothes for this special occasion. By 6 pm Maria and Giovanna are outside the convent ready to pick us up.

Wait! What's this? None of the ladies is dressed up. Maybe they'll do this after they take us to their home. I felt embarrassed right away, although they did their best to make us feel comfortable. I feel like I did a *brutta figura*. A "faux-pas." Totally out of place, out of sync.

We have been introduced to Sr. Alberto Ranieri, as well as to Maria's siblings—Giulia, Maria's younger sister, and Andrea, their brother. Everybody made us welcome and included. Dinner was amazing although unpretentious. Italian style, family cooking. Lentils with fresh pork sausage, with a creamy, mild flavour. It's called *Cotechino con lentiche* and it seems to be an Italian New Years' Eve tradition. Delicious. The entertainment part consisted of singing mainly Christmas carols. We all joined in. My part of the entertainment consisted of showing slides. The family had a slide projector and a screen, so all the slides I brought with me from Romania were projected on the large screen. For the first time I was able to show how beautiful my home country was. All the trips we have taken throughout the past years had been stored as memorable moments on those beautiful slides. I could finally show them how proud I was of my country of origin. It was just the communist regime that had cast a dark shadow over the beauty of the nature and the historical sites Romania had to offer.

We rang in the New Year with songs and cheers and a glass of champagne. After all the hugs and kisses and good wishes for the New Year, Alberto suggested we call Greg in Canada, if we wanted. Wow! If we wanted? Of course! This was going to be quite a present for Greg. Obviously, my heart and my mind were with him, wondering how he was going to spend this special night away from us.

"Hi, Greg!" He's definitely taken by surprise. He sounds happy to hear me and emotional at the same time. Obviously, my call is coming out of the blue. It is midnight here in Italy, but he is eight hours behind us, so it is only 4 pm in his part of the world.

"How are you? Are you celebrating New Year's Eve in any way?" His shaky and soft voice, halting over words denotes an utter disbelief.

"We are doing very well; we have been invited to spend this special night with an Italian family."

"Did you just meet them? You are with them right now?" Indeed, it seems unreal and I have to admit that it really is a miracle.

"Did you not receive our letters? We met this family about a week ago through one of their daughters who came to the convent. You will find all the details in our letters."

"Oh, I'm so happy for you. Nothing special is happening here. My aunt and uncle will probably go to bed before midnight…I expect a dull ringing into the New Year." Greg's voice slips into sadness.

My heart is sinking, too. I wish I could lift up his spirits, but I have to keep the conversation short. I don't know how much an international phone call like this would cost this family.

"I miss you…" Greg's voice is cracking with extreme sorrow. I can tell that he is holding back some tears. All I can do is to utter some words of comfort.

"I'm sure the New Year is going to bring us some good news. If you can just hold on for a little while…I don't know what January is going to bring to us, but one way or another, there will be a solution. You want to talk to the girls?"

"Definitely." I pass the phone to the girls as I make a gesture of keep-it-short. I cannot take advantage of this family's kindness. The girls' talk is brief, but hearing their voices is unquestionably lifting their Dad's mood on a night like this.

To say that our celebration continued would be an overstatement. Our moods have changed. Greg is in a different situation from ours. Yes, we do live in a convent in totally precarious conditions, and he is with his remote family in Canada, but he's alone while I have our girls with me.

Buon Anno! Happy New Year! Wishes of happiness left and right, hugs and kisses, all the best! Ranieri's family is offering us to sleep at their place. How wonderful and how caring. Of course, Pietro would not have opened the door to the convent for us at this time of the night!

1991 started on the right foot. January 1st—we continued to enjoy the festivity at Ranieri's place with their family during a nice breakfast, with panettone and espresso! Ah, espresso…

We're just about ready to leave. Giovanna will give us a ride back to the convent "Signora Maria, I understand you are looking for a job. I don't want you to feel insulted, but if you're willing to do some housework, some cleaning and tidying up at our place twice a week, I would like to offer you the possibility to earn some money." Giovanna seems to be almost embarrassed while she's making this proposal. She knows about my teaching career back in Romania, about all my degrees all the way up to the doctoral degree, and she doesn't feel at ease.

"I'd love to. I am absolutely happy to work, so I can make a living and provide for the girls."

"Perfect. It would be twice a week, Tuesday and Saturday for four hours each day and we will pay you 10,000 lira per hour."

Wow! That's $40 a day, $80 per week to start with! Of course I accept.

"Would it be possible I start mid-January though? I need to enroll the girls in schools and for now I need a little flexibility." I have located the schools, basically the buildings, but Christmas break is a holiday for everybody. Talking with the principals is my first and utmost priority as soon as the holidays are over.

"Definitely. Here is our phone number. You can give us a call as soon as you know about your availability."

It seems almost unreal what Christmas has brought to us. First, we met Maria; then Maria brought along her mother. New Year introduced us to their entire family, and now I have a job, too. Everything in one week. This is a true miracle. God truly works in mysterious ways!

*December 20, 1990—first days in the convent.
Happy to have a roof over our heads.*

I SHALL NOT FAIL

December 25, 1990—first Christmas in Vatican. Pope John Paul II is on His way out of St. Peter's Basilica to give His benediction to the people gathered in the Vatican Square.

7
WE'RE GOING TO SCHOOL!

Carogna! Stronza! Figlia di puttana!!! Marianna's morning routine started on a bad note! I have no idea what she's saying, but she sounds so mad. She must have not slept well last night, or maybe she woke up on the wrong side of the bed. The Italian - Romanian dictionary that I brought with us should help, but judging by how irate Marianna sounds, those words didn't even make it into my basic dictionary.

"Mom, she's swearing." Amanda seems to know already more Italian expletives than I do. They're both laughing at me. "You won't find these words in your dictionary…" Yes, I was assuming so…

Well, Marianna's mood will not spoil our day! Christmas holidays are over, school has started today, so we are going to visit the schools and I'll try to enroll the girls. The morning convent routine, breakfast included, is a starting point. Panettone and hot chocolate—nothing better to start the day. Dishes aside, table clean, and we're all dressed up, ready to leave. Pietro opens the door and off we go. Pass by Circus Maximus on the left and then Colosseum, keep walking across Via Labicana and here is Ruggiero Bonghi School in Via Guicciardini. I take a deep breath and walk in. In my mind I already rehearsed a scenario. Now I'll see if it works.

"Buon giorno."

"Buon giorno, Signora. What can we do for you?"

"I would like to talk to the principal, if it is possible."

"Please have a seat; she'll see you in a few minutes." Wow, that was easy.

A nice lady, professionally dressed in black, approaches us a few minutes later. The conversation that followed gave me the perspective of how warm-hearted, kind and caring Italian people are. Although I made clear that we were immigrants waiting for a clear status to be granted to us along with the papers, the principal accepted Evelyn in grade five on the spot! She'll be in school six days a week. Monday to Friday, 9 am to 4 pm, and Saturday from 9 am to 1 pm. Lunch is provided by the school and even a *grembiule* will be fitted for Evelyn. Apparently, the kids have to wear this little apron (*grembiule*) at school to prevent staining their clothes. And just like that she is taken to her class by one of her teachers who had just joined us. Absolutely amazing! Totally unexpected…A few signatures later, papers filled out, and Evelyn is a student in the fifth grade at Ruggiero Bonghi School!

This event created a perfect momentum for us, and now Amanda's school enrollment is next. A couple of blocks around, in Via Ariosto, here is the secondary school for Amanda, Silvio Pellico. The previous rehearsed conversation had led to a positive outcome. I was hoping for the same. Not so easy and not so fast! The principal was hard to be convinced of Amanda's capabilities and strengths. It's true, her knowledge of Italian language is based on what she has absorbed and managed to learn during the past three weeks and yes, the students are very advanced, also given that Italian is their mother tongue. The principal suggests I should enroll Amanda in grade six. That would be one year behind. No way! NO WAY!! I know Amanda will pick up everything at amazing speed. I know what a fast learner she is. I am a truly believer in full immersion (my study during the two years of preparation for my doctorate degree, my research work back in Romania have provided me with a clear understanding about how easily children learn a language once they are fully and truly immersed). I am not going to give up.

"Signora Preside, please give her a chance." My voice is altered by the tears I am trying to stifle. Amanda has just turned 13 a month ago. I do not want her in grade six.

"Signora Preside, she will catch up. Please accept her. If anything, she would fail at the end of the school year." In fact, the school year is organized in three three-month terms (trimesters), the fourth one being the summer vacation. So, this is the second trimester. Two thirds of the school year still left.

Half an hour later we scored! The principal's heart melted, and she eventually gave us the approval. All I was required was to provide documents from Romania to prove that Amanda had indeed been a grade seven student when we left, and evidence of certain vaccinations. Also, we needed to submit proof showing that we had at least a permit of stay in Italy.

Two difficult objectives to reach. Both dealing with authorities, in Romania and Italy. How can we get our permit of stay in the first week of January when our appointment is scheduled for the end of February? Maybe Gino would have a suggestion. We stopped seeing him after we got accepted in the convent. We had an excuse! Today though I need his advice. Of course, Gino is at his usual location at the railway station.

"Buon giorno, Signor' Gino."

"Ciao, ragazze! How are you! Just the two of you?"

"Yes, my other daughter is enrolled in school already."

"Benissimo! That was fast. What can I do for you today?"

"Well, we seem to have hit a little bit of a dead end. At least for now. Maybe you have an idea." I'm telling him about our need to obtain a permit of stay as soon as possible.

"Well, you can go to *Questura* tomorrow as early as possible, as you already know, and try to obtain the document tomorrow, if you can find an official to talk with. Tell him why you need the documents and maybe you'll get them."

"Is that easy?"

"I'm not saying it's easy. I'm saying it's worth trying and you might succeed."

I "might" succeed? I will have to succeed! Although Gino's suggestion has a disconcerting feeling of uncertainty, I have only one choice: try and hope for the best. No need to continue engaging in a more elaborate discussion. Gino is always in the mood of talking, but we have better things to do. In fact, I have an answer to my question and that will do it for now. I need to concoct a plan so I can obtain the permit of stay as soon as possible.

At 4 pm Amanda and I go to Evelyn's school to pick her up. I can still consider this as being a successful day. I stop to talk to Evelyn's teachers so I can excuse her for tomorrow. We need to go to the Police station to obtain documents. No problem.

"So, how was school, Evelyn?"

"It was amazing, Mom. I have played with the other kids, we have two teachers, and everybody seems so cheerful and I feel so included. I loved the whole day. The teachers are so nice. They were continuously trying to make sure I was understanding everything."

"Did you eat anything?"

"Yes, we had lunch. They gave all the kids a big sandwich and some fruit."

"Do you have homework?"

"Not yet, but I was told that I would soon. We also need some notebooks and pencils and other type of stationery."

"What exact stationery do you need?"

"Crayons. Pencil crayons. Washable markers. Erasers. Notebooks. Lined paper. A couple of glue sticks." Evelyn is giving me a complete list of supplies that she needs for school. That is an easy task.

I need to call my mother in Romania. She will have to get some documents for Amanda to prove that she was a grade seven student when we left Romania. Also proof of the girls' vaccinations—polio, chickenpox, measles, mumps and whooping cough, and I don't know what else.

"Where are we going now"?

"In Via Dandolo to eat. The convent is not open yet until 6 pm."

Located in the Trastevere District, the St. Egidio soup kitchen (*mensa*) is a space of welcome and inclusion, a sweet and warm expression of the universal family where the poor people are served at the tables by numerous volunteers including seminarians, priests, students, teachers, men and women alike. Not only are they providing food for poor people, but the atmosphere is one of respect and hospitality.

On our way we stop to make a phone call to my mother in Romania. All of a sudden I feel overwhelmed. Supplies for Evelyn. Documents for Amanda. Our permit of stay that needs to be issued as soon as possible. Trying to organize my agenda on the go doesn't leave much time for conversation with the girls. They know that when I am not talkative, it's better to not interfere. My mind is overloaded.

"Hi, Mom." I'm rushing to explain briefly to her the reason of my calling. My mother's reaction to my voice gives me a feeling of reassurance. I need my mother, too! She sounds so happy to hear me. I cannot speak for too long because it's quite expensive. I'm telling her what we need her to help us with: documents from the girls' schools and proof of vaccinations. I don't need to explain. My mother is a go-getter! She is a woman of few words, and 'action' is her name! Never a procrastinator, always ready to take life by the horns! I pass the phone to the girls to say hello to her and exchange a few words. I knew this was going to make her day, their day! Mine as well.

Back to the convent, the evening rosary ends our day, and the nuns go around turning the lights off at 8 pm. It's early, but we have no choice at this point. I don't even care whether or not Marianna is going to finish the evening prayer with her usual swearing. I must admit, I am pretty tired.

Good night!

8

"MAMMA, HO FAME!"

Knowing how big the crowds gathering in front of the police station are, at least an hour before they even open, we leave the convent at 7 am. It's early, it's dark, and it's cold. Still, we have to walk the almost two km. Three tickets per day, for all the three of us is the equivalent of $2.50. I don't know what tomorrow is going to bring, so, until I have a steady, daily job, walking is the only option. The girls are not complaining. I am truly fortunate; we are in all this together.

Half an hour later, we arrive. Not many people yet. This is good, but what the day is going to bring on is very uncertain. They open at 9 am. Ninety minutes of waiting outside…

This reminds me of the late 80's when food had become scarce in Romania and everything was rationalized. We could get two litres of milk per day, but the milk supply was never enough. There were times when I was waking up at 3 am and I was going to the store and secure my spot in line, placing two empty bottles on the pavement, in front of the door, one set of bottles for each family, placed in sequence, one behind another. People were making arrangements: who was going to watch over all the lined-up bottles and who was lucky enough to go to bed for a few more hours and come back when the store was going to open. We were taking turns. It was extremely tough. Disgusting. Why? Because our brilliant communist leader, Ceausescu, had vowed to pay all the debts the country owed, mainly to the Soviet Union, by starving his own people while he and his witch of a wife were living lavishly. People were extremely unhappy, but we were all living in fear. Fear of the Secret Police, the "Securitate" agents who could have been impersonated by anyone. We could not have open discussions on any political topics with anybody, or the next day we would have run the risk of "disappearing." One evening, as I recall, I was coming home with another colleague of mine. The 30-minute walk was an opportunity to exchange with other people some words and feelings of dissatisfaction. However, never with more than one person at a time! Talking with just one individual gave us some confidence that the beans would not be spilled. The fear was, however, insurmountable.

"I am fed up! I hope that one day we will be revenged. We cannot take it anymore. How is it possible to not being able to put bread on the table? To be afraid to speak openly or choose to not speak at all out of fear! To not have enough heat in our homes! Shortage of electricity! Filling the gas tank of our cars just once a month. Hot water in our apartments a few times a week, mainly in the evening, and only for two hours. I am disgusted!!" My voice is picking up. The volume gets higher and higher. I am on the brink of collapsing. My entire family is, and so many more like us.

"Shush…Don't say anything. I don't want to hear this…"

Yes, my colleague was not even willing to hear. She knew what the repercussions could have been, but that was exactly why I was sharing my feelings only with her, without being concerned of anybody's overhearing us, secretly listening in. I needed to vent. Still, the fear of "disappearing", of being apprehended by the secret police (the "Securitate" agents), being taken to the police headquarters, interrogated, physical harm inflicted, and not being able to come back to my family, to my children—all that fear was muffling us. We had been reduced to silence. For how long? The discontent of the people had almost reached a boiling point…and then the communism fell apart!

* * *

The doors to the Police station open a few minutes after 9. It's almost typically Italian to not be punctual…It doesn't matter. We are inside and it's warm. Luckily, we get three chairs to sit on. I truly don't know how to go about this. I need to approach an officer, and what am I going to tell him or her? And how? I'm watching them going left and right, and I am trying to read their faces in an attempt to figure out which one is more approachable. There are hundreds of people in the large room, some sitting, some standing, all waiting for their numbers to be called. All of them with a valid reason to visit the police headquarters. Refugees, asylum seekers who had fled their countries for fear of persecution and were consequently asking for protection in Italy, some of them stateless, as well, migrants, maybe illegal immigrants, too. The room was already full.

Today we are number 12. At least the wait is not going to be as long as it was the first time. It shouldn't. I keep my hopes up. I have to. I make my first move.

"Buon giorno, signore." He mumbles something in response, but I can't get discouraged. "I have a special request, if you don't mind. We have applied for a permit of stay three weeks ago and we have been scheduled to obtain it at the end of February. However, I need to enroll my daughters in school, and I need documents to prove that we have a status in Italy, that we are here legally." Did I approach the wrong person? He looked rather "friendly", but they do have a difficult job here.

"Signora, all these people here are applying for similar documents. They all need to submit their applications."

"I understand, but we came here earlier, and we have a number, too." I don't know what else to say.

"Have a seat, please, and wait." And just like that I'm being dismissed. It's not going to be easy, this is sure. Everybody is in a state of some sort of emergency. We all need documents, so why should I get a "special status"? I have been scheduled for next month, we have legal documents, albeit temporary, but others do not. Unfortunately, I cannot give up. Survival prevails. It's about my children.

It doesn't take long until our number is called. I approach the desk and I repeat the same story, this time to another officer. I am told to wait, again. Wait…for how long? It was our number, our turn! Why wait longer? Why can they not deal with our request? I don't seem to have a choice, but sit again and wait…At least, if we wait, will we get what we need today?

Two more hours later and nothing is moving. Nobody is calling us. I feel powerless, lost. I have a couple of oranges with me and two bananas. We cannot leave this place. The girls are hungry. Oranges will do for now.

Lunch break. The officers are disappearing, taking turns, who's leaving and who's staying…Just two of them left to assist the crowd behind me. I'm determined to ask another officer if there are any developments in our case. I am told to wait and sit…Again. I feel defeated. Overwhelmed. There seems to be no end to this nightmarish situation. Every day is presenting us with something unexpected, unpleasantly disturbing.

Three pm. The bananas are gone. The girls are losing their patience. Evelyn is completely restless. Sometimes she goes outside, just to get some fresh air.

My thoughts are going back to Romania and the fall of the communist regime. I don't know why…Maybe because I need to keep my mind busy with something? Or maybe since the reason we are here today is because of everything that happened after December 1989, just a year ago, when all our hopes had been crushed…I am thinking about the "Revolution" that toppled Ceausescu's government…

I continue to believe that the 1989 "Revolution" never really existed per se; in fact, to my knowledge and understanding, it had been a coup, secretly planned and well mastered behind the scenes by high-ranking communists, which had just happened to fall in the organizers' lap at the right moment. It was also a momentum that followed the spark which had ignited in Germany, and Poland, and Czechoslovakia, and Hungary…travelling east into Romania. The European political movement at the end of the eighties was the right moment for all the communist countries on the old continent to get rid of a political system that had been imposed on them through unfortunate fate games. For almost half a century the Romanian people had been destined to endure the "Red Plague," inflicted by the Soviet Union and the so-called "Iron Curtain" acting as a barrier between the Russian country and the rest of Europe, and unwillingly accepted. The fear of harsh repercussions never ceased to loom. Nevertheless, at least 200,000 people had lost their lives as a result of the communist regime imported from the East between 1948 and 1964 alone.

I remember when the Berlin Wall was opened on November 9, 1989 after masses of people clambered up on the barrier and jubilantly chipped away at its concrete with pickaxes, shovels, and their bare hands. It was a unique political movement, one to relish. Astoundingly, nonviolent citizens' protesting helped topple Soviet restrictions. Sheer ecstasy for an entire nation. High hopes for all the communist countries. Yet, we couldn't openly share the elation of the German people who had taken an active part in making history. The two hours of TV each day that we were allotted and allowed through "thoughtful" consideration and care of the Ceausescu regime said nothing about the memorable historic moment. The free flow of information had been banned by the government authorities. Our only link with the "outer" world was through the clandestine radio station, Radio Free Europe, that was broadcast from somewhere in Germany. We were trying to listen and make sense of the news, in spite of hearing only bits and pieces of information, short-circuited by the communist censorship. Something was going on in the world, but we were afraid to make any open comments.

Towards the end of November a peaceful student demonstration in Prague was suppressed by the police followed by a series of popular demonstrations from November 19th to late December. Barbed wire and other obstructions were removed from the borders with West Germany and Austria in early December. The Velvet Revolution was in full swing in Czechoslovakia. Was Romania going to be next?

There was a certain political fever, a kind of unprecedented unrest that was looming around entire Eastern Europe. We were hoping that the revolt sparks would catch fire in Romania, as well. Ears glued to the radio, we were listening to the Radio Free Europe broadcast, in spite of the late hours. There was news about one of Romania's few dissidents, László Tőkés, a pastor in the Hungarian Reformed Church, who had dared use his pulpit in the city of Timisoara to condemn the communist regime and who had been evicted from his church. We learned that the Hungarian parishioners joined by ethnic Romanians surrounded the church to prevent his removal.

By mid-December the entire city of Timisoara in Western Romania, where, for the first time, crowds of people shouted "freedom," was on strike and the protesters tried to outwit tanks and armoured vehicles. The word spread like a shock wave across the country, encouraging more people to go out onto the streets to protest against the communist regime. Although we could hear on the radio the frequent slogan, "Without Violence!" we learned however that over 60 people had been already killed in Timisoara alone and more than 700 had been arrested. Altogether, more than 1,000 people died on the streets in Timisoara, Bucharest and other cities of Romania in those days. However, nobody dared to tell Ceausescu how serious the Timisoara rioting was, so he had no worries about calling a counter-demonstration in Bucharest on the 21st of December. He came out on the balcony of the "People's House" in Bucharest to deliver a speech. The "Securitate" forces bussed in factory workers to make the turnout seem bigger, but in the anonymity of the crowd, some people started booing. Ceausescu froze in mid-speech, his mouth open: he had never been heckled before.

This was a broadcast that was "allowed" on our TV stations. Our leader was talking, so we were supposed to listen to our leader. I am sure everybody watching that live television broadcast saw his sudden vulnerability. It was about time.

That night the Revolution broke out in earnest. The next morning, December 22nd, Ceausescu and his wife Elena clambered into a helicopter just as the crowd was breaking into his headquarters, and he headed north. But the pilot soon landed, claiming he had run out of fuel. Really!! The Ceausescus' bodyguards melted away. Both Nicolae Ceausescu and his wife got off the helicopter and decided to try the highway. Elena, tougher than her husband, pulled out a gun and hijacked a passing car. In the end, though, they were captured. This was history that was happening in our own country, under our eyes. The usually censored Radio Free Europe radio station started to broadcast in clearer voices.

Watching and hearing all these events rolling out in our own country was unprecedented. Shivers of jubilation were making me shudder. Finally! The Romanian people dared do something about their fate. Or so we hoped…

* * *

It is almost 5 pm. We've been here for the past 10 hours, almost. I have no food left for the girls, and we are all starving. Waiting for so long was totally unexpected. In spite of having approached a couple of officials a few more times, nothing worked. Still, I cannot give up. Amanda needs documents to be properly enrolled in school. I am determined to not leave this place without a resolution.

Evelyn has completely lost her patience. It's amazing it lasted this long! She's wandering about the large room where some people have left but many more are still here, everybody waiting for papers.

This is weird! What is Evelyn doing behind the officials' desks? She decided to start conversations with some of them! Nobody seems to be bothered…Interesting. I am not going to intervene. Worse come to worst, she will be disciplined somehow, and maybe sent to sit down next to us. One officer is saying something to her. She looks at me, she gestures something, but then she keeps talking to him. There is some movement at that desk, but I can't quite see what is going on from where I am sitting. What is that? I hear a girl's giggling voice, like a bird chirping. It's Evelyn speaking on the microphone!!!

"Mamma, ho fame!" My heart is melting. She is hungry. I know she is… but she is saying that out loud, and in Italian?! And the officer has given her permission to use his microphone? I am speechless. Or ashamed. Or relieved. Maybe this is going to help…

Twenty minutes later I hear my name. I am approaching the main desk in sheer disbelief, but with a certain apprehension. This is the police headquarters! Not a stage for a comedian. They might as well kick us out and refuse our documents altogether.

"Signora, your documents are ready. Good luck!"

Our famous *permesso di soggiorno* that we hoped to obtain all day, waiting more and more impatiently at the *Questura,* totally famished and exhausted, has been finally issued and it was being handed to us.

"Grazie." I am sure Evelyn's "intervention" helped. Italians do have big hearts…

We are out. All of us hungry, but the fresh air feels good. Success!

9

NEVER AGAIN!

January 25th, 1991

Dear Greg,

Your letters are worrying me. From what you're saying nothing seems to be moving in Canada. What can I say? Wait until March when you're scheduled to appear in front of the Immigration and Refugee Board, or whatever it's called, and present your case. You have a strong story and enough material to explain why you left Romania and what your reasons are to ask for political asylum. I don't think I need to remind you of anything. We have all gone through tough times and you have definitely suffered more than I did. Remember when you were a student at the Military Academy and you stood up against the communist policies, how they reprimanded you, lowering your rank? And later on, how they fired you from your military position because you dared to continue being a dissident? And then all throughout the past years you suffered because of not wanting to become a member of the Communist Party, just as I didn't either? Yes, the communist regime was toppled last year, but when we showed our right-wing political affiliations, and became members of the conservative party in 1989-1990, things did not improve, and we became dissidents again. You have to show that nothing much has changed in Romania. In spite of the so-called freedom we achieved, there is still chaos, and voicing our political beliefs cannot be done without still being fearful. Remember all the reasons we decided to leave Romania for! You know it was not for economic reasons. We had a solid material situation, and we would have continued to do well provided that we would have complied with some obscure forces and their demands. I trust that you will be successful. Maybe that Romanian family who immigrated to Canada a few years ago and whom you recently befriended might be able to help you. From what you're telling me, they seem to be nice people.

I know you're missing us. We miss you, too. We will be together soon. As for us here, for the time being, we are just following our regular routine: taking the girls to school one at a time, dropping them off, going to work etc. I found two more families that I help with house cleaning, so I'm working every day. At 1 pm I pick Amanda up, we go to a food bank/soup kitchen to eat lunch, at 4 pm we pick Evelyn up, and then the evening schedule follows as usual. The hardest part is Amanda's homework. She has started Dante Alighieri and his famous "Divina Commedia." Can you believe it? Amanda's enrolled in an Italian secondary school, fully immersed, studying a 13th century poet. Not only is Italian language new to her and to all of us, but that kind of language is so different from today's Italian. The only dictionary I have is not helping much. She also studies mathematics, geography, history etc. On top of this, at 8 pm, the nuns go around the convent and turn the lights off. Everybody is supposed to go to bed. Sure! Amanda has homework and plenty of it! The nuns seem to have a hard time accepting that. So, we do homework in the hallway, using a flashlight! Well, it is what it is.

What worries me the most now is this Gulf War that just started, and I don't know what to make of it. I don't know if the Italian media is making too much drama out of it, or is this really going to be the end of the world? Well, we'll see what happens next. At least, you have a heated place where you live with your relatives in Canada, while our convent has no heat whatsoever. The mosaic floors and the thick brick humid walls are not helping at all. When Amanda does her homework, her hands are quite often frozen. Sometimes she has to wear gloves while sitting at the table and writing.

Please don't feel guilty for anything! Going back to Romania is not an option! I understand you're desperate but remember why we left. Returning to our home country is ruled out. We will manage and will eventually be successful. Please excuse the girls from not writing to you. Amanda has a lot of homework and Evelyn is at school all day.

Stay strong!

We are in this together!

Love you.

    I feel discouraged and emotionally drained. The Gulf War is really scaring me. I don't know much about it. No TV, no radio. I can't afford to buy newspapers and I'm reading the news while I am on a tramway, on my way to work, and since most of the time I'm standing, I surreptitiously read the news on the newspapers of the people who are sitting because it's easy to read over their shoulders. Besides, graffiti everywhere make a big issue of this war. All I know is that, apparently, at this point in time, this operation is called Desert Storm and it is in its combat phase, deriving from a war waged by coalition forces from 35 nations led by the United States against Iraq, in response to Iraq's invasion and annexation of

Kuwait, basically arising from oil pricing and production disputes. Still, I don't have enough details. I can't put two and two together.

* * *

"Signora, what are you doing here?" Glancing up, guilty looking and all, I manage to mutter one single word: "*Compiti*."

"*Compiti?*"

"Yes, we are doing homework."

Amanda has no place to go after she finishes her school days at 1 pm every day. We tried everything. We have a window of three hours between the time her school day is over until 4 pm when I pick Evelyn up, and that is a good time for her to do homework. But where? We tried everything. We went to churches. Santa Maria Maggiore is one of our favourites. Sitting in pews, but still cold. Dark too, most of the times. We also tried the public library, but we needed a pass, and we couldn't get any. *Questura*. The Police Station was worth trying for a few times, or as long as we could go inside and sit "unnoticed" or just ignored. There was a table in a corner and a few chairs close to the main entrance where people were sitting while they were filling out their questionnaires and their paper forms. It was warm and we hoped to get unobserved…it seemed to work, but only for a couple of days. Now what? The officer didn't ask us to leave; judging by the look on his face, he seemed amused. I know Italians have a great sense of humour. I bet nobody has ever come to the police headquarters to do their…homework! I feel embarrassed, but as long as we're not kicked out, we'll stay. At least today. I can use this time to write a letter to my parents.

> *Hello, my dear parents,*
>
> *Thank you so much for the documents that you sent us, as well as for the package with all the school supplies and also the newspaper clippings. We can definitely use them to make our case when we have our interview for the political asylum. It's better to send everything to the post office. That way it's certain we will receive everything. The convent is not that safe in this respect.*

Nothing much is going on here. Our days are falling into a routine. Taking the girls to school, my work, coming back, homework for girls etc. Same schedule almost every day.

I am not going to tell my parents about the crude reality of our living conditions. They're worrying too much anyways. Mom writes to me long letters almost every day. Eight pages or more. All sorts of details. Political. Family-related. Friends asking about us and all agreeing that our leaving Romania was the best thing to do under the present circumstances. My Mom is also trying to lift our spirits up while they are truly devastated. How can she do that? She is also concerned about Greg's state of mind. I know, I am, too. He seems to be at the end of his rope. Depression. Panic attacks. Hopelessness. Despair. All I can do is to write him letters, every day or every other day. Trying to encourage him and keep his spirits up. I am mentally exhausted.

My mind gets a break from the daily emotional trauma only when I go to work. Two of the ladies whose houses I clean four times a week engage me in conversations. This is good exercise for me to keep practicing speaking Italian and improving it. The best moment I spend in their homes is when I get to dust their huge bookcases with hundreds and hundreds of books. Something very usual in most European houses. I miss all those books that I left behind…. Hundreds of them. Mostly Romanian, but also world literature books in different languages. I still took quite a few with me. Whether I am ever going to read them or not, that's a different story. For now, I am happy to keep dusting each shelf and read the titles of each book.

I'm constantly learning. Today I discovered a new plant that one of the ladies had on her balcony. A plant from the citrus family, judging by its leaves and fruit. They look like little, tiny oranges, the size of olives.

"What are these?" Kumquats, I'm told. I've never heard of them. I tried one, skin and all. It tasted good.

My work is allowing me to earn some cash, so, Mom, you mentioned in one of your letters that you would like to send us money. NO! I get paid every day. By the end of my four hours of work, I get paid 40,000 lira which equals

$40. With my first paycheck I decided to buy myself a small present, so I got a $10 guidebook about Rome. Now I can get more information about everything we see around us, every day. That was the only "luxury" I decided to buy for myself. It may sound cheap, selfish even, but I need to save everything. All the money goes in my waist pouch, on me all the time, under my garments. There are pick pocketers everywhere. On tramways, on buses, on the metro, in crowded places, shopping centers, tourist sites. They have some tricks and lots of people are falling victims. One day we'll need to move to a rental place, but everything is so expensive. So, Mom, there is no reason to worry about us. We are doing just fine. Stay healthy, that's all that matters.

Love you.
Maria, Amanda and Evelyn

Today I am very tired. Walking back to the convent seems to be more exhausting than usual. We need to take a tram, but I have used all the tickets I bought last week. I'm determined to take a chance and see if we can ride a tram for a few stops for free. I know I feel like a thief myself. Karma kicked in…

"Signora, biglietti!" As luck would have it—or bad luck, for that matter—three transit officials boarded the tramway, each of them through one of the three doors. There is no way anybody can sneak out of the tram since all the exits are blocked. I'm caught. We are caught. What is going to happen next? Will they throw me in jail? I'm extremely scared.

* * *

My mind takes me back to Romania. About six years ago we were coming from a two-week vacation we had spent in a seaside resort. Greg could not come with us, so I took my kids with me, a friend of mine and her son, and we headed out to our beautiful sandy beaches on the Black Sea.

On our way driving back home, we passed by some beautiful sunflower fields. The kids were looking at the tempting helianthus flowers, all in full bloom, wondering if they could get some seeds. I stopped the car, I sneaked out and I surreptitiously tried to snitch one of those flower crowns, all full of seeds. I knew I was trespassing. It was not a private property, though. Everything was belonging to the government. Through collectivization, the state took people's properties and turned them all into public ones, run by governmental institutions. Stealing just one sunflower was not going to be the end of the world. However, before I even had the chance to detach that stunning yellow hat off the plant, two guards popped up from the field. How was it possible? How many of them could have been in that field? Were they employees paid by the government to keep an eye on those huge crops? Was that a real job? They rushed to immobilize me. I made several attempts to explain to them that my kids craved some sunflower seeds. To no avail. Sheer panic was taking over me. It was brutal. I was trying to smooth things out. Nothing seemed to work. Evelyn started to cry, "Sir, please don't kill my Mom, please!" They were threatening to take me away, arrest me. Twenty minutes later, which seemed like an eternity, they let me go. I got back in the car and we sped away. I was shattered to pieces. Hands trembling, feet uneasy on pedals, I took off. Extremely traumatic. Ah, communist Romania, living in fear, oppression everywhere, abuse of power…

* * *

Here we are today, in Rome, in a trespassing situation. I am definitely breaking the law. Two of the traffic officials invite us to get off the tram at the first stop. We descend. I am thrown in a panic again. Tears flowing on my cheeks, scared that I'll be imprisoned, leaving my children behind, all sorts of scenarios are flooding my mind in one single instant. However, preserving my equanimity undisturbed in dark hours of danger is paramount. Luckily, this is only a warning. It will serve me better.

NEVER AGAIN!

10

IT'S MAGIC!

The days are getting longer and warmer. It's almost mid-February but it feels like spring. Today is Sunday, our only day off. Why not explore Rome into more detail? We have covered quite a bit since we arrived here, but we can adventure further. After all this is Rome. ROMA. Undoubtedly one of the most romantic cities in the world, although there is nothing romantic for us. In general, the whole city, with its millenary history, its majestic monuments and its unique atmosphere has something romantic and distinctive. It represented the first great metropolis of humanity, the heart of one of the most important ancient civilizations, which influenced society, culture, language, literature, art, philosophy, religion, law and customs for many centuries. Capital of the First Republic and then of the Roman Empire, it extended its dominion over the whole Mediterranean basin and most of Europe. We'll be tourists today!

"Girls, what do you think about going for a walk on Via Appia Antica?" The girls shrug. They have no idea how far the Appian Way is. Neither do I. I know it'll be quite a walk—because we will walk—but how far we'll go, I'm not sure.

"Let's get dressed! It's a beautiful day, let's get out of here!"

A few slices of *panettone* and a hot chocolate later, all morning convent chores fulfilled, and we are out.

It's a warm day. February 10th. Spring-like weather. The parasol-shaped Mediterranean pine trees seem to curve upwards their emerald green branches, blessing and caressing the primaveral skies. Apparently, these pine trees, also called stone pines, with edible nuts, are typical to this zone.

We have also seen even a few palm trees, definitely not native to Italy. Street vendors here and there sell flowers, and the ones taking front stage are the yellow mimosas. I have never seen mimosas in real life. There're so many little bouquets of this delicate yellow bloom. Apparently, this is the traditional flower in Italy for Valentine's Day, coming up in four days. Valentine's Day? Never heard of it. Lovers' day. How sweet! A little mimosa bouquet and some chocolate seem to be the perfect combination of a symbolic gift. Beautiful. Greg is not here for this romantic celebration. I'm sure they have it in Canada, too, but where he is right now, in Saskatchewan, winter is in full swing. Will I ever have the chance of celebrating a real Valentine's Day? With yellow mimosas flowers? Oh, well…

"Girls, do you realize that these cobblestones we're walking on are 2,000 years old?"

"Yeah, Mom." My excitement is met with a certain ennui. Who can blame them? We have been walking for the past three hours. Still going. We passed Porta Capena, went down on Via delle Terme di Caracalla, passed by Porta San Sebastiano and here we are on the Appian Way. The famous catacombs: San Callisto and San Sebastiano on our right. We take a peek inside. I cannot afford to pay the entrance fee. I feel somewhat parsimonious, but this is still a bit of a luxury. Not yet. It is something we can live without for now. We can look around, from the outside. The guide I bought with my first paycheck allows me to learn more. I read out loud:

"In these catacombs (or rather tunnels), the early Christians buried their dead and, during the times of persecution, they held clandestine church services. Inside the catacombs there are tens of thousands of burial niches. Early Christians referred to each chamber as a *dormitorio;* they believed the bodies were merely sleeping, awaiting resurrection. In some of these the remains of early Christian art are still visible."

My excitement is met with a perfunctory attitude. The girls do not seem to show any interest. They are tired, I understand, but I am not giving up.

My final point is the tomb of Cecilia Metella that I hope we can reach. I'm trying to enlighten the girls. "Cecilia Metella was the daughter of a consul in 69 BC (Quintus Cecilius Metellus Creticus), and she was also the wife of a questor, son of famous Marcus Crassus who served under

Julius Caesar. The Tomb of Cecilia is one of the most well-known and well-preserved monuments along the Via Appia."

The girls continue to look annoyed. On our way back we stop in the Appia Antica Park, which is a popular Sunday lunch picnic site for Roman families. I have some food with me, and we can call it a picnic!

About five hours and 14 km later, we're back in Rome. It's time I reward the girls with a treat. After all, a lot of energy has been burnt and sugar is in low supply!

"Would you like a gelato, girls?"

"Yes," and their large smiles lighten up their sombre faces. A "gelateria" pops up right on our way, as if it was called for! The girls pick their selection. I can't see any price posted, but it cannot be more than maybe $3 apiece.

"Tre gelati per favore."

Three big cones and different flavours. Mine is mainly vanilla. It's my favourite. What? Did he say 30,000? $30?! I feel almost thunderstruck, maybe because I'm exhausted, but I cannot argue. I'm handing out the money. 30,000 lira! Three ice cream cones. I'm still perplexed, totally befuddled, and my feet refuse to move. As my mind is on pause, my mouth opens to say something to the vendor. He's gone! He disappears in the back of the little store. It's useless to wait. He's not coming out and I won't win this battle. Another lesson learned! Ask before you pay! It doesn't matter. It's less than my one-day paycheck. The girls deserve this. Walking all day and no complaints; they are worth it.

Time goes by. My interview for political asylum is coming up. My parents keep sending me newspaper clippings. The political situation is not getting any better in Romania. Lots of clashes, people are discontent, their requests are not met. The National Salvation Front, the new ruling party, composed mainly of former members of the second echelon of the Communist Party, immediately assumed control over the state institutions, including the main media outlets such as the national radio and television networks. They used their control of the media in order to launch attacks against their political opponents, newly created political parties that claimed to be successors to those existing before 1948.

At that time, massive protests erupted in downtown Bucharest as political rallies organized by the opposition parties during the presidential elections, with a small part of the protesters deciding to stand ground even after Ion Iliescu was re-elected with an overwhelming majority of 85%. Attempts by police to evacuate the remaining protesters resulted in attacks on state institutions, prompting Iliescu to appeal to the country's workers for help. Infiltrated and instigated by former Securitate agents, in the following days a large mass of workers, mainly miners, entered Bucharest and attacked and fought with anti-government protesters and gathered bystanders.

While other former ruling Communist parties in the Soviet bloc reconfigured themselves into social democratic or democratic socialist parties, the Romanian Communist Party melted away in the wake of the 1989 Revolution, never to return. However, a number of former communist politicians continued to remain prominent on Romania's political scene.

We have met a very nice family in Via Dandolo where we have our daily evening meals (should I call them dinners?). We talked about our political situation and our status in Italy. They've applied for political asylum, too. I'm told that, although I have a strong case, I still need to prepare it properly. Apparently, there is a nice Italian lady holding a certain position with the Ministry of Internal Affairs of Italy who sometimes gives advice to immigrants and assists them with making their cases. Why an Italian official would do something like this is beyond my understanding. It's worth trying though.

Ministry of Internal Affairs. *Ministero dell'Interno*. Right on! I've located it in Piazza del Viminale, close to the main railway station. How do I get to meet this woman? She's an employee and I don't know her. Where would I find her? How? It takes me a few days to come up with a plan. Will it work? The only choice is to try. For a whole week I'm walking up and down the street, early in the morning, before I go to my work. The building has five stories and hundreds of windows. Obviously, offices. A large staircase leads to the main entrance.

Girls in school, I can start doing my research. Watching employees going to work every morning. My eyes are on women. What are they wearing? How do they go to work? When? It's funny to observe their routine. Everybody comes to work before or around 9 am. Professionally dressed up, heels and all, the women walk in, mostly in groups of two or three or individually, but a few minutes later they come down the main entrance stairs and they all go out, somewhere. Ah, some of them haven't had their espresso yet! I get it! A few espressos later they are back to work.

The big day has arrived. I'm taking my chance! I have to find this lady! What if she has a day off? What if my plan fails? I refuse to take any more what-ifs! I'm on my way! Dressed up, black skirt and a nice grey blazer, black sheer pantyhose and decent high heels, a mini business folder under my arm, nicely coiffed and makeup on, poised and confident, I'm ready to approach the main entrance. A pair of eyeglasses (that I don't need, and I never wear) will make me look more professional, or so I hope. At least, the probable insecurity in my eyes may be hard to be easily identified. I am an "employee" and I'll play this card with aplomb! There's a guard on the right, as I walk in. I'm trying to blend in with a small group of women, so it looks as if we are going into the building together. I notice that they have just said "Ciao" to the guard and they keep walking towards their offices. How do I know where this lady's office is in this huge building? No idea! Action!

I'm in. Wow! I keep going. Right in front of me a double impressive staircase splits up in two, one to the left and the other one to the right. No clue where I'm supposed to go, but I'm taking the right staircase. I need to blend in. Once out of the guard's eyesight, I ask somebody where I can find Signora Falcone.

"Second door on the left." That was easy. I knock on the door. I hear a "Si" and I walk in. Three women sitting at their desks. How do I know which one is Ms. Falcone?

"I'd like to talk to Signora Falcone. Is she here today?"

"Yes," a voice coming from my right brings hope and relief to my heart. "What can I do for you?"

"I would like to talk with you for a few minutes, if you don't mind." Although we have never met, she seems to be so cooperative. Why? She's a tiny little lady, probably in her fifties, wearing sunglasses, very kind features. How can I explain why all these people are so helpful? The more I'm getting to know Italians, the more convinced I am of their kindness and compassion. She comes around her desk and we walk out in the hallway. How does she know that the conversation should rather be private?

"Signora Falcone, my name is Maria, and I am a Romanian refugee, scheduled to have an interview for political asylum in two weeks. I was told that you might be able to give me a few hints, some suggestions so I can make my case. I'm here in Italy with my two daughters, aged 11 and 13. Do you think you could give me some advice?"

"What are your main points to sustain your argument?"

I'm telling her about our life in Romania, our malaise and our suffering.

"Do you have documents to prove?"

"Not exactly. All I have are some newspaper clippings, showing the continuous state of unrest, the ongoing political turmoil."

"You have to write everything down. Put everything you are telling me on a piece of paper, obviously in Italian. The more details, the more solid your case. It would be helpful if you can bring this paper and give it to me, the sooner the better."

I promise her that I will have it in a couple of days. She wants to see me again.

I am truly amazed. Funny though, she is not even asking me how I managed to get in here. Well, I'm not asked, so I won't volunteer answers! Now I know the drill.

Two days later, I'm repeating the same scenario. Success! I'm an "employee," no doubt! I'm giving the paper to Ms. Falcone. She reads everything right on the spot, always in the hallway.

"It's good. When is your interview?"

"On February 28th."

"Your case looks axiomatic, so I don't think you need more evidence than this. It seems solid to me. Just answer the questions the best you can, the more details, the better. Make sure you explain all the hardships you had to endure during the communist regime, but also focus on the present situation. Explain why it is dangerous for you to go back to Romania, and take this paper with you. It's great that you can speak Italian and you don't need a translator. I'll also give you a guide with instructions regarding your request and the criteria and regulations you need to take into account, but I feel that you will be truly credible."

"Yes. Grazie mille." I am speechless in front of this wonderful woman and her willingness to help us. Why? How is this happening? Is it real? Am I dreaming? I'm on my way out. For whatever reason I feel some sort of protection, from above. I can't explain. It's magic.

11
THANK YOU, MOM!

Our dear girls,
We hope you don't mind that I write to you so often.
No, Mom, why would I mind? We'd like to hear from you. We are constantly thinking about you.
I wouldn't lie. We miss you dearly. We miss the girls and John is suffering the most. Life is totally different without them around, their playfulness…
I know we broke their hearts when we left. Their only grandchildren—my daughters and their only daughter, myself—we took the fate in our hands and we left…almost abandoning them.
We were thinking about applying to get visitors' visas to come to Italy to see you. Maybe this summer?
Well, Mom, we'd love that, too, but where would you stay? You don't even have money to buy plane tickets.
If nothing works, remember that you can always come back home. You can start all over again. At least here in Romania you live with people you know and who speak the same language.
Same language? Yes, Romanian, but is that all it takes? We may speak the same language, but that alone doesn't make for a decent life, unless honesty and rightfulness are the norm. No, we will not go back to Romania. NEVER!
It's unfortunate that you left your apartment. We could have bought it. The actual government allows people to buy the apartments they lived in before.

Yes, indeed, we truly abandoned that apartment. It's true we had obtained it from the government, rent-free. All we were ever paying for was water, electricity and gas. It was quite luxurious. Three bedrooms, two bathrooms, a large living room and kitchen, and two beautiful long balconies that we had turned into fancy patios. Everything on the fifth floor of a building in the downtown area where we were living. Greg and I had revamped it all. Hallway dressed in mahogany panels all the way to the fancy ceiling, expensive hardwood floors, tiles in the bathrooms and kitchen, lavish indeed. We had invested a lot of money and work in it. High-end furniture and Persian rugs. I guess we could have kept it before we left Romania. We could have bought it, or my parents could have purchased it for a modest sum of money. We could have, but we didn't. We didn't want to own anything in Romania. We also sold our car. No personal possessions left behind. I knew that once we had something to come back to, that might have been an option. No going back! We had only one direction: ahead!

Do you have warm clothes? Do you have good food? Where do you eat? How is the girls' school going? Do you have chocolate, coffee?

Yes, Mom, we have everything. I make money and life goes on. Poor Mom. It's amazing how much soul my mother is pouring into her letters. She has always come across as a tough woman who would never take a no for a no. She hardly let anyone see through her emotions, who hardly gave me a kiss or a hug, yet she was so sensitive, showing emotions that I had never seen or never knew she had. I have to admit she was closer to my daughters than she had ever been to me or so it seemed to be. Appearances are deceiving. All I can do to soothe their open wounds is to write them reassuring letters.

We still hope we'll come to visit you one day. The other night we were watching a TV show from Italy. A concert. Huge audience. We were hoping to see you somewhere in the crowd.

Really, Mom? We can't afford to go to concerts. We hardly afford to buy bus tickets to use the public transit. Oh, Mom…I realized that writing letters is not the same as actually talking to them. From the money I earn from my jobs I will put some aside to call them once a week. That will give them some peace of mind and bring some cheer in their dull days.

Another Sunday coming up. Another day spent in the Vatican City would be lovely in this primaveral weather. This has become almost a regular Sunday activity. Besides, it's the last Sunday of February, and the last Sunday of each month the Vatican Museum is open to visitors, free of charge.

Although we get there early, the crowds are unfathomable! A real zoo! The moment the museum opens, hordes of visitors are allowed to get in. I certainly didn't expect this. There is no way of stopping in front of certain exhibits, trying to admire them for a few minutes, spending more time in front of them while indulging in taking in details of these masterpieces. We are being swept away with the crowds. If anybody stops, an *embouteillage* is created, leading to a bottleneck effect. Guards everywhere keep yelling at us: keep moving! And we all are! Just like sheep!!! What can I say? It's free. After all, we can at least have a glimpse and try to understand what all of this is about.

We will come back another day, pay the entrance fee and stop in front of all these marvels: Roman sculptures, tombstones, inscriptions, an early Christian sarcophagus; the Raphael rooms with his many works, along with his famous masterpiece *The School of Athens* included; the *Niccoline* Chapel especially notable for its fresco paintings by Fra Angelico; the Gallery of Maps displaying topographical maps of the whole Italy, going back to late 1500's, commissioned by Pope Gregory XIII; this gallery seems to be the largest pictorial geographical study in the entire world.

The Bramante staircase is very famous. The spiral stairs of the Vatican Museums, consisting of two parts: a so-called double helix of shallow incline, looking more like a stepped ramp than a staircase; the red marble papal throne that was initially in the Basilica of San Giovanni in Laterano (the oldest and highest in ranks among the four papal major basilicas), and last but not least, the famous Sistine Chapel, including the Sistine Chapel ceiling, cornerstone work of High Renaissance art. We would like to stop and admire Michelangelo's Last Judgment on the sanctuary wall, or at least the wall paintings done by several leading painters of the late 15th century, but the only choice we have is to keep moving with the masses.

A few hours later we are outside. It has been a mesmerizing experience, in spite of the huge, moving crowds. Well, we can't have everything in life! After all, we can claim we have visited the Vatican. We shall be back!

I think it's fair we call my parents. Actually, I'll have the kids talk to them and that would make their day! After having saved money from not paying the museum entrance fees on a free-visit day, I can afford to talk on the phone with them.

"Hi, Grandma! How are you? Guess who's calling you!"

"Hi, Evelyn! What a surprise!" I can tell my mother is elated. I can hear her voice as Evelyn is holding the phone so I can also listen to what they are saying.

"How are you?" Evelyn fills her in with a trove of details, all positive. Her perspective is excellent. This will give my parents some peace of mind. School is great, living in the convent has become a "regular." Mainly the place where we sleep, but also extremely important for Evelyn and her… toys as well as the ton of clothes she collects from the basement of the convent. "Grandma, do you know how many suitcases we have? About 16!"

Yes, about sixteen, different sizes, all disposed of by previous travellers. We have clothes and dolls stuffed in those bags that we keep hiding under our beds!!

I signal to Evelyn that she has to cut it short. It's Amanda's turn, too.

I realize that my parents' phone is on speaker because I can also hear John mumbling something in the background, but mainly sniffling. I know he's hardly holding back those tears. Amanda's way of describing our life in Italy and our daily routine has a different angle. School is challenging but making progress every day, students and teachers very welcoming, making her feel very included, and spring in Italy is simply beautiful! My turn is next.

"Hi, Mom. Hi, John." I can hear my stepfather muttering a choked "Hi."

"So happy to hear from you, to hear your voices. I think Evelyn has an Italian accent already."

"Really? That's interesting." However, I am not surprised. I hear the girls speaking Italian between themselves, more and more often. The full immersion works. I can swear by it!

"Thank you, Mom, for all the newspaper articles you sent us, as well as for the parcels with all those school supplies. We can buy anything here, as well. I am working every day, but I am basically saving for bad days."

My mother is updating me on all the current events, political and social and family or friends related. She is glad we are in a convent. Sure…I never quite told her about the real conditions we were living in and the level of austerity around us. Not necessary.

"We are quite concerned about this Gulf War." I know. I read the news every day. I have learned a little more about what happened. So, apparently, earlier in January large quantities of oil began to spill into the Persian Gulf. Some initial reports from Iraqi forces claimed that the spill had been caused by the United States sinking two oil tankers. Sure. Why not blame another country, especially the U.S.? It was later revealed that in a desperate military move, Iraqi forces had opened oil valves of a certain pipeline, releasing oil from numerous tankers. The goal of this spill was to impede the U.S. troops from attempting beach landings, but in the end the spill simply resulted in hundreds of million gallons of crude oil being dumped into the Persian Gulf. Is this ever going to end with a peaceful resolution, or will this be the end of the world? Judging by the way the Italian media is portraying everything, I am more and more fearful every day. In fact, I am starting to lose appetite. I cannot eat, I can hardly sleep, and my weight is down. However, this is not something that I am going to share with my parents.

"How did you manage to obtain those papers from the school board and my school?" I'm sure Mom had a heck of a time.

"Well, not as easily as I would have liked it, but we made it. It's interesting to see who your true friends have been and what a different face some of them are showing now."

"What do you mean?" I am not sure I understand.

"Well, some of your "friends" seemed to be visibly hostile when I was trying to obtain all those documents for you. I don't know if it was out of jealousy or what…Some others seemed to show some sort of compassion, although I have never told them anything."

My mother doesn't want to expand on the topic. I understand and I am not surprised. There is an old saying in Romania which, in literal translation, refers to some neighbours' metaphorical goat that should die…or something along the lines that "your goat should also die, now that mine has already died!!" ("*Dacă moare capra mea, trebuie să moară și capra vecinului!*"). It runs deeply in the Romanian culture and it seems to be a means of coping with all the disappointment in our history. It's no laughing matter: rancour and spite are exhausting, and hard times made people more vulnerable. They easily compromise relationships and, what's worse, they leave you feeling miserable. It is an aggressive form of envy that keeps people from achieving their potential. It is not something that concerns me right now. I won't lose sleep over this.

"Anyways, very few people have remained loyal to you. Most of your colleagues at your school, including the principal, admitted that you did the right thing leaving. They sent you their best wishes and they all said they were missing you. Greg called us the other day, too."

Oh, he did… "What did he say?"

"He was incredibly devastated. He sounded like he was going crazy in Canada, waiting to go through his interview and be over with. He said that he was ready to return to Romania any time. Are you writing to him?"

"Yes, twice a week at least. I am trying my best, but returning is not an option!!" I feel overwhelmed, almost like I'm falling apart. Here I am, between two worlds: in the west, my husband in Canada, 8,000 km away, feeling lost and distressed, anxious and depressed, losing hope and trust, and my parents, east of me, closer but still unreachable at this moment, also worried and bothered for not being able to help us more. In between, here I am, trying to juggle with their disposition, mindsets, moods and unhappiness, while dealing with my own misery. I feel I'm being stretched too thin.

Our conversation ends up on an optimistic note, or at least I am trying to make it sound positive. I promise to call them every Sunday from now on. It's the least I can do for them. My mother has been so supportive during the last few months since we left. Truth be told, she has been supportive all my life, although she was occasionally too harsh on me. I will never forget a very dramatic scene from the time I had finished high school and I was supposed to enroll in university.

The story is long and goes all the way back to my early childhood years. Since my grandmother had taught me to read and write at an early age, I was frequently getting bored, so occasionally I liked to visit my mother at her work. There was always a typewriter on her desk. It was fascinating. I must have been seven or eight years old, but my fingers were all over the keys. The sound of the typewriter keys and the product of my typing were exhilarating. That was "playing" for me!

That memory stayed with me for many years. So much so, that after I finished high school I did not want to go to any university, although my mother had always pushed me to have a degree in languages. I didn't want a university degree! All I wanted was to have a secretarial job in an office where I could use a typewriter!! However, my mother sent me to try the university admission exam. In those times the competition was brutal. There were a limited number of seats and a large number of candidates. I went only because my mother wanted me to, but I was still not convinced that I wanted to have a university degree and pursue a career in languages.

Still I had to obey, so I did the written part of the admission exam, and, rebellious and independent as I was, I left the university in search of a technical school where I could enroll in a typewriting and stenography kind of program. It took me a couple of days to go all around Bucharest in search of such a school.

Meanwhile my Mom lost track of me and, since there were no mobile phones at the time, she couldn't locate me. I was supposed to go for the oral part of the exam which had been moved earlier by one day. My mother was frantically looking for me! She was desperate. I was missing my opportunity. Eventually, just by chance, we found each other. She gave me a good earful! My turn had already passed. I had been scheduled for that morning, it was 2 pm now and I was late for this exam.

We arrive in front of the door where the oral examination is held. The door opens and I see inside five candidates, already sitting at tables, preparing their oral presentation. At the front of the classroom, three professors were sitting at their table. One of them comes out and asks for another candidate so they have an even number. My Mom physically pushes me inside, so here I am in front of these three professors. (I found out later that one of them was the dean of the faculty, and the other one was the chancellor!) They ask me for my name. Then they look down on their papers and their facial expressions denote some confusion.

"Miss, your turn was this morning. You missed it. Where have you been?"

I don't have time to think, so my mouth just utters the first response that comes to my mind.

"I was wandering around…"

This is not the reply they are expecting. It sounds insolent.

"Miss, you are either a little cheeky or you are very well prepared and ready for your exam."

"Both." I'm saying without blinking.

Without any further discussions, I'm invited to sit at a table to prepare for my oral examination. When my turn comes, my confidence comes through and my oral presentation is flawless, judging by the 100% I'm receiving! Combined with the mark I already received in the written part, I'm acing the exam. Sheer jubilation! I am one of the 100 candidates, accepted for one of the 10 available seats.

* * *

I owed it to my mother. If she had not factually pushed me into that examination room, I wouldn't have been here today. My Mom has always been a woman of character, true to her word, respectful and correct, always holding on, no matter how rough the times. She has been a veritable role model, and I was realizing that I had always looked up to her, but never acknowledged it.

Thank you, Mom!

12

LA VITA È BELLA!

February 28th

The "big" day is here. Our interview for political asylum is scheduled for today. *Questura di Roma—Divisione Stranieri*. The immigration department of the police force in Rome. Amanda is with me. I'm not sure if she is going to be of any help, but I needed someone on my side. Evelyn had some rehearsal at school today, so I didn't want to interfere with her program.

It's been over two months since we applied for our *permesso di soggiorno*. At that time we had been given a couple of receipts stapled to a flimsy piece of printer paper. The paper, which looked like it was printed in the 1980s, indicated the date and time that we needed to appear at the *Questura di Roma* for our in-person appointment.

That day is today! We need to go to the office in Via Rebibbia. Metro line B and a bus will take us to the destination. Once arrived at the last station—Rebibbia—we come out of the station, we take the stairs and turn right. We curve around the building, and a few steps later we see the bus stop. It's our bus. There are a lot of other people looking slightly worried and clutching folders full of documents, just as we do. I'm glad I came here to locate this place about a week ago. I don't like to leave things to the last minute, and taking a chance on a day like this is not an option.

Interestingly enough, the bus literally empties when it arrives at the *Questura*. It's an orange building, part round, part rectangular. We follow the crowds and join the masses. We take a seat, waiting to be called for our appointment.

I believe I have properly and solidly built my case. As a for seeking protection from the Italian state, I am insisting on our fleeing the country for fear of persecution, and I am ready to justify in my application the circumstances that motivated our escape.

I already submitted the application to the *Questura* which issued us a document certifying the request and the date of the appointment. Ms. Falcone advised me to have a written record of my case at the time of the interview. I also have some documents to prove what I declared (newspaper articles, photos, official documents, everything my mother sent me recently). I do not have a passport (because I declared it "lost" as per Gino's suggestion), so in order to prove my Romanian identity, all I have is my Romanian ID card.

I hear my name. Both Amanda and I stand up and we approach a desk. Three officials are sitting on one side. Two men and one woman. We are invited to sit—opposite of them.

The preliminary interview starts. We are asked to identify ourselves and to explain how we arrived in Italy. I introduce myself; I mention that I have two daughters, and I signal to Amanda who introduces herself.

"Where is your other daughter?"

"At school."

"Can you please tell us why you chose to come to Italy?"

Frankly, because by the time we realized that going to Canada as a family, all the four of us, was not possible, other countries in Europe were no longer issuing visas to Romanian people, so Italy was the only choice, the last one. I am not going to lie. We needed to leave the country, no matter where in Europe, and Italy was the last chance.

"You have mentioned that you were in danger. Can you expand on this issue?"

Sure. I start by telling the three officials about our political views during the communist years, before the 1989 Revolution. Our struggles to stay politically "afloat" while being obvious that we were refusing any affiliation with the Communist Party. I keep telling them about the fear we lived in throughout all those years, about the repercussions we had suffered from plainly refusing to join the Communist Party.

"We understand, but this was before. Hasn't the situation improved after 1989?"

"No. The actual ruling party is still a socialist organization that emerged as the leader during the anti-Ceausescu revolution, and consequently decided to run as a party in the elections it was set to organize. Further discontent was brought by the fact that many of the leaders of this new party, including its president, were former members of the Communist Party. So, nothing has changed for the better. Hundreds and hundreds of people have been killed in the 1989 Revolution. For what? We have the same wolves, but dressed in sheepskin.

The whole country continues to be in turmoil even today. The ruling party got involved in squashing the ongoing protests by sending groups of industrial workers and coal miners, brought to Bucharest by the government to counter the mounting violence of the demonstrators. Many of the miners, factory workers, and other anti-protester groups, fought with the protesters and bystanders. The nefarious aggression resulted in a lot of deaths and many injuries, again. The miners had been told that it was their "duty" to protect Romania and the new democratic system. Few, if any, of the miners had any association with or information about the protesters and their demands, so they followed the direction of individuals they believed represented the government. There is proof, according to recent inquiries showing that the Romanian Intelligence Service, the successor to the former "Securitate" was involved in the instigation and manipulation of the June 1990 miners' revolt."

"How is this affecting you?"

"It affects us in different ways. The Intelligence Service, the successors of the "Securitate" agents are still active. We fear for our lives. We lived in fear before and nothing seems to have changed. Politically wise we are affiliated with a conservative party, and we are also monarchy supporters. Romania had a king who was forced to abdicate in 1947. King Michael attempted to return to Romania to visit his home country, only to be arrested and forced to leave upon arrival. So, if the king is arrested, what are ordinary people like us supposed to expect from the current regime?"

I feel distressed. I hear myself speaking in a firm tone. I am not trying to impress, and I am not playing any role. I am revolted. All the memories from the past are awakening strong emotions in me. My eyes are swelling up with tears. I wish I could stop them from rolling down my face. I am explaining to these officials how the government inquiries showed that the miners had indeed been "joined" by vigilantes who were later convincingly identified as former officers of the "Securitate," and that for two days, the miners had been helped in their violent confrontation with the protesters and had been actually encouraged by former "Securitate" agents who were conspicuously playing the role of instigators. In addition to these accusations, there was also evidence that during this period the Secret Service was involved in distributing fake Legionary flyers claiming that a fascist take-over in Romania was about to happen. Just the thought of the atrocities the "Securitate" forces performed in Romania make me shiver. This was before, but this is also now. NOW!!

I open my folder and I pull out different newspaper articles that my mother sent me. They are in Romanian, but all these images speak for themselves. Brutal reprisals. The officials look over them and seem to have run out of questions. Amanda is sitting next to me all this time, without saying a word, witnessing the whole interrogatory. What is she thinking? Did she ever realize the fear we had lived in during the communist years, back in Romania? Unlikely. We never wanted to get them involved in any way. We were protective of our children, on the one hand, but also pretending that life was normal, good, reasonable.

We are told that the authorities would review our application and decide if the acts of persecution and reasons for persecution that we claimed will be accepted. So, if our application is approved, we will be allowed to have the refugee status recognized. According to the Geneva Convention our claim has to be serious enough, to represent a serious violation of fundamental human rights. In order to recognize the refugee status, acts of persecution must be traceable to "political opinion" grounds.

If we are granted refugee status, this will allow us to have a residence permit issued which will be good for five years; we will also be issued travel documents in case we need to go abroad, and within 5 years of living in Italy we can also apply for citizenship through naturalization. We will have legal access to employment, to education, health and social care on an equal basis with Italian citizens. Just the thought that we will be able to apply for a job and work legally is encouraging. If…

We will find out in a few days. Since we do not have an actual physical address, we are told to check with the *Questura* in a few days.

We are out. The spring day is even more beautiful. Sunny day. Spring is a delight. It's a sparkling boost, an overflowing bottle of effervescent happiness. Flower buds glow in the sunlight, turning into lively blossoms of yellow and pink and purple. Mimosas and wisteria and tulips—-abundance. Spring soars, with an unambiguous precision, the yawning wounds winter leaves on the land and in our hearts.

It feels like the world just woke up to an azure sky and the brightest sun. A sun, shining for us and on us. It is a continuum of joy that salves both spirit and soul.

Spring is here. Spring is in our hearts, too. The thrusting heart of nature is beating again, like a high voltage pacemaker that jump-starts life into the land. This is hope. It's life, too. I have no doubt that we will have good news. Life is beautiful! *La vita è bella*!

13

THE CANADIAN DREAM IS OVER!

Mid-March. We have news from Greg. His request for refugee status was denied. Why? Hard to say. From the phone conversation I had with him a couple of days ago I could feel a mix of disappointment and disgust, sorrow and despondency, failure and frustration, and sadness…Enraged and distressed, depressed and angry.

"Don't worry", I said. "Heads up! The good thing is that you are not sent back to Romania."

"That's right. I can take a flight to Italy."

"That's great news. Come on over here and we'll build our life again, together. If Canada doesn't want you, Italy will accept you, for sure. We just received a response from the Italian officials. Our application has been approved. We have a legal status, and this is a new beginning for all of us."

I don't need to ask him what went wrong. I don't have money for a long phone conversation, but I can also fathom what happened. Apparently, he had the right to an interpreter, but he wanted to represent himself, personally. Probably not the best idea. Emotions interfere with words and not always for the best result. While my tears during the interview were coming from sorrow, from open wounds, and they came across as sadness and despair, I could see why Greg's misery put into words misled the audience. His anger was not something the Canadian authorities wanted to hear. Maybe his choice of words, too. Well, everything happens for a reason.

"Girls, Dad is coming to Italy!"

"Yaaaay!! When?"

"Probably next week. We'll have to give him another call in a couple of days to find out what the exact date is."

"Where is he going to stay?" Amanda's mind is anticipating some extra stress.

Extra, indeed. How do we go about this? The convent is out of question. It's disquieting to see the men living outside the monastery in makeshift tents. Some of them are the husbands of the Albanian women living inside. The convent has a high off-the-ground main floor, creating a sort of a vault outside, right under our windows. They built beds made out of wooden pallets, or simply wooden slats and pieces of cardboard, covering themselves with filthy blankets and newspapers. All winter we could see them gathered around a pit fire they kept making in the yard, right in front of the main façade of the convent. Covering themselves with the same blankets they were using at night to protect them from the damp cold. It was a sad picture. No, Greg will not stay here. It's out of question.

I need to start looking for a rental apartment. Not an easy task. Everything is so expensive. I'm making almost $900 per month, working six days a week in three houses, going in three different directions every other day, crisscrossing Rome. It's more than we can afford to pay for one-month rent. We need to eat, too…Then I will be left with no money for food.

Life is getting complicated. Easter is approaching, too. No mood for celebration! In addition to the problematical situation we are in right now, the newspapers are mentioning every day the imminence of a World War III. No…I'm glad Greg is coming. I hope he'll make it. If we cannot live together, at least we can die together…

I'm falling apart. The girls keep comforting me every day. Now it's the other way around. They are my support. Wonderful daughters. I lost so much weight. Clothes are loose on me. I have to keep going though, and find my strength. The other night, as we were reciting the Rosario—counting our prayers, one bead at a time—I had an "apparition." Was it real? I don't quite believe in visions of this kind, but immersed into the holy world as I was, looking out the window into the dark sky of the night, I "saw" a white silhouette…She seemed to tell me "Don't worry. You will be fine. "Who was she? Was she real? Or a product of my imagination?

Was she Madonna? She looked like any of those "Madonna" paintings everywhere. Did my mind create that image? Maybe I was in a state of meditation. It came at the right moment, though, imagination or product of my meditation. I felt a sensation of peace covering me, taking over my entire heart and mind, serenity and calm and a feeling of reassurance. I couldn't describe it in words. Still now, it doesn't do justice to that emotion to be put into words. As the sensation of peacefulness came over me, the pressure was off. I knew we would succeed.

The 40 days leading up to Easter are sacred for the Italian Catholics. Lent is a spiritual time. The weather is warmer and there's an air of hope and celebration. The flowers are in full bloom and the sun shines, and it seems like God is speaking to us through nature. It is the right time to look forward to rebirth in nature and life.

Palm Sunday today. *Domenica delle palme.* Palm Sunday is the celebration that begins Holy Week—the final week of Lent that culminates with the Easter Triduum (three days) of the Mass of the Lord's Last Supper, Good Friday Crucifixion and Easter Vigil or Easter Saturday.

It's right we go to the Mass today in the big church, adjacent to the convent, San Gregorio Magno. Not only is this a very holy day, but the nuns have advised us that Mother Teresa is here, spending this week in Rome, so she'll definitely come to visit us.

This is very special. I'm quite excited. Since we've been living in one of the shelters belonging to the congregation that she founded around the world, we've learned a little of her life and accomplishments. I know she was born in Macedonia, (one of the countries fighting to obtain independence from Yugoslavia) to parents of Albanian descent, lived in India where she received Indian citizenship, and apparently she began her missionary work at the end of the 1940's. She directed her efforts at tending to the poor, the hungry and the homeless. Her first Missionary of Charity was opened in India and it expanded throughout the world, but when Eastern Europe experienced increased openness in the late 1980's, Teresa extended her efforts to communist countries which had initially rejected the Missionaries of Charity but were now accepting her assistance. We had been fortunate to find shelter in one of these places.

Palm Sunday Mass in San Gregorio Church. Apparently, it is part of a monastery of monks of the Camaldolese branch of the Benedictine Order. At least this is what I am told by one of the Italian women sharing the room with us, my "next-bed-over" neighbour. She seems to be quite educated, but I have no idea what her family situation is and how she ended up in this convent. It's rare that I get to see her sober. Most of the time she is inebriated, but today she is totally clear-headed. I enjoy listening to her. She keeps telling me that in the 1970's, the Camaldolese monks allowed Mother Teresa to set up a food kitchen for the poor of the city in the building we are staying in, attached to the monastery, and she set up one of her Missionaries of Charity. So, the convent we are staying in right now has a historical significance, too. Interesting.

It's a very festive day today. Palm Sunday is celebrated by the blessing and distribution of palm shoots representing the palm branches the crowd scattered in front of Christ as he rode into Jerusalem. However, the palm branches are replaced by olive stems which are plentiful in Italy, and we all receive a little olive twig as we enter the church.

The Blessing of the Palms precedes the Mass, including Gospel reading. I didn't have the chance to understand much of this procession. We were born Orthodox, and my grandmother used to take me with her to that church when I was little, back in Romania, but later on we had to give up attending any church celebrations because of communism…Still, from what I remember, the Mass celebrations seem to be quite similar. I have not retained anything from the Gospel readings. As a child, the only thing that comes to mind is boredom! The Mass was always too long, and we were all standing! I always wished it had been over so I could go home and rest my little tired feet.

Even today I remember the times when, as a child, my grandmother used to take me to the church, mostly before Easter. Taking communion was part of the ritual, but without admitting that I had "sinned," communion was not possible.

According to the Orthodox religion, we were supposed to kneel under the priest's black stole and repent. While the priest was asking me questions, all I was looking at were the laces of his shoes.

"Have you lied?" His rather hostile voice had an unwelcome and disconcerting accusatory tone to it.

"Yes…"

"Are you disobeying your parents?"

"Yes…," I had to admit. I was often disobeying my grandmother because she seemed unreasonable in all her requests.

"Have you ever stolen?"

"Yes…" although I didn't remember to have stolen much, other than maybe fruits from my neighbours' fruit trees.

And the questions were going on and on, making me feel unwanted and unloved by God. I had always been told that He will punish me for misbehaving. Punishment was not the word that was resonating positively with me. So, as a child, during my confession under the priest's stole, my eyes were on his shoes and the laces that I would have liked to tie across. What would he do if I had tied the left shoelaces to the right ones? Misbehaving? Yes. Right there!!

After the confession I was given the communion. Throughout my very young life, back in Romania, when my grandmother was taking me to the church, all I could hear was: "If you behave badly, God will punish you!" I was tired of being reprimanded. If God loved me, why would He punish me? That never worked for me. Fear of being admonished, scolded, chastised—was detrimental to my mental and emotional development, to my becoming confident.

*　*　*

Only a couple of months ago, soon after Evelyn discovered the hidden treasures in the basement of the convent, one day she came upstairs with a Barbie doll. Her big smile and lively eyes were usually a happy indication of her new and precious possession. In that very moment, however, the looks on her face were hiding a mix of shame, guilt and fear. A few steps behind a nun showed up.

"Maria, your daughter was scouring through our donations and she ran off with some toys." The nun's voice was not completely accusatory, there was no malevolence to it, but although I was fully aware of Evelyn's "pastime" in the basement, that was the last thing I wanted to hear, out loud, in front of the other women. I felt ashamed, put on the spot. What kind of mother was I? What was I teaching my daughters? One of them had been caught stealing, but I was also caught by surprise.

"Evelyn, that was not nice. God will punish you for misbehaving." Those were the only words I could come up with.

"No, Maria. God does not punish us. God loves us all." In a soft but determined voice, the nun was giving me a lesson in God's love, right there. A precious lesson. I learned in that very moment that, when you love somebody, God included—or God in the first place—you will not do something wrong, you will not hurt that person or that being. It is a form of disloyalty to betray someone fully knowing that he or she loves you.

The political mess came later, during the Romanian Communist regime, when we learned that some Orthodox priests were also collaborating with the agents of the "Securitate." So much for sinning.

* * *

I understand that today's Catholic Mass will be long, but we are sitting for most of the time. At least, part of the Mass is in Latin, and my mind is trying to connect Latin to the Italian and Romanian languages and find the similarities. In spite of my mind playing tricks on me, taking me back to my childhood, and later on, to my high school and university years and the languages I studied, I am still aware of the entirely blessed atmosphere around us.

Mother Teresa is up at the pulpit.

Lord God,
I give You thanks, for You are good, and Your mercy is endless.
Here I stand, at the start of this holy week,
This week in which Your church remembers Jesus' passion and death,
I bless You, Lord, for shining your light upon me,
And for sending Your Son to us, in human frailty.
To walk the road we walk.
Open my eyes that I may see Him coming,
And may praise Him with a pure heart.
And may walk in the way of His suffering,

And share also in His resurrection.
Through Jesus Christ our Lord, who lives and reigns with You and the Holy Spirit, one God forever and ever.
Amen.

The entire congregation joins in.

It's very solemn. Incredible how this tiny woman is able to conquer the church audience…. *Benedetto colui che viene nel nome del Signore!* . . . *Osanna nel più alto dei cieli*! The singing feels majestic. All Glory, Laud, and Honour. Hosanna. Rejoice, the Lord Is King.

The Mass is over. Reality kicks in. We have a full agenda today despite the almost divine atmosphere. Newspaper and map in hand, I take the girls with me. We are out on a mission: a few more rentals to check out. Location and price are the main important issues to consider. We need to call Greg in Canada, too. It's likely we will wake him up. It's 1 pm here, so it's 5 am in central Canada. Let's do it!

"Hi, Greg. Sorry to wake you up. What's new?" Sleepy or not, this call is exactly what he needed.

"My aunt bought me a plane ticket to Rome."

"Wonderful! When are you arriving here?"

"Wednesday at 12:30 pm."

"Which Wednesday?"

"This Wednesday."

"That is great! We'll be at the airport to meet you!"

It's right the girls say something to him, too. I'm passing the phone to Evelyn, but I touch the speaker push button so they can both hear him.

"Ciao, Dad! So, you'll be here on Wednesday! We're so happy to see you. We'll spend Easter together…" He sounds delighted to hear them.

"Go back to sleep now, Dad! We'll see you in a few days."

So, he is coming on Wednesday! This coming up Wednesday! This is in three days. Three days! My mind switches into emergency mode. I refuse to accept panic!

We have two more chances today. Here is one of them. It looks like a two-story building. Ring the bell. A lady comes out.

"I understand you have a place for rent. Is there any chance we can see it?"

"Yes, of course." She opens the door large and waves us in. We go up a couple of flights of stairs. Where are we going? Oh, this looks like an attic. An attic room with bunk beds. A double bed on top, and one on the bottom. So, we as parents, we are supposed to sleep on the bottom "shelf" and the girls on top. Interesting. There's a ladder leading to the upper bed. This is right under the roof. If the girls sleep in this bed and they sit up, they will hit the roof!

"How much is it?"

"900,000 lire a month." It's the equivalent of $900. That's my monthly earnings and then we'll have no money to pay for food, transportation or anything else.

"Can we give you an answer later?"

"Of course. However, if you don't come by 5 o'clock this evening, I'll have to open the offer again for other people."

"Sounds good. Grazie."

No, this is not good. This is not an option. We have to move on.

Last chance. Via di Boccea. We can take the metro line A. Thirty minutes, a little walk and 10 metro stops later, we arrived. Here's the building, a high-rise. It's a student residence. Called Sporting Residence. No more choices.

"Buon giorno. We found an ad in the newspaper and I understand you have some rooms for rent. How much is the rent?"

"We have one for $800 and one for $1,000 month."

"Is the $800-one available right now?"

"No. It'll be vacated on Tuesday."

"How about to the $1,000 one? Can we see it?"

"Sure." He takes us up one flight of stairs. There is an elevator, too. Is it working? He opens the door, and the room is large. Three beds; I'm told it can accommodate four beds, too. This is fine. A small bathroom and a little electrical stove and a fridge box in a corner; it also has a balcony. Still, $1,000 is more than I can afford.

"So, the $800 one will be available in two days?"

"Yes."

"Why the difference in price?"

"Because it's on the main floor and it doesn't have a balcony or even a patio. Also the bathroom is smaller." I wonder how much smaller. This is already very small! The receptionist seems to read my mind: "The bathroom has a shower, a sink and, of course, a toilet. No bidet, though."

Ah, right! No bidet! We have a bidet in our only bathroom in the convent, and it has always been used as an alternative to the toilet!! It was always filled to the top with…everything! I am not sure I have ever seen that bidet clean, not that I would have ever used it. In fact, one early morning we woke up to a terrible stench. We soon discovered what had happened, or rather we guessed…Anna had a bowel problem during the night. Since she could never reach the toilet properly, she spread feces everywhere around the convent. On the floors, shuffling her socks around, leaving brownish traces behind her on the mosaic flooring, even on the walls and on the door…On the walls? Did this woman ever wash her hands, at least? Thinking that she was "helping" in the kitchen, cooking our meals…It's a true miracle we never got sick.

So, we don't have a bidet in this room! We will survive!!! It was not a "must-have"!

"Is this residence safe?"

"Yes. We haven't had any incidents. Maybe some students may get ahead of themselves sometimes and become too noisy, but it doesn't happen very often."

I have no choice. At least, overdrinking in Italy does not seem to be an issue, from what I have noticed, so, alcohol may not be involved. Italians are loud enough, though. The younger, the louder, too!

"How can I get this room on the main floor? Do we have to pay for it now?" I'd prefer to not pay, but I need to secure it, too.

"You can leave a deposit of $200 today."

I'm ready to take a chance. How can I trust this guy?

"Are you going to give me a receipt?"

"Sure." I wonder if that would make a difference in case we are being driven into a scam. I look at the girls.

"What do you think?" We exchanged a few comments in Romanian. Amanda seems to be skeptical. Evelyn seems to look hopeful. I decide to make this deposit. I need to secure the least expensive room.

On our way back to the convent, we are rethinking everything.

"So, Dad is coming in three days."

"Yes. Three days. This is getting complicated. Well, if Canada doesn't want him, maybe Italy will!"

Greg's Canadian dream is over. Ours, too!

14

MADRE TERESA

On our way back to the convent I am discussing with the girls about how we need to organize ourselves during the next couple of days. It is getting very tight. We have to reorganize our suitcases and then probably take a few trips to this place. Challenging, to say the least.

"Evelyn, you seem to have collected a lot of toys, Barbie dolls and everything else. Do you really need them all?" I stress the word "need."

"Yes, Mom…" Her voice doesn't leave room for negotiations. Back in Romania, after she was born, those years had been the toughest. Even toys for children were in short supply. Barbies? Never. Other sorts of dolls, yes, but never Barbies. I remember Greg went on a two-week excursion to Russia (Soviet Union, at the time) in the 80's. When he came back, he had two big dolls that he had purchased in USSR for our daughters. The Russians had everything we didn't. Of course, they did. Ceausescu was starving us while paying the country's debts to the Soviet Union, while also he, his family and all his acolytes were living a life of luxury, starving the population. However, I never quite understood why he was trying to "pay the debts"…Which debts? What was Romania owing to the Soviet Union? Then, assuming that we would have paid whatever we were owing them, what was he thinking we would accomplish as a country? Break away from their communist influence? Get rid of communism?

Of course, I cannot oppose to Evelyn's taking all those toys with her—half received, with the nuns' acceptance. The other half—she had just made away with!! Same with clothing. Anyways, we will be out of the convent soon. Palm Sunday ends with hopes for a new day, new week, new start.

We are all very tired, and Marianna seems to behave tonight. Lights out. Good night!

* * *

Monday morning. It's Easter vacation, so no school. I'm lucky in this respect because the girls can help with this moving process. It is going to be tough. Everything is happening this week. The Holy week! We have to move our stuff to this new place, and Greg is arriving on Wednesday. Anyways, I'm glad he's coming to join us here in Italy. I feel that a load will be taken off my mind. Or will it…?

There are some rumours going around the convent and I hear that Mother Teresa is coming to visit us. That sounds great. Meet her in person. I feel honoured to have the chance to see her, to greet her personally. This is a unique moment. Everybody's in a frenzy. Cleaning up, left and right, tidying up—the rooms, the kitchen, the bathroom, the refectory, everything. I've never seen the bathroom so clean as today. Even the bidet!

Here she is, walking into the main hallway of the convent, accompanied by a few nuns. She's checking everything out. Checking for what? Some of the women are not in the convent today. A couple of the Albanian women are around, but most of them are out, especially the younger ones. She's asking the nuns why there are so many young women around here. That doesn't sound good.

About 15 minutes later we are invited to gather in the refectory for an announcement. We are all lining up, not very many of us around. The Italian women with whom we are sharing the room are gone, except for Anna who is probably helping with cooking upstairs. (Did she wash her hands, today?). The youngest Albanian women are all gone; only four of them are around, still not old at all…

There are about eleven of us left. Mother Teresa is walking slowly, stopping in front of us. We curtsy. The nun accompanying her is informing her about the countries we are all from. As she stops in front of each of us, she extends her hand. I bow and kiss her hand. This is Madre Teresa. She is tiny—I would say five feet tall, wearing her typical white sari with the three blue stripes on the borders, one thicker than the rest, but in spite of being of a petite stature, she looks energetic and determined. Especially determined. For whatever reason, she seems to be somewhat irritated. There is something very stern in her voice. Her face is quite wrinkled, but her dark eyes command attention, shining in an intense way, radiating an aura of piety and intelligence. It feels like a divine moment.

She goes to the next room occupied by the mothers with their small children. Some are out, but most are still around, tending to their babies or toddlers. About 45 minutes later she leaves. We are going back to our normal activities. However, "normal" for us today is packing up. I need to sit and think. That apartment that we are about to rent is extremely filthy. The entire residence looks like it is in need of some major cleaning, even sanitization. I wonder what the newly rented $800 room looks like. I would like to do some serious cleaning before we move in.

With noon approaching, we are all setting the big table in the middle of the dining hall. Fettuccine pasta topped with tomato sauce, a few sprinkles of Parmesan cheese and chopped nuts is our today's lunch. Figs for dessert. Fresh figs. We have seen fresh figs around, but never bought any. Saving money may sound selfish or stingy, but we must stay prepared for all sorts of surprises, not all good. Evelyn seems to enjoy the figs the most. They are so delicious.

Lunch is over. A couple of nuns—the ones we now know that are "higher in rank"—come into the dining hall while we were just about to say the "thank you" prayer. There is something formal to their appearance. Official, but in an unlikable way.

"Attention, everybody. We are here to bring an announcement from Madre Teresa. Tomorrow she is asking all the women who are young and in good health, and who do not have small children to leave the convent."

What?! Mother Teresa is asking us to leave this place? She's not asking, actually. It sounds like an order, almost. At least, this is how the nuns formulated the announcement. It is not a question. It is a request. Any probability that the nuns gave Madre Teresa's words a different twist? Truth be told, they're too many young women around and it doesn't make sense to use these beds that otherwise would be needed by people who are really in need. I have to admit that she's right. Yes, some of us are homeless, the girls and I included, all these young Albanian women, the Serbian ones and a few in the other room with older children. So, what are we supposed to do?

I am looking at my daughters. We are looking at each other, speechless, reading each others' minds, trying to make sense of all this entire situation.

So, what do we do now? Where are we going? Where will everybody be going? In fact, all I should care is about the three of us. Well, this is a new addition to our already stressful situation, and it's making things feel even more exhausting than they already are. Luckily, we seem to have secured a place to stay, but it sounds like we have to leave right away. It's almost noon and there's no way we can leave now. We have to pack everything and get our suitcases and bags ready. How can we leave right away? The only choice is to leave tomorrow! Where?

This is another element added to our already stressful situation. We truly didn't need this now. We have amassed so much stuff during the past three and a half months. Clothes and toys and God knows what else. I don't even have time to do a selection among all this s***. This is an emergency.

"Girls, let's get out of here now. We need to find a hotel for one night."

"But, Mom, we can move in on Tuesday, can we not?"

"Yes, Amanda, but I am not comfortable moving in that place without a proper cleaning job. We have lived in precarious sanitary conditions for the past almost four months, mice and ants and all, besides Anna's poop all over, and I am really not willing to repeat anything like that. So, we need a hotel room from Tuesday to Wednesday." Hopefully the $200 I left as deposit at that students' residence is not wasted.

Wandering around the historical center, looking for decently priced hotels, hopelessness is almost taking over. Where can we find a hotel at a reasonable price and which is not very far so we can take our luggage from here, and then from that point to the residence that we visited yesterday?

"Mom, let's check some hotels around the railway station. We know that area pretty well now and I'm sure we'll find something for a decent price."

"Good idea, Amanda." The girls are of enormous help. We start walking towards the main station, checking hotels left and right on our way. It's an eerie feeling of a déjà-vu. Only four months ago, just arrived in Rome, we were looking for a place to stay. So little time has gone by, so many events have taken place.

Finally, we find a hotel and we book it for tomorrow morning. This one will charge $70. It is the perfect location. There's one more detail. We have too much stuff and we cannot take many trips to this hotel, given that time is of essence.

"Mom, do you remember that man that we met a few weeks ago in Via Dandolo? That Romanian fellow who was showing us that he had a car? Maybe if we can find him, he can give us a ride?"

"Yes, I remember. That was quite a car, if we can call it that way!!! A wreck! I'm sure somebody disposed of it; he may have found it in a dumpster!! I'm sure he's not even driving it legally. But, frankly, I think that's not a bad idea, Amanda. Maybe this might be a solution. We have to find him tonight. Do you remember what his name was?"

"I think Peter…" So happy to have the girls with me.

All set. Luckily, Peter is showing up for our evening meals at the food kitchen in Via Dandolo. He agrees to help us. We have a ride for tomorrow.

Back to the convent. It's a warm evening. It's surprising where God's ways are leading us. We knew we were supposed to leave the convent one day. Greg's coming this Wednesday, on such a short notice, precipitated the things, but this "saintly" visit threw us in a real spin.

Grazie, Madre Teresa!

15

HAPPY EASTER!

Tuesday Morning. Last breakfast in the convent. Probably last slices of *panettone*. Actually, this is a *colomba*, the Easter variety that tastes almost the same. Easter dove bread. Our last cups of hot chocolate, too. From now on we are on our own in the morning, as well as lunches, and dinners…for all the four of us. We will miss these breakfasts.

Peter is here with his dilapidated car. It is in such a decrepit state, that it makes me wonder how he can drive this wreck. Rusty and old—it's a wonder it's accepted to be on the roads.

Anyways, beggars can't be choosers! Our entire luggage is out in front of the convent. I'm counting 18 bags and suitcases and all. We've been here for almost four months and we have accumulated so much stuff. We came here with only two suitcases and today we have 18 pieces of luggage!

We managed to load everything in Peter's car, kids included! There's no room for me. I have no choice but send them with this man to the hotel. I have no idea who this man is. I only met him a couple of times. Yes, he is another Romanian fellow, but I know nothing about him other than that he is just as lost and homeless as we are. How can I trust that he's going to take my girls to the hotel? Am I too credulous? Do I just trust people too easily, or is it my gut feeling that we would be safe?

My only choice is to walk to this hotel. They will get there before I do, which is just fine. I hope they will. I hope he's not going to take off with my children.

Forty-five minutes later I join them. The luggage is in the hallway of the hotel, and the girls are sitting in the lobby chairs, waiting for me to come and take them to our room. Thank goodness!

This is ironic. It's the holy week, the week before Easter, *la settimana santa*, and we have been kicked out of the convent tonight by the very Mother Teresa! I can't complain. She was right in so many ways. There were too many young women doing nothing but pretending they were too "sick" to be able to help with any convent chores. The role of the *Missionarie della carità* of Madre Teresa was exactly that: to help people who were indeed in need, older people who could not work and had no shelter. Or, with some of these women, that was not the case. Anyways, it just complicated our situation on too short of a notice.

Evening already. I need to fix something to eat, and then I will have to leave the girls at the hotel. At least there's a TV in the room. We haven't watched TV or even listened to a radio since we left our home country. Besides, a comfortable bed and a decent bathroom, a shower and hot water make it for a lovely night…Hot water! It sounds like a regular commodity, but in the convent we had a warm shower only twice, and that was only on the second floor, the men's "quarters"! I never understood why they had a decent bathroom while we, the women living on the first floor, did not. For the last almost four months of our staying in the convent, the water in our only shower was cold, or if we were lucky, maybe lukewarm.

"Mamma, do you want us to come with you? Maybe you need help to clean the place." Amanda's show of support is invaluable, but no, they both need to rest tonight.

"No, girls. Thank you. You need to sleep. Tomorrow is going to be another tough day."

A couple of hours later I'm on my way to clean up our new place. Luckily, the young fellow behind the reception desk acknowledges that I paid indeed a deposit of $200. He gives me the key and I go to check the room. It is totally unsanitary. Dirty. Smelly. Disgusting. Words are not enough to describe the condition of this room. Included with the rent, we have sheets and blankets and pillows. Clean? Not sure. I cannot trust.

"Is there a washing machine around?"

"Yes, there are two of them at the end of the hallway."

"Am I allowed to use them?"

"Sure. No money, but you must have your own detergent." I have detergent. Luckily, I bought a huge supply of soap and chemicals on my way to this place. I knew I needed a large quantity of cleaning solutions. This should not be too difficult. However, the condition of the room is despicable. The bathroom is so small. Really tiny. Yes, there is a shower, but it is so small and so mucky. The door to the bathroom doesn't even open all the way because the sink is in the way and the door opens only halfway! At least there is a sink! Also, a toilet. The filth surpasses any imagination. The kitchen, or rather the so-called kitchen (*angolo cottura*) is right at the entrance, on the left. In Italian it's described as a place to cook in a corner. That's exactly what it is. It features a hot plate and a tiny little fridge underneath. Two small cupboards above. The hot plate has a thick layer of grime on it, sticky and revolting. I open the closet and the cupboards. Cockroaches and all sorts of bugs around. One cockroach is crawling out of the small fridge, sluggishly moving its frozen legs. Yuck! This is pure contamination. A real dumpster. It makes me shiver, but what choice is there? I accept the room. At least there are four beds, as per previously discussed. One next to the other, all lining up with one end against the same wall. No privacy!! A window opens to the yard leading to the entrance. No patio. No problem. Here starts my night cleaning job! I'm glad I have a broom and a mop, a lot of different kinds of detergents and disinfectants. Washing the bed sheets and pillowcases, even the window curtain. There is nothing I can do about the pillows. They may have germs, but at least the pillow covers are clean.

Six hours later, I can declare myself somewhat content. There is nothing else I can do. It's 4:00 o'clock in the morning. I have worked non-stop. The room looks fairly decent. There is no comparison to the condition in which it was when I took over last night. If anything, I am grateful for one thing, at least: the hot water. Now we are really on our own. We will manage. I'm going back to the hotel. It's about 5 am. If I could only get a couple of hours of sleep. I am exhausted.

Wednesday morning. The girls are sleeping.

"Ciao, mamma! What time is it? We didn't hear your coming. When did you get here?"

"Last night…this morning…I don't know…" It's almost 8 am, and my mind is still sleeping. Still, we don't have much time. "Get dressed, please. You have some slices of that Easter bread, the *colomba*, and there is some milk we bought yesterday. This is going to be your breakfast for today. Maybe lunch, too. We'll think about lunch after we pick Dad up from the airport. First, we need to take a few trips by metro to our new place to carry over all our stuff."

We are on the way. A few pieces of luggage at the time and a few trips later, we have taken everything into this dormitory. We hardly have the time to put everything away. In fact, there are no closets, so everything will have to stay in the suitcases. We'll sort everything out one of these days. We need to go through everything and dispose of everything we don't need. There's no space for storage. No closet. Just a little rack for some clothes, a table and two chairs in the corner by the window. At least that's where the girls will do their homework.

"It's almost noon. We have to go to the railway station to get on the train to Fiumicino Airport. Let's move!"

"How long does it take to get to the airport?"

"About an hour, I believe." Never been at this airport. Greg should be here around noon. We'll make it!

The flight seems to be in time. We find a visible spot where the exit from the arrivals is. My heart is pounding with anticipation.

* * *

"Hi, Dad!" The girls have just spotted him. He's here. Finally reunited. Hugs and kisses and tears. It's an emotional encounter. He is here! We are here together. We are a family again, all the four of us. We will be able to pull something off and together we'll find a way. He looks tired, but happy.

"Hello, girls! Hello, Maria…I missed you all…"

"Welcome to Rome! If Canada didn't want you, maybe Italy will. For the time being you just need to relax your mind." Everything is new to Greg. He had learned about Rome from history books, but never visited it.

The metro will take us to our new place. In the meantime we are giving him a few updates on the most recent events that occurred during the past couple of days. I'm trying to prepare him for the shock he might have once he gets to see this place.

Here we are! Open the door. It's clean, according to my recently "adjusted" standards.

"This is where you live? This is definitely not something I was expecting." His pained expression and raised, arched eyebrows show more than just surprise. He seems to be in shock.

"What do you mean?" I am bewildered. What am I to make of his comments?

He is avoiding my eyes, while looking around in confusion.

"It looks dirty." His eyes are squeezing shut for a moment.

"Dirty? You have no idea what it looked like yesterday. I worked all night to get it as clean as you can see it." I know he doesn't mean to offend me, but I truly don't understand what he expected.

"Dad, you have no idea what the convent looked like." Amanda is trying to bring some justice into this discussion. "This room is really clean as compared to the convent. Besides, we have a bathroom for just the four of us."

"Anyways, make yourself comfortable. You must be very tired. While you catch up with the girls, I'll run to the corner store and buy some food. The important thing is that you are here. Next week we'll go to the police station and ask for papers for you."

* * *

Our first night together after almost four months. Gulf War, World War III—it doesn't matter anymore; we can die together if we cannot live together. We have four days left of the Holy week, including Easter Sunday. Actually, the Italians have the *Pasquetta*, too—the Easter Monday. Five days of enjoyment and celebration.

Thursday is a day of decompression. We take it slowly, allowing Greg to catch up with us. A beautiful spring day to enjoy in Rome. As tense as this week has been, today is the perfect day to relax and talk. We tell him about every single event, big and small, since we came to Italy. He is truly in awe. The three of us, completely on our own have achieved more during this time in comparison to him who—presumably—had some support in Canada. It doesn't matter. We're together again.

The girls are happy to take their father around, to play the role of a tourist guide for him, showing him everything we have seen for the past almost four months. We stop, take pictures, sit on benches, revelling in everything, soaking in every single moment. We go up the Park of Oranges—*il Parco degli aranci*—for a panoramic photo of Rome. Evelyn wants an orange picked right from the tree. The tree is pretty tall, but Greg manages to get her one. Big disappointment. It's bitter. These are not edible oranges…

Holy Friday is here. Easter is certainly the most important celebration in Italy, and tonight we will have the opportunity to see live the *Via Crucis* (Way of the Cross) event which takes place in Rome in one of the most evocative and unique scenarios that only the Eternal City can offer, and is personally and publicly celebrated by the Pope John Paul II as he journeys from the Colosseum to the Temple of Venus. The *Via Crucis* depicts the latest dramatic events related to the Passion of Jesus and refers to the Gospel stories; it is also called Calvary from the name of the mountain on which the torture of Christ occurred. It initially began in 1750 with Pope Benedict XIV who decided that 14 Stations of the Cross should be placed inside the famous Flavian Amphitheater, the less common name of the Colosseum.

In Rome the *Via Crucis* is carefully organized. So much so that on the last stretch an enchanting atmosphere is created, at the Convent of St. Bonaventure on the Palatine Hill. Among the ruins of the ancient city we have the amazing opportunity to participate in a real show.

We arrive at the Colosseum a little early so we can get a decent spot from where we can watch, obviously standing. There are a few extremely large screens around, so people won't miss anything. It's 9 pm. We cuddle to be close to one another, to make up for the time we missed being together. There are thousands and thousands of people gathered around Colosseum. The ceremony starts. We hear the Pope, and we can also see him on the screen. He is inside the ancient arena. No matter how close we are, it is impossible to see the whole procession.

"Forty days have passed since we started the Lent journey. Today we have relived the last hours of the earthly life of the Lord Jesus until, suspended on the cross, He cried out his *"consummatum est."* Gathered in this place, where thousands of people suffered martyrdom in the past for remaining faithful to Christ, we now want to walk this painful way together with all the poor, the excluded from society, the victims of the powers and laws, of blindness and selfishness, but above all of our heart hardened by indifference, a disease which we Christians also suffer from. May the Cross of Christ, an instrument of death but also of new life, which holds together in an embrace earth and sky, north and south, east and west, illuminate the consciences of citizens, of the Church, of legislators and of all those whom they profess followers of Christ, so that the Good News of redemption may reach everyone."

The first *"Via Crucis"* presided over by John Paul II was in 1979, accompanied by meditation on the texts of Paul VI's speeches. Tonight we will have the opportunity to witness this advent chaired by John Paul II. The Pope personally carries the cross from station to station. Every year a person or a group of people is invited to write the texts of the meditations that will be read at each station. It gets more and more difficult as the Pope goes higher and higher, carrying the cross on his shoulders. We can see on the large TV screens the images of his shoulders, curved under the wood of the cross. He is getting older and more fragile, and the cross is heavy, but he has always insisted to carry it himself. The pontiff was experiencing his ascent to Calvary.

The atmosphere is particularly fascinating, especially during the representation's finale, near the Convent of St. Bonaventure on the Palatine. Amidst the ancient ruins and Rome's typical parasol pines, pilgrims and worshippers, tourists and locals alike, we all witness this breathtaking display.

The celebration ends with a candle-lit cross illuminating the night sky in front of the Roman monument.

* * *

Easter Sunday. The Vatican is the place to be today, inside the St. Peter's Basilica.

"Dad, maybe we get to see the Pope again! We saw him on Christmas, from up close." Maybe, but I doubt it. It doesn't matter. Thousands of people are gathered in the large Saint Peter's Square where the Mass is celebrated in the morning, and gives the entire ceremony a stadium feeling. Here is the Pope up on the well-known balcony. He will deliver the blessing known as the "Urbi et Orbi" ("to the City and to the World') from the balcony on the facade of the basilica. His benediction follows, in over 30 languages.

Happy Easter! *Buona Pasqua*!

16
SCHOOL IS OVER

A couple of weeks have gone by since Greg arrived. Spring is in full swing. Blooming oleanders are gleaming in hues of romance and everlasting charm. Greg is still in the tourist mode, for now. We are trying to help him relax his mind. During the week I am busy with work, and the girls go to school, but on Sundays we walk everywhere. Vatican City has become a "regular", but today we are crossing the Tiber River, and explore the Baths of Caracalla, that used to be the city's second largest Roman public baths (*Terme di Caracalla*), built during the reigns of emperors Septimius Severus and his son, Caracalla.

A few hundreds of metres away it's the pyramid of Caius Cestius (Piramide *di Caio Cestio* or *Piramide Cestia*), an ancient pyramid, initially built as a tomb for Gaius Cestius, a Roman senator and general who was active during the Principate. It stands at a bifurcation between two ancient roads, the Via Ostiensis and Via Marmorata, and it is one of the best-preserved ancient buildings in Rome.

We cross the river back to the other side, taking the Sublicio Bridge this time. What better way to end the day than with a visit to a happy place?! We go by the Porta Portese city gate and here we are, walking into a popular flea market, held every Sunday in this area, Porta Portese Market. There is nothing of historic importance, but as the most famous market in Rome and the best known, it's a good place to lift anybody's spirits up. (It's also—unfortunately—the most notorious for pickpockets!!)

Porta Portese is the most famous Sunday market in Rome. You can really find everything: furniture and objects from all eras of course, household and personal linen, used and new clothes, vinyls and CDs, books and prints, historical newspapers, shirts and underwear, watches and shoes, jewelry, leather jackets and suitcases, beads and toys. And the list could be endless. On the other hand, Porta Portese surpasses the imagination of any traveller who arrives in Rome, so it is on our list of things to see. The atmosphere is beautiful, truly happy—Italians singing while showing off their merchandise in an attempt to lure people to buy. We don't need to buy anything, but it invigorates our spirits.

Letters from our parents keep coming with firm regularity. The political situation is still shaken by the continuous unrest, but we are in a somewhat steady state of balance right now. My parents are calmer, reassured that we are back together, reunited as a family, but they keep missing us. Occasionally, they still remind us that going back to Romania is still an option.

No, Mother. That is no longer an option, especially now that we do have a legal status in Italy, at least the three of us, the girls and I. As refugees, the last thing we want to do is go back to the country we fled from! Then why did we leave in the first place if not because of political reasons? Yes, we are "poor" now, materially speaking. We moved from having-a-lot to "having-not," but personally, I feel really rich from a spiritual point of view. Material things may be important, but life is more important. Family, love, the feeling of togetherness, freedom, peace of mind…

Mid-April. Amanda's school is organizing a trip to Florence. It is a unique occasion. Who knows if we will ever have such a chance? We may not be in a good financial position, but we can afford the $100 for a two-day trip. A couple of days later, as soon as she returned, she filled us in with all the details of her school trip. Amanda's recounting of the entire experience was proof of a right decision. She was so excited that she kept going on and on, sharing with us everything she had seen and visited.

"It was fabulous! We went to *Palazzo Pitti* (Pitti Palace) which bears the name of its first owner, a Florentine banker, Luca Pitti who commissioned the construction of this palace in the 1500's at the foot of the Boboli hill beyond the Arno River, but it is a symbol of the Medici's power over Tuscany."

"Did you go inside?"

"Yes, and it was truly stunning as compared to the outside. Then we went to the Uffizi Gallery and we saw an impressive art collection, including Raphael's Madonna and Child and young Saint John. There is also amazing furniture showing how the rich and powerful the Medici family lived."

"What did you see outside? Where did you go?"

"We walked around, and we saw *Fontana del Nettuno* (The Fountain of Neptune) in *Piazza della Signoria* (Signoria Square), and then we crossed the *Ponte Vecchio* (Old Bridge) over the Arno River and did some window shopping—there were so many small shops, mainly jewelry, on this bridge—it was amazing! Did you know that during World War II this was the only bridge across the Arno River that the fleeing Germans did not destroy? Instead, they blocked access by knocking down the medieval buildings on each side of the river."

Amanda is so excited that we don't need to ask her any questions. She keeps going and going and has photos to prove everything she saw and visited.

"Once on the other side of the Arno River, we went to visit *Palazzo Vecchio* (Old Palace), made of marble and bronze, located in the Signoria Square and at its entrance we saw sculptures of Adam and Eve, and a copy of Michelangelo's David."

"Why a copy? Where is the original?"

"It's in the *Galleria dell'Accademia di Firenze* (Gallery of the Academy of Florence), to protect it from weather, so the one in the Signoria Square is only a copy, majestic, nevertheless. Did you know that Michelangelo was only 26 years old when he started working on this famous statue? We learned that the block of marble he carved David on had been tried by other artists before him, but the block had a lot of issues because the material was fragile."

"Impressive." We are so glad Amanda had this chance. "What else?"

"Did you know that *Palazzo Vecchio* is located in the most important square in Florence?"

"No, we didn't! We know now!"

"…and in the *Palazzo Vecchio* there is a series of hidden passages which had been built by the Medici Family to escape their enemies and to store valuables?"

"How long did it take to Michelangelo to finish the statue?"
"Apparently three years."

* * *

The days go by—fast enough for me, but too slowly for Greg. I am juggling my work—same six days, same three different locations—taking the girls to school, picking them up, lunch at the soup kitchen in Via delle Sette Sale (newly "discovered"), back to "our" residence apartment in Via di Boccea.

Greg went to *Questura* a couple of days ago and tried to apply for a resident permit in Italy, but he was told that he had no grounds! He applied for political asylum in Canada and was refused, so that option is ruled out. Once refused in another country, one is not allowed to apply again anywhere else. Visitor? No visa…

This is really weird, though. How was he allowed to come to Italy when he arrived about a month ago if all he had was just a Romanian passport? Yes, he was joining his family in Italy, but still…Maybe because his Italian visa was still valid. Well, there is nothing we can do at this moment. Life goes on. He will be happy though if he can find some work, anything. He seems to be more and more concerned every day. As much as he likes Italy and the Italian people, he doesn't "see" a future for us in this country.

To make things worse, we just received a letter from the American Consulate. They rejected our application. Chemical engineers are not needed in the U.S. That's too bad!! If Greg was not successful applying as an engineer, what can I say about my qualifications? They will definitely not need an English teacher, or a French one!

We still have hopes. The Australian Embassy still did not respond. There are days when Greg seems to have regrets for not having been accepted to stay in Canada. I feel lost, disconcerted…He just arrived, about a month ago. I understand it's hard for him to feel "useless." Hopelessness and helplessness combined. Should we give Canada a try again? As a family this time? It's a possibility…

* * *

On a positive note, the girls are doing extremely well in school. Their mastering of the Italian language is amazing. It is incredible to hear them conversing in Italian between themselves, or even when they talk with us, sometimes, or even with their grandparents over the phone, once in a while. It seems to come natural to them. In fact, my mother keeps mentioning to me every single time we call her that Evelyn has an Italian accent when she speaks Romanian. Funny…

Amanda's homework continues to be demanding. Italian grammar and literature occupy most of her time. Verb tenses and moods, articles and prepositions and combinations of both, noun cases and endings everywhere—I know it's difficult, she never studied Italian in Romania, but she's doing an amazing job. Her classes in Italian literature are the most challenging. As a fully and truly immersed student in the seventh grade of an Italian middle school, the first author she is studying is Dante. Dante! Dante Alighieri, the 13th century poet and his famous "Divina Commedia."

Engaging Amanda in conversations, usually at the end of a school day, on our way to find a place for the daily homework, gives me the chance to learn about the Italian education system and makes me feel somewhat connected to my teaching career.

"So, what are some impressions of your studying Italian literature?"

"Oh, Mom…There is a lot to talk about. So, the teacher wants us to read, sometimes out loud. She wants us to hear the words we are reading so we can feel and live the emotions they are conveying, to absorb and savour the beauty of the language…"

"Does the teacher engage the students in discussions?"

"Yes, all the time. Today, for example we read in class the first canticle of the Divine Comedy, a song after another, and then the teacher stopped and asked us to put ourselves in Dante's shoes…What did we think Dante felt? What happened to him? What did we feel as readers?"

I'm frankly perplexed to hear Amanda's detailed descriptions of her literature classes. Overwhelmed, too. Back in our home country she would have studied Romanian authors, but at least that would have been our mother tongue. I'm encouraging her to keep going. She is definitely on a steep learning curve, but so am I.

"In canto XXXII the damned are compared to frogs that put their heads out of the quagmire, and to storks…"

"Do the storks have a particular symbolism attached to them?"

"Yes, in medieval texts these birds are apparently a symbol of love for children. Here is a question for you, Mom: what do you know about a hendecasyllable?"

Is Amanda trying to test my knowledge of medieval literature?

"If I remember well, I think a hendecasyllable has to do with a number of syllables, eleven, if I am not wrong."

"Yes, it is a line of verse containing eleven syllables."

I realize that in her classes the students not only read, but they have to analyze, compare, make hypotheses. It is fundamental, in fact, that in addition to listening and reading, they talk about literature, they have to show that they understand the meaning as well as the feelings of the poets, dwelling sometimes on the sensations.

"What is your homework for tomorrow?"

"I have to compose a sonnet in hendecasyllables."

"Does it have to rhyme?"

"Luckily, no…The teacher wants us to dwell on some specific words."

"And then…?"

"Then we will have to read our lyrics in class and then reflect on the path that we have taken."

"What do you mean by that?" I am still struggling to understand where all this strategy is leading.

"We have to focus on the meaning of making poetry."

From everything Amanda is telling me, I am wondering what the high school curriculum will look like if this is what she is studying in grade seven.

"However, Mom, I think maths and physics were more difficult in Romania."

Maybe. I know that she had great teachers in Romania, too, both elementary and middle school. They definitely helped.

Amanda's first report card was remarkably reassuring, to say the least. Her teachers had only words of support, congratulating her for her continuous effort and hard work.

***

It is truly amazing to see how well the girls have been accepted and integrated in their classes. Both their teachers and classmates have been so accommodating, making them feel included, part of their teams and everyday activities. Amanda is part of the school volleyball team, and she is truthfully ecstatic about it.

Evelyn, on the other hand, is getting ready for the end of the school year which seems to be a real celebration since it's also the end of the elementary cycle. She has a role in a few shows that her classmates are putting together under the direction of their two teachers. So, I have to work on a few costumes…No sewing machine…Well, I am grateful that when I was just a 7—8 years old kid, my grandmother taught me how to sew, knit, crochet—basically use needles and thread and…my own hands and imagination! It's paying off today and, as much as I hated it when my grandmother was hardly allowing me to play, today I am grateful. I remember the times when, as a kid I wanted to play with dolls. I must have been 6 years old or maybe even younger. "What are you doing?" my grandmother was yelling, trying to locate me, hidden in some remote part of our house or backyard, or garden. I was, of course, playing, yet saying that out loud, acknowledging to what any normal kid my age would normally do, was not an option. I was not allowed to play! At least not play per se. So, I had no choice but lying sometimes. However, my playing consisted in making outfits for my dolls, crocheting or knitting, anything useful was supposed to be my playing.

"Mamma, you have to make me a pretty outfit for the Tarantella dance, please!"

"Oh, do I? What is it supposed to look like?" Evelyn is giving me some details. I think I can pull something off.

"Mamma, do you know where the word Tarantella comes from?"

I have to admit I don't.

"It was first used in the 14th century and its name presumably comes from Taranto, an Italian town in the south, where the dance originated as a weird response of field workers to the bite of a spider whose name is also related to Taranto—the tarantula."

It is obvious that she learned this at school. I am also learning from them every day. I find that although life in Italy under our present conditions is extremely challenging and difficult, it's also enriching in so many ways. Maybe I am too positive, but it helps.

* * *

Month of May is here. Greg's first day of work. The Ranieri family have a house in the countryside, about 60 km north-east of Rome, on Via Salaria, all the way into the Province of Rieti. They purchased this beautiful villa, featuring a big garden, but also an olive grove that has not been properly maintained by the previous owners. Greg's first "job" is to take the bus in the morning, go to this place and remove all the rocks so the soil would be more manageable and suitable for the olive trees. At least this will make him feel useful, giving him a purpose, and a way of making some money for our family.

Amanda's enjoyment for being part of the volleyball team was not to last very long. One day, as I went to pick her up from school, to my surprise, her left arm was in a cast!!!

"What happened?"

"I broke my wrist."

"How?"

"I just fell in the gym."

"How did you get the cast on?"

"The teachers took me to the hospital."

Oh, how much more caring than that? It's true that this happened while Amanda was at school and everything happened on the school premises. It was also true that there was no way any of us could have been contacted (no cell phones at the time…). No more volleyball for this year.

* * *

End of the school year. As parents, we are invited to be spectators to our children's celebration of the elementary cycle. An entire presentation, very artistic and "very Italian." All the outfits that I had sewn by hand were on the stage now.

The dance of the vestal virgins. Girls dancing around, pretending to be part of a ritual where a sacred fire, Vesta's fire, was supposed to be preserved, so Rome could never be destroyed...Pink silk, flowing dresses, with sashays in a darker shade of pink. All the girls are so beautiful.

Next comes a little play. Evelyn is a teacher this time, and she is presenting Rome to "her students." Wearing a black dress, with white polka dots, a hair piece covering her head—this "professional" outfit is giving her an air of...importance. "*Roma è una città bella, piena di storia ed antiche rovine...*" (Rome is a beautiful city bursting with history and antique ruins). Good job, Evelyn!

Three more dances—one classical with the girls wearing white Roman short costumes all adorned with "golden" belts and hair ornamentations, another one performed by countryside women engaged in daily chores while chatting away, and then here is the tarantella, the liveliest of all. Parents are ecstatic. Our children have been true performers. Many thanks to the teachers. Excellent job! The end of the show marks the end of the school year. Summer vacation is here!

March 31, 1991—celebrating Easter in Vatican. Pope John Paul II is delivering the "Urbi et Orbi" message to the thousands of people gathered in the Vatican Square.

June 1991—enjoying a Sunday stroll through Rome. Delighted to wear a t-shirt featuring the Canadian maple leaf that my husband brought from Canada. A quick stop in front of the Arch of Constantine.

June 1991—time for a short rest in Colle Oppio Park, adjacent to the Colosseum.

17

FIRST PEACEFUL NIGHT

"Buon giorno. I would like to talk to Signora Maria-Concetta."

"Speaking. Who is this?"

"My name is Maria. I am a Romanian immigrant and I'm in Italy with my family. It is my understanding that you are part of a volunteering program doing some community work, helping immigrants to adjust and adapt to life in Italy. I was wondering if I could have the pleasure of meeting with you one of these days." To my surprise, it didn't take long for Maria-Concetta to agree to meet me.

I had obtained her phone number from other fellow immigrants whom I met at the soup kitchen where we were having our daily lunch, in Via delle Sette Sale. I really didn't know what I wanted from her. At this point we were pretty much all set, except for Greg's work. I was hoping she would have some connections that would allow my husband to find a real job.

"Where would you like to meet?"

Well, that was a good question. I have never been out anywhere and I had no idea where to meet someone. A café, but where? There were thousands of them! Besides, I was all the time on the move, on and off buses, tramways, metro—going in all directions, work, children's school, home.

"The only place I can think of is the food kitchen in Via delle Sette Sale where we eat every day." Nothing else comes to my mind.

"Sounds good. Can we meet tomorrow?"

"Yes, what time?"

"What time is convenient for you?"

"2 pm?"

125

"Great. See you tomorrow."

* * *

It's almost the end of June. School is over now, so I don't have to worry about the girls' school. For the last couple of weeks the level of noise in this residence has become unbearable. Students seem to be in a euphoric state, as the academic year is approaching for them, as well. What can I say? At least, we have a roof over our heads. Greg has finished his work in the countryside. Luck is on his side, though. The Ranieri family has started to do some construction work at their home in Rome. They are restructuring their condo unit and, although experienced workers have been hired for this job, they are also considering giving Greg something to do, some labourer's work. He's really happy to be able to make himself useful and make some money, as well.

June 25th, 1991. Maria-Concetta shows up at the meeting point with very little delay. (It's almost customary to be late for appointments and meetings in Italy). A very nice lady, apparently in her 50's, wearing glasses with thick lenses, squinting as if the diopters of the lenses are not helping with her noticeable myopia. Our conversation goes very well. I am telling her about all our story. She is visibly affected by the repulsive living conditions we had to endure while living in the convent. What can I say? It's over. At least we had a shelter, a roof; we didn't have to live in the streets. She doesn't seem to be too religious, but she likes helping people in need. Politically wise, she is obviously left oriented. I don't care about Italian politics. Our Romanian "left" has become extremely abusive to the point where socialism turned into communism turned into a plain, obnoxious and cruel dictatorship.

"So, where do you live right now?"

"In a student residence, a dormitory of sorts."

"A dormitory? How many rooms do you have?"

"Rooms? We have only one room, with four beds, one next to the other," I don't get to give her a full description of our living conditions, because she is cutting me short.

"Listen! I have an apartment in a new area of Rome, called EUR. It's a residential and business area, south from the city centre, about 45 minutes by metro from the main railway station. It's part of a condominium, all furnished, two bedrooms, bathrooms, kitchen, etc. I wouldn't charge you anything, other than gas and electricity, which is not expensive at all. I hope you don't feel offended."

Offended? I almost feel like I have to pinch myself to believe that this is real. What prompted this woman to offer us help? We just met. How can she trust me? Why? We continue our discussion for another hour or so, and I am learning that she occasionally spends a few months in different South American countries, mainly Guatemala, helping people in need, helping them to build their communities. This woman is a total inspiration. We say good-bye to each other, and she offers to come pick us up, on Sunday, June 28th, luggage and all.

I wish I could grow wings to fly to our apartment in the residence right away and share the good news with my family. The girls are happy. We start packing up, including Evelyn's collection of dolls that didn't subside in volume or number. Maybe it's time we give some unnecessary items to a charity…Greg will be home, too, in a couple of hours. I'm sure he will be in disbelief to hear the good news.

*　*　*

Sunday around noon, Maria-Concetta showed up at the address I had given her. Our luggage was ready, but her car was too small.

"We can send the girls with you, and we—Greg and I—will take the metro."

"No, no! I can take one girl and one adult with me and come back for a second trip later in the afternoon to pick up the other two of you." Sounds like a great alternative. I offer to go with Amanda and the luggage. Once we get to this new location, we can already arrange everything around, so everything will be ready when Greg and Evelyn join us.

In the evening we are all set. Welcome to a new home! It's the most decent place we've lived in since we left Romania. There is a phone in the living-room, too! We thank Maria-Concetta. She has been of a huge help and her offering us to stay in this place that she owns gives us a feeling of hope. My understanding is that she inherited this condo from her parents after they died. She is definitely a kind soul.

* * *

We slide smoothly into July, so we can afford to relax a little. Peacefulness taking over. What a great feeling! One of these days we have to go to the Canadian Consulate to check what the procedures to apply for immigration to Canada are. I love Italy and the Italians, but as the days go by, I realize that we may never have any chance of getting some decent jobs, owning an apartment, having a car or two, sending the girls to continue their education at a higher level. We will never have enough money to afford all these amenities. In fact, one of the families whom I help with cleaning has a twenty-seven-year-old daughter who has a degree in languages, just like I do. She has been unemployed for over four years. Occasionally she gets a job as a substitute teacher, but at her age, she still lives with her parents in a two-bedroom apartment! No, we did not leave Romania to be content with crumbs. We will have to give Canada another try. An "official" one.

* * *

Almost end of July. Drama again! Maria-Concetta has just called us. She was very worried. I didn't know what to make of all that conversation, but she said she was coming to see us as soon as possible, because she had some bad news.

Bad news? There seems to be no end to our misfortune. One step forward, one backwards! We don't seem to make any progress.

"Buon giorno. What's going on?"

Almost trying to catch her breath, as if she had come here running, she spilled the bad news:

"You have to leave."

"What do you mean? What did we do? What happened?"

"You didn't do anything, but the owners of these condo units who belong to a condominium association have complained to the management that I rented my apartment."

"Yes, but we still don't understand…"

"I'm afraid I've made a mistake. I should have advised the association, but it's very likely they would not have approved of my renting this place.

Tenants have rights in Italy. If, for example, you do not want to leave, I cannot force you, and this creates a problem for all the condo owners."

"But, Maria-Concetta, we are not going to live here forever. It's just temporary while we are in this transitional stage…"

"I know. I understand. I believe you, but I cannot convince the management and I cannot change their rules."

We look at one another. What choice is there?! Maria-Concetta agrees to give us a few days until we find something else. What? When? Where? How much the rent again? How fast? I feel totally desperate. We are all shocked, at a real loss for words. Greg is wrapping arms around himself, looking down, totally avoiding eye contact, in utter disbelief. Maria-Concetta had good intentions, but it was not meant to be.

*　*　*

I have nobody to speak with other than the Ranieri family, and the other lady who's helping them with cooking the family's meals, Carmelina. Maybe one of them knows somebody who knows somebody who… Everything is happening on such a short notice. When I was just thinking that we would have some quiet time this summer…

July 22nd. Monday. I'm back to work. Greg is, too. The girls are enjoying their summer break at Maria-Concetta's condo. There is no school until mid-September, so they can enjoy their homework-free days. The day goes by too slowly today. Will we find anybody to help us any time soon? Around 3 pm Giovanna is home. Distress is plastered all over my face. It doesn't take long until I start pouring all my misery out. Tears rolling down, eyes swollen, nose sniffling.

"Give me time until tomorrow," says Giovanna. "We'll think of something. Just go home, both of you, and try not to worry too much. We'll find a solution."

July 23rd. Giovanna is at work, so is Alberto. Carmelina is not working today. I am all alone. There is a note on the table, written by Giovanna:

"Maria, you know the house we have just bought at Fara Sabina, in the countryside. The house is uninhabited, but it is all furnished. We can offer you to move there as soon as you need to. Please let us know if our proposal sounds acceptable to you."

If it sounds acceptable? It's definitely more than we ever dreamed of. Or thought of. It is about 60 km north-east of Rome, but there are buses several times a day. Greg has already worked in their garden and he knows how to get there.

Once we get to Maria-Concetta's condo, we give her a call to update her on the new developments of the situation. She is offering to give us a ride. Why not?! She's relieved we are not creating any problems for her. However, her car is still small. We'll figure something out, again…

Saturday, July 27th—we are moving again. The fourth time in four months! We have a key to this house from Ranieri family and off we go! We manage to squeeze all our bags and suitcases in Maria-Concetta's car (eventually we got rid of the unnecessary stuff, clothes and toys and all disposables, so we have so much less to carry with us around); the girls make some room for themselves in the back seat, among some other pieces of luggage, and I am sitting in the front seat. Greg is coming by bus. He knows how to go about it.

An hour later we arrive at the destination. We say good-bye and thank you to Maria-Concetta and, as we are unloading our possessions, dropping them in a big pile right in the driveway, we realize that we need to take a deep breath! What we see is almost unimaginable. We are truly amazed. This is a mansion, not a house!

Another hour later Greg arrives from Rome, as well. Time to wind down and take in the magnificence and the peacefulness of this place. The lush green pastures spreading down the hill, slowly transitioning into the olive groves, are all blending in the horizon line. The sense of inner peace and harmony is unsurpassed.

Evening melts into a tranquil night, all adorned with shimmering stars twinkling above us, a borderless stream of clarity; a vast, seemingly clear sky stretching out for a time without end, a perfect midnight velvet curtain, an invisible splendour of God, expanding His soul in elation in the midst of the universal radiance of creation.

A beautiful night of sleeping in peace. Hopefully this will last for a while. Thank you, Alberto and Giovanna! *Mille grazie!*

18

COMMUNISM IS FALLING APART

The first two weeks of August have gone by in a blink of an eye. *Ferragosto* on August 15th is a day when most Italians are taking a couple of weeks off. It is also a religious celebration, the Assumption of Mary, a dogma of faith (established recently, only in 1950) according to which Mary, mother of Jesus, at the end of her earthly life, went to heaven in body and soul.

Going back in history, the *Ferragosto* was a day whose origins were dating back to the Roman period and the pagan calendar, and it means "Augustus' rest" (*Feriae Augusti*), in honour of Octavian Augustus, the first Roman emperor (from whom the month of August actually takes its name). Octavian Augustus made the 1st of August a day of rest after weeks of hard work in the agricultural sector. This way, people were given a well-deserved rest after the hard work of the previous weeks. In ancient times, the Ferragosto was celebrated on August 1st with horse races, festivals, floral decorations, but the break days were many more, so much so that the celebrations were extended until August 15th. However, the festivity was initially created for political reasons, and later on the Catholic Church decided to move the festivity to the 15th of August which is the celebration of the Assumption of Mary.

"Mamma, can we go to Montegrottone village tonight?"

August 15th was here and the next village down the road was celebrating this religious festivity in a very jubilant way.

"How are you getting there?"

"We are walking."

It was not too far—about 30 minutes walk, but it was late in the evening, and we didn't know how long it would take, when it would be over or when they would be back home. The curfew was not a concept. Not only was the village extremely safe, but all the neighbours seemed to be constantly on the watch. Alcohol consumption was not an issue. It was simply not customary for teenagers to drink. Neither in the Italian culture, nor in the Romanian one. There was no "drinking age." It had never been. Actually, back in our home country, whenever we were having a family reunion or a celebration of any kind where alcohol was served, parents were offering their children the chance to taste the drink—either by dipping their fingers or simply taking a sip. Their curiosity was met with acceptance, and since the alcohol was not a "forbidden fruit," drinking never became an issue.

"Please, Mom, Dad…" It was difficult to say no to the girls especially since four of their friends had come over, so we were outnumbered! We knew it was safe.

Different concerts and a colourful display of lights added a festive note to the religious ceremony that had taken place earlier during the day, and by midnight the celebrations ended with fireworks. Golden ribbons of sparkling arc-shaped rockets were soaring skywards, and, as if shattering against the sky, they were falling downwards in a burst of sparks. Barrels of bonfires, some shooting straight up before exploding, others whirling down in a spiral, but all exploding into thousands of sparks, tumbling down like a scarlet waterfall.

Soon after midnight the girls came home, also accompanied by their friends, our neighbours.

* * *

Since we moved to this residence in the countryside, we finally had the "luxury" of relaxing a little in the evenings after the long hours of commuting and work, and since we also had a TV, we started to "indulge" ourselves in watching the "Telegiornale."

However, tonight I am busy in the kitchen, trying to prepare a nice dinner. It has been a tiring day. Mondays always seem more strenuous than other days of the week. Maybe because Sunday is our only day off, and we never have enough rest. The ride to Rome in the morning is one hour long by bus. It is long, but the ride is comfortable. Greg usually goes to his workplace in construction, close to the Spanish Steps, and I go to my regular cleaning jobs. Obviously, once arrived in Rome, we still need to take a metro or a bus or a tramway to our work, so the time is always long, and the public transit is always extremely crowded. In the late afternoon or evening we follow the same route coming back home and then we join the girls in this beautiful countryside home that Ranieri family allowed us to live in for the summer.

We have this entire house for our sole use. Obviously, we restrict ourselves to occupying as little space as possible, while enjoying the privacy of two of the four bedrooms—bathrooms included—on the upper floor which is connected with the main floor through a beautiful winding staircase, spiralling down into the main hallway. The main floor is not off limits, by all means (although we always respect our boundaries, so the master bedroom and the ensuite bathroom are of unique use by the owners). An extremely large and well-equipped kitchen and the adjacent expansive, elegantly furnished living-room along with the dining-room, everything covered with terracotta tiles, they both have doors opening onto a beautiful terrace, leading into a lavish garden, continuing with the olive grove that Greg worked in about two months ago. This is not a simple house. It is a real villa, a magnificent property, tastefully restored with luxury finishes, offering a unique and magical panoramic view over the hills and valleys extending all the way to Rome, at a considerable distance.

It didn't take long until our neighbours started to drop by, bringing a homemade loaf of bread, or a pizza, or some "dolce" (dessert), and spending time with us, socializing in the well-known Italian-style. To our girls' joy, the few teenagers in our neighbourhood became their friends, making them feel included, and taking them along to participate to the different summer activities in our village.

*　*　*

"Did you hear that?"

"Hear what?"

"Mikhail Gorbachev resigned from the Communist Party of the Soviet Union."

Greg was watching the news in the living room.

"That's interesting. How did that happen? What led to his resignation?"

The political situation in the Middle East had somewhat quieted down, but latest news about the Soviet Union and their leader, Mikhail Gorbachev, seemed to be quite alarming. As transitional as our status in Italy was, we were relieved to know that we could truly enjoy our freedom. Our feelings were still raw and memories from the past were still occasionally haunting us. Tonight, however, we were learning that earlier in the morning the Soviet Union woke up to Tchaikovsky's "Swan Lake" being broadcast on television combined with journalists reading an announcement. It was an attempt made by members of the government of the Soviet Union to take control of the country from Soviet President Mikhail Gorbachev. This was apparently a coup orchestrated by hard-line communists who were opposed to Gorbachev's reform program.

In the late 1980s Mikhail Gorbachev had begun the democratization of the Soviet Union by implementing open discussions of political and social issues, the so-called *glasnost* (transparency), along with introducing fundamental reforms, which became known as *perestroika* (restructuring). We were still in Romania at that time and this unexpected openness of a solid communist regime, coming directly from Gorbachev, initially came as a surprise. A positive one, as seen by the people. Personally, when we were secretly trying to discuss these issues with our close friends in Romania, I remember the feeling of temporal relief we were experiencing, a ray of optimism, a shred of hope that seemed to be lurking in the horizon. I liked to think that Gorbachev's reforms led to the weakening of the communist regime in Eastern Europe, culminating eventually with the fall of the Berlin Wall.

It was only recently, after we moved to Italy that we learned about Ronald Reagan's speech from June 1987. Obviously, our communist regime under Ceausescu never made public that famous speech that almost set ground for what was to come. "Mr. President, tear down this wall" had been Reagan's famous words from his speech in Berlin, at the Brandenburg's Gate. He was asking Gorbachev to open the Berlin Wall which had separated West and East Berlin since 1961. There had been debates whether that speech had had any influence on the wall coming down. I believe it did.

The wall did come down in 1989, and here we are two more years later, on this day of August 19th, 1991 the coup leaders end up by removing Mikhail Gorbachev as president of the Soviet Union. The Soviet Union would continue on *de jure* for another four months, but *de facto* it already ceased to exist. Would those 16 republics gain their total independence? Or will the Soviet Union become a confederation of sovereign states?

As the days went on, we learned more news from Russia (or actually, still the Soviet Union). The attempted coup destroyed Gorbachev politically. The republics rushed to be free of Moscow's control. Latvia, one of the three Baltic countries, declared its independence from the USSR on August 21st, and Ukraine followed on August 24th, the same day when Gorbachev dissolved the Central Committee of the Communist Party and resigned as the party's general secretary, thus signalling the beginning of the end of the USSR.

This is happening under our own eyes. The end of communism is finally here, but the future of Europe is far from being certain. What's next? Will the ex-communist European countries be integrated in a larger Europe? Will there be a European Union any time soon? Much of everything that has already happened is behind us now, but more is yet to come. We are witnessing history being made, day by day.

19

LIFE GOES ON

August has been a truly peaceful month, and we are slowly moving into the first week of September. The beginning of a school year is around the corner. Luckily, both girls are going now to the same school, always in Rome, but September comes with a new move! Fara Sabina has been just our temporary summer "residence." It is time we move again! The Ranieri family has a condo apartment right on the Tyrrhenian Sea, another 65 km away from Rome, going north-west this time, always by bus, following the popular Via Aurelia, another famous Roman road constructed in approximately 241 BC.

The first school day is Monday, September 16[th,] which coincides with Evelyn's birthday. We cannot leave this place before we celebrate her turning 12 years old. Back in our home country we never missed a birthday. Cake, candles, happy singing, presents and all—no matter how sombre the times or the political situation was, we always did our best to celebrate each passing year in our children's lives, immortalizing the moments by taking pictures, black and white, but unforgettable, nevertheless.

Ranieri family are all here today, and Alberto is ready to give us a ride. However, a nice festive lunch ending on a singing note, cake included, makes Evelyn's day feel special. It is her last pre-teen birthday.

Celebration over, we pack up our belongings into Alberto's car. They kindly help us load our luggage into the vehicle and here we are on our way to the new temporary residence on the seashore this time. We say a temporary good-bye to Fara Sabina and to all the new friends we have made among the neighbours, and we are off to another beginning…How many more "beginnings" will there be, going on and on, over and over, and for how long?

At least we know that we are allowed to stay here until the end of June, next year. For the next 10 months we are going to be "stable."

Once arrived at the new destination, I wouldn't be wrong to admit that we are totally surprised. The entire building, two stories high and two entrances, counting probably 12 apartments altogether, is empty! We are going to be the only people living here. This entire building is another private residence of the Ranieri's, the apartments belonging to the different members of their large family. Alberto opens the main entrance door into the building, and then the apartment door and here we are, being offered a beautiful accommodation, complete with all amenities, everything for our sole use…Just incredible. Again, no rent. No fees. Simply God's love…

"Mom, we have bedrooms for all of us…and two bathrooms…"

"Did you see the kitchen? It opens onto a beautiful balcony surrounded by bay leaf trees! It opens onto a patio!"

"Oh, look at this other balcony! We cross the street, and we are on the seashore! We can go to the beach tomorrow!"

"We have a TV, too!"

The girls cannot contain their amazement. Indeed, we have everything we need. An hour later, our belongings rearranged, we are on an exploration spree!

"Look at those cacti! They have fruit…"

We have recently learned that the fruit belonging to that type of cactus are called *"fichi d'India,"* a typical Sicilian fruit (we are about to learn later that in English it is called "cactus pear"). We are locating the grocery store—very important, and then the bus stop for the bus that will take us to Rome; next, we are checking the main beach and the "downtown" area, and extremely pleased, we return to our condo a few hours later.

However, in spite of the comfortable lifestyle we have been offered, our souls are still on edge. This is a temporary situation. Every day going by without a response from the Australian Embassy or Canadian Consulate is killing our hopes, little by little.

* * *

Letters from our parents are still coming with regularity. However, we have a phone on the premises, so once a week my mother is calling us. It may sound totally bizarre nowadays, but international phone calls at this point between Romania and other countries are still managed by switchboard operators, although local calls can be dialed directly. Making long distance calls facilitated by operators is time-consuming, as all of them have to be manually operated. Sometimes, either because of short staffing, shortage of phone lines or simple the lack of switchboard operators' willingness and professionalism, the time between placing a call and actually talking with someone at the other end of the line can be as long as two to three hours! So, my mother is "placing the order" around 9 pm and the phone is ringing at our end around mid-night…It seems like Romania was a third-world country!!! Maybe it still is!

The political turmoil is still ongoing. The unrest did not come to a stop in 1991, nor did it calm down. People are still discontent. The riots are continuing on and off, and throughout these turbulent times, the newly elected president, Ion Iliescu, is vowing to restore the order and democracy while making promises for better conditions of living and working, for better salaries, and for, basically, everything! A year ago, in 1990, both in February and June, the government's response was to defeat the protesters by manipulating thousands of miners from the coal mines and sending them to the capital to interfere with the demonstrators and crush the protests. Government agents and former employees of the "Securitate" (the ex-Secret Police Service) had been infiltrated and disguised themselves as miners. Thousands of miners from the Jiu Valley had been trucked into Bucharest by the government forces to confront the demonstrators. Romanian people as well as the entire world were watching the television broadcasts of miners viciously fighting with students and other protesters.

All the demonstrators are asking now is the official recognition of a 13-point document called Timisoara Proclamation, whose signers are expressing liberal-democratic goals, among which, the best-known requirement—the 8th Point—is calling for all former Romanian Communist Party officials and "Securitate" cadres to be prevented from holding official functions for a period of 10 years.

How can this requirement be ever implemented when the new regime, in spite of claiming that they are restoring democracy, consists of officials who have all worked for the previous regime, who have been Ceausescu's acolytes, sycophants, a second echelon of communists, wolves in sheep's skin?

The demonstrations became truly violent when Iliescu appealed to the miners to "defend" the country. Special trains brought around 10,000 miners to Bucharest, where the clashes became brutal. Several people had been killed and later on buried in a common grave near Bucharest, and thousands more had been wounded.

These anti-communist manifestations continued to lead to rebellion and civil unrest, and the government decided to crush them rather than trying to meet people's expectations or finding alternatives.

However, here we are now, a year later, September 1991—nothing has changed. People are unhappy; there are looming rumours of a civil war. This time the miners have had enough of their demands not having been met; they are tired of continuing to live in poverty, while the politicians are making promises that they are failing to put into practice.

At the national level, this miners' revolt of 1991, the fourth one, called the "mineriad," has a negative effect on the population. The television is broadcasting directly from the very confrontation places, showing miners armed with sticks, axes, picks, chains, beating anyone who seems suspicious of them. They are violent, threatening everybody in the way, and hitting in all directions. Hundreds of people end up being wounded, of whom some seem to be in need of hospitalization, and a few have been reported as being killed. After almost two years since the 1989 revolution, the Romanians are still fighting against communism, against corruption. Nothing has changed. Eventually, the government is forced to resign.

* * *

My mother is updating me on all this news, and I can't tell if she is saddened by what is going on in our home country, or happy because we have left, trying to forget the past, leaving everything behind us, running towards freedom, away from a disorganized regime which is still leading a country thrown into chaos by years of communism.

"We have decided to open a business." Is my mother talking about starting a company, opening a "business"? It sounds incredible in so many ways. It is a little hard to comprehend. My parents have been accountants for their entire life, they had comfortable jobs, and they are now retired. All they have waited for during all those long years of working was a "happy" retirement. Well, the retirement is here. My mother is almost 60 years old, but they are far from being happy, one of the reasons being our departure.

"Business in what?"

"We are thinking about opening a home business in accounting, assisting people with their taxes."

"Really? Is it possible?" I know that Romania has become a little more open to business, and that private companies, big or small, are being encouraged, but I am stunned to hear that my parents are now able to change their lifestyle and they are already adopting an entrepreneurial attitude.

"Yes, it is possible, and it is something that would give us something to do, and will keep our minds occupied."

"Who will be your clients?"

"There are some businesses that have opened around the city and they need help when time comes to submit the tax forms to the government. Besides, we can earn some extra money. The Romanian currency has devalued drastically, and our pensions are not enough."

I don't know whether to be happy for them or sad. The fact that they don't have enough money obviously makes their life more difficult. They can hardly make ends meet with their small pensions, and it is extremely sad to know that they have worked their entire life hoping that one day they will enjoy the retirement. Here they are, both retired, almost 60 and 65 years of age, and they have to start a business because money is scarce. I also feel guilty in a way. If we had stayed in Romania, we wouldn't have been able to help them much. We would have been physically there, but occupied with our jobs and our children.

"We're also thinking about coming to see you one day," says Mom.

I'm wondering if this is the actual reason for their opening a home business because they need to keep their minds busy, to just stop thinking about us. It breaks my heart, truly breaks my heart. Oh, Mom…So many hardships she has encountered in her life, but I have never heard her complaining. No matter how hard and no matter how many times she tried to achieve different things, she never gave up and she kept going, in spite of the difficulties and hardships. Luckily, my stepfather was an amazing man, too. (Unfortunately, my parents had to divorce when I was seven years old, and my birth father was not in a better situation either.) However, my Mom had been a true example of resilience. She definitely inherited it from her mother—my grandmother—and then she passed it on to me. Never give up. Never surrender. Never take a No for a No. A door closes on you, but a window will open somewhere. Pick yourself up, brush yourself off, and keep going. The only option is ahead. Yes, my mother has truly created a model for anyone around her, but especially for me. Being harsh at times, but still without imposing it. Just by showing that she had to cherish herself exactly as she was, and not beating herself up over little things.

"You'll be successful, Mom. I know you both loved your jobs." Not only did my mother like her job in accounting, but her bright mind was always computing and doing math at any time, sometimes even without writing down. They do not have a computer with software, of course. All their accounting was—and, I am sure, still is—on paper, lots of sheets of paper, and their only "tool" is a small calculator. Brilliant minds. I have always been fascinated to see my mother bent over their sheets of paper, spread around on their table. Eyeglasses on, pencil in hand, erasers and even rulers around and, of course, sharpeners handy at all times.

It is late at night. The children are already in bed. Tomorrow is a school day. Life goes on…

20

EUROPEAN HISTORY IN THE MAKING

Amanda is working on history tonight.

"Dad, was Yugoslavia a kingdom?"

"Yes, King Peter II was the last king and he abdicated in 1945." Greg has a solid knowledge of history. "Why are you asking?"

"We learned in class today and I was surprised, because I don't remember learning that in Romania."

"It's because maybe you didn't get to that part of history while in Romania or maybe because history was taught in Romania through communist lenses. It's what the communist government wanted us to know, so certain historical facts have been either "omitted", or simply twisted…" Greg wanted to throw in a few more details so he could offer Amanda an overview of European history, but he realized that he would have probably engaged in a long diatribe against the communist regime. The wounds are still too raw. Time has not completely healed them.

*　*　*

1966. I'm in grade seven. A new schoolyear has just started, and history classes are not enticing me. Contemporary history. Communism. I'm only 13 years old but something is not right. The teacher has a bored look on his face and no matter what he is trying to teach us, the message doesn't quite go through. He is not convincing. Nor convinced either. However, we are supposed to memorize everything he is lecturing, and then regurgitate whenever we have oral questionnaires or quizzes. I'm thinking that maybe my grandmother would be able to help me.

"Grandma, how old were you when Grandpa died?"

"42. Why?"

"Just asking…So, at the age of 42 you were a widow?"

"Yes, and your mother was two years old, and I had six more children, seven altogether, all different ages. Why are you asking? Don't you have homework to do?"

"Yes, that's exactly why I am asking! So, how did you manage? Today, in our history class we learned about the Great Depression. Were you affected in any way?"

"Yes, but what choice was there other than rolling up my sleeves, taking care of my children and keep living!" My grandmother's stoic demeanor doesn't let any show of emotions on her face.

"Did you manage to recover after?"

"Kiddo, after that depression, it took a few years for the economy to improve, but in the meantime, the Second World War was around the corner, so the recovery was anything but…!"

"So, how did you manage to stay afloat?"

My grandmother is not answering. Obviously, my questioning is making her uneasy. After a short pause, she picks up with a pensive look on her face.

"During the Second World War your mother was younger than you are today. She was about 12 and she was the only child that was still in my care. All the other six ones were married or living on their own. I remember sending your Mom by train to take some supplies to one of her older sisters, so, at some point during this one-hour trip to Bucharest, an airstrike took them by surprise, bombs dropping from up above." Grandma's voice has a sad tone to it.

"So, you sent Mom alone? All by herself by train?"

"Yes, there was no choice."

"And what did Mom do?"

"She did what everybody else was doing. Got off the train and ran to a nearby bunker. We learned later that this was called the Operation Tidal Wave; it was an air attack by bombers of the United States Army Air Forces on some of the oil refineries about 60 km away from Bucharest…I remember to this very day…It was August 1, 1943. Your Mom was one month short from turning 12…"

"And then…?"

"When everything seemed to be safe and the aircraft were out of sight, everybody came out from underground and got back on the train, so your Mom just followed the crowds… She had a job to do, so she kept going."

My mind is working on putting things together. I'm trying to make sense of my grandmother's story, but something is not adding up. So, my Mom was 12 at the time, I am 13 today…My mother had some freedom, albeit imposed by the circumstances, while I do not have any freedom today. Still, I'm too curious to hear my grandmother's story. She is not easily opening up.

"And then, after the war, did you manage to get your life back and rebuild something?" A deep frown throws a large shadow on my grandmother's face.

"No. We lost everything."

"What do you mean? What happened?"

"Communism took over, Russians took over, and all our possessions were taken away. Properties, land, everything…" My grandmother is sighing. She stops. The grim expression on her face and the cold look in her eyes do not leave any doubt about her emotions, still painful 20 years later.

**

I remember the conversation so vividly as if it were yesterday. It was very rare that my grandmother was willing to share with me some of her heart-breaking past, the sad story of a well-off family who lost everything and became poor overnight.

Collectivization, communist promises, brainwashing, fear, people "disappearing", dissidents trying to express their discontent with the new regime being taken away, never to come back, thrown in prisons, where some of them were killed.

My mother being the youngest daughter of my grandmother became co-dependent. As my mother was growing older, my grandmother remained constantly attached to her. In her twenties, when my mother met my father and they fell in love with each other, my grandmother didn't seem to approve of their marriage. After I was born, however, my grandmother, who had just turned 60, decided to become my caretaker, so I almost became her eighth child!

And here we are today, after half a century of communism, history in Europe is constantly changing under our own eyes. New events are making headways every day. As a matter of fact, the political unrest is still going on. News coming from one of the countries that was part of Yugoslavia is truly alarming. The war in Croatia is making the headlines. Is Eastern Europe falling apart? It appears that the fall of Berlin Wall triggered a chain reaction.

Was communism a power holding together these countries, albeit by force? The Soviet Union is disintegrating, and previously independent republics are breaking away, achieving their new independence, one at a time. However, Croatia seems to have been going through hard political times recently. A lot of turmoil, unrest, upheaval…Crowds are out in the streets, demonstrating, fighting, a lot of casualties. From what we heard, it appears that a majority of Croats wanted Croatia to leave Yugoslavia and become a sovereign country, while many ethnic Serbs living in Croatia, supported by Serbia, opposed the secession and wanted Serb-claimed lands to be in a common state with Serbia. Croatia just declared independence, but this did not come without a lot of bloodshed. Over 20,000 people were killed in the war, a quarter of Croatia's economy was ruined, and refugees were displaced on both sides. This war ended with Croatian victory, and although the Serb and Croatian governments began to progressively cooperate with each other, tensions still remained.

I remember the 1980s, back in our home country. Every single day seemed to be worse than the one before. We were running out of hopes every single day we were lining up for the rationalized kilogram of flour or sugar per month, or the just one-time-per-month trip to a gas station when we could fill up our cars with gas. We were getting increasingly desperate: food was more and more scarce and there was the cruel uncertainty of what the next day would bring. Greg and I were often talking about fleeing the country, somehow, some day, but where? And how? I was suggesting to Greg that maybe he should do what other men were doing, basically taking their lives in their hands. We could hear occasionally that another man said goodbye to his family, taking his chance, swimming across the Danube into what was Yugoslavia at that time. Freedom, but most often than not, this freedom came with the attached risks. Drowning was very possible.

However, many men had managed to flee Romania via the dangerous and turbulent waters of the Danube around the straight called Iron Gates. Once arrived on the other side of the Danube, Yugoslavia seemed like a better choice and the first step out into the free world. Desperate as we were, this seemed to be a plausible solution, but Greg never wanted to leave us. He never wanted to leave his family behind. So, we continued to suffer as a family. Nevertheless, just across the Danube, Yugoslavia was just another socialist country that seemed to do so much better than Romania. Why was Yugoslavia different from what our country was? How did Tito manage to keep Yugoslavia united? Six separate republics somehow cohesive? How did he manage to break away from the Soviet Union? Or was it just an illusion?

At the beginning of the Cold War, after the Yugoslavian monarchy came to an end through the deposition of King Peter II, and after the Tito-Stalin split of 1948, Yugoslavia pursued a policy of neutrality. Its unique geopolitical situation allowed Tito to maintain an internal cohesion while suppressing nationalistic movements among the six republics that had been separated from one another along ethnic lines after WWII, so different from one another from cultural, religious and sometimes racial points of view. However, economically speaking, Yugoslavia transitioned to a market-based type of socialism, but how did Tito manage to make his country independent from the Soviet Union? Under the socialist system in Yugoslavia, the factories were worker cooperatives, and the decision-making was not as centralized as it was in Romania, which may have led to a stronger economic growth. Still, so different were our countries that Romanian communist dictatorship forbade us from travelling to Yugoslavia because they knew that once arrived on the other side of the Danube, we were free. Yugoslavia was denied to us, just as Hungary later on became a denied destination as well.

On May 1980 President Tito died. It was a time for mourning. What was to become of Yugoslavia now? Unemployment, inflation? Economic collapse? Inter-ethnic wars started to affect Bosnia and Herzegovina, Croatia and later on Kosovo, and here we are today, in the midst of a political unrest, a cruel inter-ethnic war.

Obviously, Amanda's lesson on the European history doesn't have to cover this ongoing political situation. However, we feel that we need sometimes to explain to the girls that we are part of a continuous historical and political movement, unravelling before our own eyes, making us sometimes feel like participants rather than witnesses. Amanda's European history is truly contemporary.

21

ROUTINE

I'm not a morning person. My brain is simply not working in the wee hours of the morning. I cannot even talk. Waking up before 5 am, preparing breakfast, coffee included, waking the girls up, getting ready to leave home so we are at the bus stop at 6 am, day in, day out, Monday through Saturday—this whole routine is challenging, to say the least. However, as a mother and a bread winner, this is the only option. I am glad that Greg has found a job on a construction site not far from Santa Marinella. He doesn't have to go to Rome anymore. His work consists of heavy-duty, manual labour, carrying loads of mortar mix, or cement, or bricks, or whatever is needed around the construction site. It is a tiring job, extremely strenuous, considering that he has to carry so many heavy loads up the scaffolding, no safety harness other than just a helmet, no insurance, nothing to protect him from falling or from any other injuries. After all—God forbid something happens—he does not even "exist"! He has no papers, whatsoever, and his work is totally under the table, absolutely illegal; he is stateless. However, for the time being, he is content. This work doesn't pay much. Considering how hazardous it is, 10,000 lira ($10 Canadian dollars) per hour is very little. He is totally underpaid. Basically, taken advantage of, literally exploited. I am paid the same amount of money per hour and my work is far from being difficult or dangerous. However, for now, this is giving him something to do for 10 hours a day, keeps his mind busy and gives him some satisfaction that he can bring home a sum of money every two weeks that looks good as a fistful of cash.

At least, the girls go to the same school this year, "*Scuola media Silvio Pellico*"—the middle school that Amanda has attended for half of the last school year, between January to June. She did perform amazingly well, just as I had anticipated, and the principal as well as her teachers were truly impressed. Now, she is in the eighth grade (the third year), while Evelyn has just started grade six (first year) of the same middle school. Same welcoming and accommodating atmosphere, wonderful and caring teachers, making them feel included, giving them a true feeling of belonging.

Our routine is the same every day and it is extremely exhausting for the girls, but they never seem to complain, not even a single time, no days off, no sick days. School starts at 8 am every day, six days a week, and they finish at 1 or 2 pm. However, our days start at 5 am, we are on the "COTRAL" commuter bus to Rome at 6 am, one hour and a half later we arrive in Rome, and we keep going with our daily schedule.

We only have time to wind down during our return commute, on our way back to Santa Marinella. The wind-down actually applies only to Amanda and me. Evelyn is too busy making new friends. She is such a social butterfly! We've already made friends with two other commuters: Signor' Romano, a 60+ years old gentleman who works in a photo shop in Rome, and Giancarlo, a 40-some years old teacher (or instructor) who also works in Rome teaching in a technical college. We are the only three passengers boarding the bus in Santa Marinella. Signor' Romano and Giancarlo board the bus at the terminus hub in Civitavecchia, about 15 km north of Santa Marinella, so they are already on the bus by the time the commuter arrives at our stop. The other passengers hop on the bus along the way, but I don't know any of them except for a very loquacious lady, who seems to know everybody around and engages in loud and lively conversations, in spite of the morning hours. Apparently, this lady is a long-time commuter. Always very elegant, heavy makeup (I wonder if she ever washes off her mascara), and constantly in good spirits. All the commuters seem to look forward to seeing her get on board in Santa Severa, so she becomes the free entertainer for our long commute.

The mornings are getting colder, darker and, especially, rainier. The lack of sunlight makes me lethargic. I'm not in the mood for making conversation, so I'm trying to sleep or at least keep my eyes closed most of the time.

For the last few days the rain has been coming down so heavily, some roads are flooded, which make the traffic even more challenging. Late or not, we make it to the Lepanto bus station, get off the bus, then take a metro for about eight stops, and after a short walk, we arrive at school before 8 am.

After half a day of work, I pick the girls up, and we are lucky to have the privilege of eating our lunch at a soup kitchen (Mensa "Giovanni Paolo II") belonging to Caritas Roma, a charity founded by the Catholic Church. Volunteers are helping with serving the meals, being of assistance on the semi-self-serving buffet line, but also assisting people at the tables, and we are so happy to enjoy not only a hot meal in great hygienic conditions, but also the familiar and dignified environment we are being offered. Our everyday lunch is an opportunity to establish a fraternal welcome relationship with the volunteers or other people who are in similar situations as ours.

The nuns are serving us the food from a buffet-like long counter table, where the main meal is served to us, but we can help ourselves to the fruit at the end of the line. Pasta is the main dish. While they are loading the plates, they look into our eyes, inviting us to ask for more, one spoonful at a time, if we need to. A sign, written in capital letters, displayed in full view right above the counter table says: "Take on your plate only what you need. Do not waste food." Some of us who may feel hungrier will need and may ask for more; some, maybe less. When one is starving, it's hard to know how much is too much. Our brains are late in asserting themselves satisfied, although our stomachs are full already. Almost regularly Evelyn is eating with her eyes! She thinks she is hungrier than she is, so she never finishes her meal. Since wasting food is not an option—for a good reason—I am supposed to clear her plate, and I end up eating more than I need.

An hour later and another kilometre of walking towards the Termini Railway station, we are following the same route back home. Jump on the metro, always crowded, get off at Lepanto station five metro stops later, up the stairs on the street, take the "COTRAL" commuter bus, and two hours later we are on our way home. It's 4 pm.

Useless to say, we're all tired, but during our long commuting back to Santa Marinella, I still have to participate a little in some conversations. It's hard to not respond to Italians' penchant for talking, always great conversationalists, engaging people in lively chats. Besides, both Signor' Romano and Giancarlo are very friendly, and conversing with them offers us different ideas, opening doors for new possibilities, and makes us feel welcome and included, just like any other regular citizen.

We've been in this apartment for about two months now, eight weeks of school days, and eight Sundays when we should relax and decompress. The afternoons are dedicated to homework—and there is plenty of it! The curriculum is loaded: Italian language and literature, mathematics, history, geography, natural sciences, chemistry, physics, English as a second language, music, physical education, and fine arts. Each of these objects is distributed over the 30—36 hours of classes per week, with a five-minute break between classes every day and having a different level of difficulty according to the grade. Obviously, Evelyn's program as a six-grader is less difficult than Amanda's, who, at the end of the school year, is supposed to pass a final exam consisting of a written test of Italian (language and literature), math, English language, as well as an oral test—the same for all secondary school students.

"Mom, Dad, do you know how many regions Italy is divided into?"

"I believe it's 20."

Evelyn is testing us on our knowledge of Italian geography.

"Good guess! Do you know how many provinces?"

"I have to admit I don't…" I can't know everything!

"You tell us!" Greg is encouraging her to share with us her new discoveries.

"There are 80 ordinary provinces, two autonomous provinces, four regional decentralization entities, six free municipal consortia, and 14 metropolitan cities, as well as the Aosta Valley region (which also exercises the powers of a province)."

"That's what you're learning about?"

"Yes, and I have to draw the map of Italy first and then the region of Veneto as my homework."

"What is the capital of Veneto?" It's my turn to see how fresh her recollection is of the first Italian city we set foot on last year.

"Venice!"

"That's right! Is there any memorable impression that Venice left on you?"

"Sure. The pigeons!"

"That's all?" Yes, she is still a child—well, a pre-teen—but is there anything else other than pigeons that impressed her?

"Hmmmm…The kiwis!"

Right! The "fuzzy potatoes!" How could I forget that?

"Anything else?" I was expecting Evelyn to come up with the canals, the gondolas and gondolieri, the Piazza San Marco (yes, the pigeons were right there…), the bridges—Rialto in the first place.

"Yes, the long walk towards a direction that we had no idea about, but you were dragging us behind you while reading those signs displayed on street corners everywhere…"

I am giving up. Yes, she is right. The impressions on a child's mind leave different memories. At least, she hasn't forgotten our Venice experience.

She continues with her geography homework: drawing the map of Italy first, showing the 20 regions and their capitals. (At this point in time, there is no computer, no internet, not even cell phones. All we have is books! Books, notebooks, pencils, paper and pens!). The girls have received from school all the textbooks they need for the entire school year, and they are extremely comprehensive textbooks! So, just by looking at the map in her textbook, and with a little of my help, Evelyn is hand-drawing a sketch first, and then more solid lines, colouring each region in a different shade, giving full consideration to scale, making sure the directions, distances, dimensions and coordinates are correct, writing the names of the cities and the regions on the map. The final product is a beautiful descriptive map, almost encyclopedic for a grade six student. Obviously, by now she already memorized the regions. Veneto is next.

* * *

Sunday is the only true weekend day, a time to unwind, to loosen the pressure accumulated during the long and tiring weekdays. Our apartment is right on the Tyrrhenian Sea; we can see the waves, sometimes calm and almost balmy, slowly undulating in the autumn wind, peaceful and gentle, other times merciless, restless and frantic, wildly banging against the rocks on the shoreline. All this beauty is just on the other side of our balcony. Once in a while we cross Via Aurelia, the main road, and we just sit on the rocks and breathe in the salty air, relaxing and trying to forget the everyday challenges. Sometimes, on weekends, we take the one-hour walk to the main beach, but we hardly have enough time to spend leisurely.

Yesterday, Giancarlo told me that there is an aquatic center in Civitavecchia that has a swimming program for children of different ages. Although the girls have a busy schedule, Greg and I agreed that a couple of swimming classes a week would bring some joy and excitement to their busy yet monotonous lives.

"Girls, we have a surprise for you!" Greg is breaking the news and is watching to see their reaction. Surprise? Amanda has a skeptical look on her face, but Evelyn's curiosity is visibly stirred up.

"What surprise? Any news from immigration?"

Right. I guess the girls' hearing us talking every day about our intention to immigrate somewhere in the world is all that would be considered as a surprise.

"No…" Greg is enhancing the suspense, but the girls have no idea what our plan is. "How about some swimming?" Greg is still teasing them.

"Swimming…? Where?" The girls' eyes glow with excitement, but they still don't know what to make of this surprise. Obviously, it's not going to be outside, in the sea water!

"Mom and I thought about enrolling you in a swimming program with the Aquatic Centre of Civitavecchia."

The girls can hardly contain their happiness. As emotionally balanced and uneasily affected by any kind of news Amanda usually seems to be, signs of happiness are visibly gleaming inside her, while Evelyn is clearly flabbergasted with joy.

We all went over details regarding transportation (obviously, by bus since we don't have a car), equipment—they had swimsuits, so all we needed were a couple of swimming caps, and we were all set. Of course, this was an extra expense out of our modest earnings, but since Ranieri family were not charging us rent, we could afford to invest some of our savings into a useful type of recreational activity for the girls.

22

JUST HOPES…

We call our parents every weekend. My mother is still writing letters. She has a beautiful way of expressing herself in writing and sometimes she writes on paper things that she doesn't seem capable of saying out loud. In her letters my Mom seems to be at ease with acknowledging all the feelings she is experiencing, all her sorrow for our missing from their lives, all the emotions that she tries to suppress during our phone conversations, so reading her letters makes me realize that my mother is actually pouring her heart out on paper. However, I know she is refraining from becoming too melancholic in her writing.

My mother always showed her tough side although I never quite realized how soft-hearted she was. Her feelings never became too apparent throughout all my childhood. Later in life, after I got married and I had my first child, she became a different person. Obviously, as a grandmother, she had different feelings, and a different view on life, a different approach. I guess grandparents acquire a certain wisdom and change some of their attitudes as they grow older and are no longer young parents involved in raising their own children. My mother and I had harsh arguments at times, mainly because Greg and I were trying to discipline our children, while she was perceiving the whole scenario as being too severe, maybe unnecessary according to her standards. She was usually trying to not interfere in our parental matches, and she was just giving me an evil eye. Sometimes, however, she was feeling the need to intervene verbally, but those were dangerous sparks igniting a brutal argument with my mother, always forced to leave our home. However, although on the brink of crying, she always managed to hide her tears before me and my children. Was that a good thing? Was that the sign of being strong or showing strength?

Tough love is all I learned and all I was taught during my childhood and adolescence years. I remember times when, as a child, I wished my grandmother or my mother kissed me or hugged me. I don't remember any kisses. I don't remember any of them saying to me "I love you." In fact, once my grandmother told me that children should only be kissed while sleeping. Why?

I have no doubt that they loved me. I was actually my parents' only child, but no, I have never been spoiled. Ever. On the contrary, my grandmother, who became my daily caretaker, completely ignoring the fact that my parents were around and could have easily performed their parental duties, considered important to instill in me a certain degree of independence, but God forbid I was trespassing my grandmother's rules! I was still a child, maybe eight or nine years old. I wanted to play sometimes, hiding in different corners of our house or backyard, when suddenly, I could hear my grandmother's shrieking voice, screaming off the top of her lungs "Where are you?!!" Where was I? "Playing" was not a word that I was "allowed" to use in my quotidian vocabulary, so quite often I had to come up with lies. "I'm reading," or "I'm making a dress for my doll," or "I'm knitting."

I was hoping that my grandmother would be satisfied, but she was continuing to throw other options at me: "Did you do your violin practice for today? Did you sweep up the backyard? Did you rake the leaves? Did you feed the chickens? Did you paint the shed? Did you…? Did you…?" There was no end to my grandmother's picking on me. I later understood that she wanted me to be self-sufficient, to be confident in my abilities, to be able to succeed in life without asking for much help or any at all. As a young widow she knew how important it was for a woman to be self-reliant, but she was also squishing my personality, crushing my freedom, killing my attempts to make my own choices.

Yes, it turned out to be useful. I probably became what my grandmother wanted me to, but the price to pay proved to be too high. As a mother myself I never quite knew how to play with my children. And I don't remember to have told them out loud how much I loved them. My love for them was becoming material, providing everything they needed in times of extreme scarcity, and eventually translated into fleeing our homeland, choosing to live in a free world where our children's rights would be respected, where they would be free to choose and not live in a corrupt society.

* * *

Swimming is going well. It is not the first time they get to swim, but we had never enrolled them in real swimming lessons while we lived in Romania. It was not out of lack of opportunities, but we didn't have much time, and I was also a firm believer in children's innate ability to…swim. Since for the first nine months of their pre-birth life they live in a fluid-liquid environment, I always thought that just by "dropping" them in the swimming pool would be enough to learn how to use their arms and legs, self-regulate their breath and just…swimming! It is exactly what we did with both our girls, under strict supervision, of course. Around the age of two or maybe earlier, they were "swimming," flailing their limbs, holding their breath, always at arm length from us, as parents. It was a "sink-or-swim" approach. Maybe one that we kept applying to real life on a daily basis. Anyways, this time it seems that the swimming program brings some excitement into our girls' lives, giving them the chance to break away from their daily dull routine.

Last week we even had the pleasure of meeting Giancarlo's wife, Anna Rita, and their seven-year-old son, Michele. To our total enchantment, Anna Rita (who works as a teacher of Fine Arts in Civitavecchia) offered to give us a ride back home, to our apartment in Santa Marinella, so we didn't have to take the bus on a cold and damp December evening. After that, for the rest of the swimming program, she continued to take us back home in their car, twice a week. Befriending this family was totally priceless. It felt like another gift from "up-above."

* * *

"Maria, do you have plans for Christmas?" Anna Rita's calm, friendly and reassuring voice makes her question sound like an invitation already, but plans? Of course we have no plans, nowhere to go, no other people around us in Santa Marinella or Civitavecchia whom we could call friends and who would ask us such a question.

"No, why are you asking?"

"Giancarlo and I thought about inviting you over on Christmas Eve, to celebrate together, to have a traditional meal and enjoy a drink, if you would like to join us." The unexpected invitation to join them on such a special occasion fills up my heart with warm feelings of gratitude. I am ecstatic. I cannot give Anna Rita the big hug I would like to as she is behind the wheel, driving us back home; all I can say is a few heartfelt "mille grazie." We say good night to one another, and while she stops the car in front of our condo building, she tells us that one of them will come to pick us up in a couple of weeks, on Christmas Eve. What a beautiful surprise!

"Dad, guess what!" Of course, Evelyn feels that she needs to be the first one to break the news to Greg. She is so excited!

"What?"

"Anna Rita and Giancarlo invited us to celebrate Christmas Eve at their home in Civitavecchia."

"Really?" Even Greg is surprised. Everything sounds so unexpectedly good.

Obviously, Evelyn fills him in with all the details.

My heart is infused with a feeling of extreme gratefulness. I am humbled. We go to bed with a big smile engraved on our faces and souls.

* * *

Two more weeks of school before the winter break. We are more and more tired with every day going by. The days are getting shorter, it gets dark in the evening much earlier, but our routine is the same every day. I am fortunate though because my work is always inside, with one little exception. Ranieri family added a "new member" to their family. A cute little female bichon frisé, named Daisy that I am supposed to take for a walk as part of my daily duties. It's pure joy. Daisy is playful and funny, and taking her for a walk gives me the chance to go out for a short stroll, as well.

However, Greg's work is definitely more challenging in this cold and humid weather. There's no getting away from it, working in construction is extremely tough. Loading and unloading of materials, tools, and equipment. Collecting trash, debris and other waste to keep the site clean and safe. Assembling and breaking down barricades, temporary structures, and scaffolding. His co-workers call him a "manuale," a short form of "lavoratore manuale"—unskilled worker, manual labourer. His work is as dangerous as it is demeaning. Long days. Heavy lifting. Low pay. No insurance. Sheer hardship, drudgery and extreme physical demands—no wonder there is always a shortage of good labourers. Still, he grinds his teeth and he keeps going. We keep praying that he come back home in the evening, uninjured and in one piece, after each long and excruciating workday. The sad look on his face leaves little room to the joy of seeing his family again. I don't know for how long he will be able to last.

* * *

Christmas break is almost around the corner. The girls' homework has become visibly more bearable.

"Mom, I have some great news!" Amanda's excitement is contagious. Without knowing what created this burst of enthusiasm, I already jump on the bandwagon.

"What is it? Did you win the lottery?"

"Right! Lottery! Actually, it will feel like a lottery. I signed up for an essay writing contest. It will take place at the end of this week, Friday evening, in Rome."

"An essay writing? On what? What's the topic?"

"I am supposed to write about an event that was the most significant for me this year, so I am thinking about describing our fleeing our home country, our long journey to Italy, about all our hardships and challenges throughout this year."

Amanda is beaming with delight, but also impatient to see my reaction.

I am astounded, but not completely surprised. Eleven months ago I was trying to convince the principal to enroll her in grade seven after the first term of the school year had already passed, while Amanda's knowledge of Italian was minimal, and today, she is going to compete against other teenagers in an essay writing contest? In Italian? It is almost incomprehensible. This is a true Christmas present.

"Well, congratulations, girl! I am truly happy for you!"

"Wait, Mom! I haven't won anything. I am not sure if I am going to win anything. I only signed up for it."

"Yes, but this is an accomplishment by itself. It means that you are confident, that you will be able to write an essay in Italian when 12 months ago we had just arrived in Italy and we were struggling every day facing all sorts of problems, and the Italian language was only one of them."

"I know. That's exactly what I'm going to write about."

* * *

Twelve months have gone by already. This time last year we were trying to adapt to living in the convent, coping with uncertainties of all kinds, with daily challenges, with an unknown that we were delving in, one day after another. Every other few months on the move again, changing places and addresses, trying to adjust to the new locations and then, it was time to move again, on and on, with no real destination in mind. The only constant in all this turmoil was the girls' school. Yes, they had to commute every day, but getting to have the same teachers, same classmates, was less challenging. Besides, our status in Italy was still uncertain. It is true that the girls and I were legal residents, but Greg was not. At least not yet. We still don't know what we want. We have some options, and we'll have to see which one becomes a valid one, a possibility that we can turn into reality. With every end of a year and the beginning of a new one new hopes are filling up our hearts. Hope is all we have for now.

23

HAPPY NEW YEAR!

Happy New Year, indeed. At least, all we can do is hope that it will be happy, or at least, happier than last one.

Last days of December 1991 brought along some delightful moments. Amanda's essay writing contest was the highlight of the season. She won the first prize! It was incredible. The ceremony took place in front of University of Washington (also known in some not-so-distant past as Palazzo Pio) which overlooks the Campo de' Fiori. It was truly festive. The marching band playing Christmas music, the prizes being awarded to the winners, the excitement of the moment—everything had a celebratory aura. Amanda received a trophy cup and a beautiful red sashay. A few pictures later we made our way out of the crowds, ready for our two-hour commute to Santa Marinella. It was a night to remember!

Christmas night and then New Year's Eve joyfully spent at Giancarlo and Anna Rita's home in Civitavecchia finished the year on a happy note. We felt included, part of a family of friends, part of the larger family of Italians, so welcoming and so accepting. Great traditional Italian meals, carols singing, fireworks and, of course, *panettone*! To our girls' delight, Giancarlo had a three-tier piano keyboard, all equipped with chords and acoustics and speakers, so both girls got to play a few tunes or just chords and sing along. (The girls took piano lessons back in Romania, enrolled in the same School of Music and Fine Arts that I had also attended during my elementary and middle school years, so the girls' playing on Giancarlo's keyboard brought back some memories from our home country, along with the joy of moving their fingers on the keys).

* * *

Two years have gone by since the communist regime was toppled in Romania. Last month, in December 1991, a new constitution was drafted and subsequently adopted, after a popular referendum. However, we continued to believe that the fighting was concocted, and that the revolution was a facade. Yes, there had been a revolution by the people, but we had been tricked to believe it was true, it was real. We were all romantics, feeling drunk with the political upheaval and the hopes we were building. It took us about a year to realize that one faction had simply removed another faction. The institutions which had run the country before still remained intact, albeit with another name, appearing like harmless lambs still draped in wolves' skin hidden underneath their deceiving innocent sheep-like coat.

My mother keeps sending us letters. I love reading them, so detailed, political stories so nicely narrated, as accurate as she could render them. Still, as life goes on and we are busy with other daily endeavours, I feel the need to stay disengaged from the political chaos making the headlines all over the Romanian media. That's why we are here today.

Greg is not very happy. He seems to be losing hope with every day going by. We have not heard anything from the Canadian Consulate which is still our last hope. We gave up on Australia; the United States rejected our application. Canada remains the only option. Continuing to live in Italy would be the last resort. As included as we feel, there is still no room for advancing in our careers. Yes, we did leave Romania for political reasons, but another element of it was the corrupt society that we did not want to be part of and live in, we did not want to raise the children in an environment where bribery was the law of the day. Still, we cannot continue our lives working manual jobs, myself continuing with cleaning and Greg doing exhausting and humiliating manual labour on construction sites. There are so many qualified Italians with degrees and diplomas who are unemployed, who cannot find work according to their qualifications, so our chances are next-to-nothing. We are still young, we have hopes for reasonable careers in our fields, I miss my teaching, my students, Greg is missing his work in chemical engineering, but Italy is out of reach in this respect.

* * *

I recently heard about a charity place that is in charge of sending documents to different embassies or consulates for people who apply for immigration. Today I finally located it. It's not far from Via Dandolo where we used to have our dinners while we were staying in the convent. It is a branch of Caritas, a world organization advocating for fair and just systems, believing in allowing the poorest people to reach their human potential.

"Poorest" people…It feels so awkward. Are we poor? What does "poor" mean? Maybe this is how my grandmother felt after the communist regime confiscated all their possessions and turned them into collectivism, where everything was under governmental authority, where no citizen was owning anything. Not owning anything? My maternal grandparents had a beautiful house, more like a mansion, a vast piece of land, they had people working for them—obviously for a pay, they had stables with a number of horses, maybe they were not rich, but they were certainly well off. I still remember my grandmother telling me a story about how she fell off the saddle from a time when she was young, riding her favourite pony, and how she broke her leg which had gotten stuck in the stirrup. Then, the Great Depression came, and the World War II after, my grandfather died, and everything culminated with our king, Michael I, being forced to abdicate in December 1947.

King Michael was forced into exile, his properties confiscated, and his citizenship stripped. Then communism took over. What my grandmother hadn't lost during the depression was taken away after. All of a sudden, she was poor. She had a pension, but very modest, definitely not enough to live on her own. Maybe that was one more reason why she continued to stay "attached" to my mother.

I was born in the eastern part of the country, on the Danube. My parents were working as accountants, and their job was on the other side of the Danube, taking the ferry across in the morning, coming back in the afternoon. Once in a while my grandmother took me to the river shore to greet my parents coming off the ferry, after a workday. I don't remember much of those times. The only detail that got stuck in my infantile memory was the colour of the Danube—if I could call that a "colour." The waters were always muddy, they looked dirty in their murkiness, so there was no actual colour to them. Later on, I learned in school that the Danube was only 120 km away from its Delta, before it flows into the Black Sea, which explained its silt deposits and all the built-up sludge.

We lived in this city on the Danube for about three years after I was born, and then we moved back to the area where my grandmother had lived most of her life. I never understood and nobody ever told me why exactly we moved from the river shore into a mountainous area. (I think the water of the big river I was born on played an important and especially sentimental role in my life. I've continued to feel the "need" of being close to water, no matter where in the world I was).

I lived the rest of my life in this city in the Carpathians. My grandmother and my mother remained "attached" to each other. It may have been a relief for my mother since she had a 24/7 caretaker for her child, but it all came with an attachment. My grandmother had never quite liked my father, and within seven years my parents divorced. Seeing my father leave the house was a traumatic scene. Many children see their parents going through a divorce, but observing my grandmother mumbling a curse as my father was loading some personal belonging on a truck marked me for the rest of my life. It hurt. It was truly painful. I knew in that very moment that no matter what, when I get married, I will never divorce my husband. I was only seven years old…

As I was growing up in this communist regime—which I had no clue about at the time—scarcity was the norm. Never enough heat (the stove needed wood constantly), food was carefully managed by my grandmother who was stretching her little pension (luckily, my alimony resulting from my parents' divorce was helping a little), we were getting monthly tickets to buy bread, oil, flour and sugar, and sanitary conditions were far from decent. Our "bathroom" was improvised in an unheated room next to the "main" (and only) heated bedroom where I was sharing the same bed with my grandmother.

Luckily for my mother, she moved out after the divorce, so I was "stuck" with my grandmother who turned me into a project! No playing per se. Learning to read at the age of four years old, writing soon after, learning to knit, crochet, make dresses (for my dolls first and for myself later), using a sewing machine, painting walls and fences, cutting wood (seesaw and axe included), even learning how to make small rugs on a loom. There was no shortage of chores or simply "opportunities" offered to me so I could learn how to use my brain and coordinate my hands accordingly.

Learning new skills was not always helpful. On the contrary, on occasions it became detrimental and my grandmother was not losing any occasion to instill shame on me. How degraded I felt when I tried to make—yes, make my first own bra! Not that I had any reason or need for it!! I was only 13, tall and lanky, burgeoning breasts just showing a little through my dresses. Making a bra out of some cotton remnants and a few ragged strips of fabric was not easy task. I knew how to use a sewing machine, but my grandmother would have found out, so I surreptitiously made my first bra by using a needle and my own hands. My masterpiece had a scandalous and dreadful ending. As soon as my grandmother noticed some rags hanging around my neck, she grabbed one of my shoulders with one hand while the other hand violently snatched my improvised bra.

"What is this?" She was holding up my first piece of self-made lingerie, hanging it up and making me shudder with humiliation while giving me a dirty look. A slap over my face with the remnants of my short-lived undergarment was the end of that story. One to remember forever. I could never figure out why she was so angry. Was it because she didn't want me to grow up? Was she afraid that I would become too independent, too fast? That's exactly what she was teaching me! Why was she clipping my wings?

In the first grade I was enrolled in a Music and Fine Arts school, learning to play the violin, and as my grandmother was always thinking that I still had too much free time, she got me a French tutor, too. Yes, this was my childhood as a single child in a communist regime!

Did it help me that I was so far advanced in reading and writing by the time I started school? No. The Romanian communist regime (imported from the Soviet Union!!) did not allow children under the age of seven to be enrolled in the elementary school. Saying that I was bored to death when my first-grade teacher was teaching my classmates to read and write is an understatement. Did my grandmother help me? In a way, yes, but I had harsh consequences to face. To kill my boredom, I was sometimes trying to read books under my desk, struggling to not be seen by my teacher. To no avail! How many times I was getting severely punished for doing that, including being slapped over my face or the back of my head—I lost track.

My mother remarried when I was almost 15 years old. In the meantime, I had finished my eight years of elementary school, I graduated from the music school, and I was admitted into the high school. It was time I started to live a decent life. Time to have proper sanitary conditions. I was a teenage girl now, and I had struggled enough trying to be clean, to wash myself (sometimes with cold water), to have regular baths. It had been pathetic enough (and extremely traumatic) when I was "hit" with my first period! I was 13 years old at the time, and I had no idea what was going on! Yes, my grandmother had taught me everything, BUT that essential detail of a woman's life. For the first two days I was trying to improvise, trying everything I could think of (no, there were no tampons at that time…), and when I had to eventually confess to my grandmother, I felt so ashamed that, if the earth had cracked open at that very moment, I would have preferred to dive right in!

My mother and my stepfather had a two-bedroom apartment, provided by the government. No rent. Just pay for utilities. I moved in with them. My life changed.

Useless to say, my parents had to become members of the Communist Party. What choice was there? Did it help them? Maybe under those circumstance they had to adapt on the go, comply with the communist rules or else…! At least, they didn't feel poor. Having a job, working every day, Monday through Saturday, earning a modest salary, enjoying a two-week paid vacation every year, and looking forward to making it into retirement.

Going through life, continuing with my education, securing a job as a high school teacher, getting married, having children, living in a regime that was imposing restrictions—this was my life in a communist country. Decent? Maybe. Yes, we had "everything" we needed, where "everything" was a subjective concept. Still, becoming members of the communist party was not an option. We never believed in communism, which meant we had a price to pay. Still, when the gas started to be rationalized in the 80's (a full tank per month!!!), when food started to get scarce again, when the shelves in the grocery stores were empty, when we had to stand for long hours in line to buy even toilet paper or wait for the Christmas season to come so we could buy two kilos of bananas and/or two kilos of oranges just ONCE a year, it was becoming unbearable. Ceausescu and his regime had stretched us too thin. And then it was all over! Or was it…?

Well, it belongs to the past. A past that it's hard to forget.

* * *

"Buon giorno."

"Ciao. What can I do for you?"

There are a few desks at this office of Caritas. Young people sitting behind their small tables, papers spread all over, piles of folders and binders of all sorts. So, this is the Caritas. These people apparently deal with large volumes of applications that they have to submit regularly to different embassies, or consulates, or other forums, as the case may be.

I am explaining what our situation is.

"Do you have your passports with you?" Once more time it became obvious why Gino told me to hold on to my passport for dear life! He knew that we would need passports once we decided to apply for immigration to another country. It was somewhat "easy" to obtain a Permit of stay in Italy without a passport, but not having a passport when applying for immigration with the consulate or embassy of another country was out of question.

"No, I don't have them with me, but I can bring them tomorrow." The young fellow I am talking with is very jovial, showing an extreme kindness and willingness to help. Obviously, they are faced with all sorts of situations every day, meeting foreigners of various nationalities, trying to assist them with their requests, representing them before different authorities all across Rome.

"Take these papers with you, fill out will all the required information and bring them back to us tomorrow along with your passports."

"And then, what happens?"

"We check the information, we discuss it with you, and then we submit the applications and your passports to the Canadian Consulate." It sounds so simple, but I am still skeptical. Submitting our passports makes me uneasy, but this fellow is reassuring me that they are in good hands.

"Grazie."

For the first time since we decided to apply for immigrating somewhere else in the world, I feel more confident. It's a new beginning, a new year, and it seems to have started on the right foot. Happy New Year, again!

24

SPRING IS IN THE AIR!

Spring brings along new hopes. Yes, the new year already started, but when birds are chirping, when trees are in bloom although it's only January, when the sea breeze is balmy, and the days are getting longer—all of these make our hearts sing with joy. Besides, each month has its own festivities.

Just as Hallowe'en is mostly celebrated in North America, Italy has one of its kind. La Befana. According to the Italian folklore, la Befana is a kind witch who brings treats on the morning of January 6 (the Epiphany). However, la Befana may be nasty if the children misbehaved, so she might just drop a…lump of coal.

According to the legend, la Befana has been flying around the world on her ragged broomstick to deliver the sweet (or sooty) treats down chimneys long before Kris Kringle or Santa Claus have become part of our Christmas stories. The witch has been in the Italian tradition at least since the 8th century, as part of the Epiphany.

In Italy, the Epiphany commemorates the day when the three Wise Men arrived at the manger bearing gifts. Every year, the occasion is celebrated with living nativity scenes, a great procession through the cities, and the arrival of La Befana.

According to the story, the Magi met La Befana early on during their quest. She generously hosted them for an evening in her modest but warm small house; the next morning, they invited her to accompany them to Bethlehem. Initially la Befana declined the invitation, but then she had second thoughts. She quickly filled a basket with presents for baby Jesus and she took off alone. Although she followed the same star, she was unable to find the manger when the Wise Men did on January 6th, so she arrives earlier, the night before—on Epiphany Eve. So, today, la Befana continues to travel around the world on the night of January 5th, searching every house for the child and leaving candies and chocolates for the well-behaved children—or just coal for the naughty ones!

In different Italian cities children wear costumes in an attempt to portray the kind witch, they gather outside, sing love songs to serenade the sun to beckon its return. The children receive candies, they jump and screech to accordion music, or sing in every key imaginable as delighted parade participants join in the cacophony. Panettone (or pandora, another type of panettone) is also a traditional food that is served around.

"Mom, Dad, can we pretend we are "Befanas?"

"What do you mean by pretending?"

"Well, we don't have costumes, but we have something in mind…"

Amanda senses that the look on my face, my questioning eyebrows are inviting to more answers, but before she has the chance to open her mouth, Evelyn pitches in."

"We are thinking about using some makeup and paint our faces to look like witches."

"And then what?" I feel like I am missing something, or maybe I'm lacking humour right now, or…or yes, I remember. I don't know how to play… (Yes, my austere childhood will continue to haunt me for the rest of my life.) After all, they still have nowhere to go! Luckily, Greg's intervention saves the moment.

"Yes, girls, go ahead!"

And just like that, 20 minutes later, we have two witches and a…wizard! It's a handsome wizard, though. Evelyn adorned her Dad's hair with a red bow. A couple of hoodies, face colours painted all over their faces, teeth blackened to make them "invisible" so they appear toothless, and we have three Befanas! No sweets. We still have panettone, so that will do. Songs and fun fill the air. Evelyn seems to play a nasty Befana. She is bugging Amanda and she seems to be doing a "good" job! Amanda is crying. Crying and laughing at the same time. Well, we can call it a fun night. It doesn't happen very often. It's Sunday tomorrow and then on Monday morning school starts again. Same routine, same commute. Better enjoy the moment.

* * *

On my way from work, once a week, I make a dash visit to Caritas. From what they are telling me, they dropped our documents to the Canadian Consulate in Rome, but all we can do now is wait. For how long, God knows. How we are going to be notified is also an unknown factor. We do not have a mobile phone. Yes, we do have a phone in this new apartment, but even if they call us, since we are not home during the day and there is no answering machine, they won't be able to reach us. Also, we don't have a stable physical address because we keep moving. The only place where we receive our letters is at the Central Post Office in Rome. All I can do is to go in person to Caritas weekly to inquire on our status.

The girls keep making progress in school. As the days are getting longer, the mornings seem to be more bearable. We are trying to find some time to relax on the seashore once in a while. The spring breeze is calming. It helps sometimes to ease up the tension arising between Greg and myself. I understand his despair. I can tune in some of his hopelessness, I can sympathize with him quite often, I understand his anxiety, but I have my limits, too. I know he is physically and emotionally exhausted, but so am I. His mood is quite often more pessimistic that I can put up with. Greg is prone to depression, something he apparently inherited from his mother. There is not much I can do about it. He lost his patience, too.

"I'm f*** tired of all this bullshit! Every day on the construction site I feel like a bucket of mortar or something is going to be dropped on my head! I'd rather go back home!!"

"Home where, Greg?"

"Back to Romania."

"You don't know what you are talking about. Are you out of your mind? Romania is out of boundaries." If anything, just the concept of returning to our home country gets me extremely furious. No way!

"Why? Just because the three of you have legal status in Italy? How about me?"

"No, it's not about that. It's about our application to immigrate to Canada."

"But nothing is happening! The U.S. rejected us, Australia didn't even bother to give us an answer; what makes you think that Canada will accept us?"

"The only choice we have is wait."

"Wait??? Wait???!" His voice reaches higher pitches. He's screaming at me. I do, too. A fighting match ensues. The girls are uncomfortable, to say the least. It's not the first time they see us arguing. We had arguments in Romania, too. Way too many. I was hoping that leaving our homeland behind, we could forget about everything that had been ugly in our marriage. I'm trying to find some reasoning.

"There is nothing we can return to, Greg. Remember? We disposed of everything we had in our apartment. All given out for free. The only thing we sold was our car, but the money devalued so badly that we will have to work all our life to recover. NO! Going back to Romania is not an option!"

Indeed. Returning for me does not exist as an alternative. There is no going back. Only forward. Greg seems to have calmed down, at least for now.

Another letter from my Mom arrived today. We call our parents every week, but Mom's letters are special, both in content as well is her calligraphy. What a beautiful handwriting my Mom has! And how grammatically correct she writes!

Our dear children,

I know we talk regularly on the phone. Thank you for calling us. We know that it costs you money, so when you call, I am trying to keep it short, but it's easier when I can put everything on paper to the last detail.

I know that Romanian politics is not much of an interest to you anymore, but I just thought I should update you on a few recent events. First of all, you probably know already that the European Union was just created on February 7th following the Maastricht Treaty. It won't be implemented right away, though.

Yes, Mom, we know. We are closer to Maastricht then you are and world politics interest me more than the Romanian ones, but thank you.

We had a census at the beginning of this year, which came to show the Romanian population had grown since the previous count in 1977. Meanwhile, King Michael I managed to see his home country after decades of exile, being welcomed by many Romanians, but not so welcomed by the current political powers.

And hear this: we have 128 legally registered political parties in Romania that kicked off the electoral campaign. Apparently, some of them formed political alliances during the campaign, but there are still too many. The National Salvation Front (FSN), the political organization governing Romania, had most candidates for both mayor and local councilor positions.

Indeed, Mom. I don't care about the corrupt parties and the corrupt regime governing our homeland. It's exactly why we left. I'm glad you remind us that we embarked on this crazy but right adventure, albeit dangerous and still insecure.

I am thinking about visiting you in Italy this summer. Coming by train is an option since a flight would be too costly.

Really, Mom? As much as we would like to see you, we have nowhere to accommodate you. Besides, you don't have enough money even for a train ticket. Not to mention that it will take you three days and three nights! We've been there a little over a year ago.

In the meantime, you will have a special anniversary to celebrate. In about two weeks you'll have to drink a glass of champagne to honour your first 15 years of marriage. So, in case our greeting card will not arrive in time, we wish you both a happy marriage, and many more anniversaries!

Right. March 7th this year is our fifteenth wedding anniversary. Actually, not a wedding anniversary. It's the civil ceremony that we had on this date 15 years ago. The religious ceremony took place in another city, because going to church in our city—Greg as a chemical engineer in the military, and myself as teacher—was totally out of question. Communism and religion were two separate concepts and attending church, even for a special ceremony like this, would have gotten us in trouble. Even the actual wedding took place a month later. Aargh…communism…

How are the girls doing in school? Last time you called, I could detect an accent when they were speaking with us in Romanian. Do they speak Italian among themselves?

Yes, Mom. Even with us!

My mother's letter was not the longest this time, but she seems to have her mind set on coming to see us. How about John, my stepfather? I assume she'll leave him home because she won't have money for two train tickets. Still, that's too big of an expense for them anyways. I wish I could send them some money, but we are saving every single penny, because we don't know what our next move will be. Besides, we don't have a bank account, and I don't even know if my parents have one. Sending cash by mail is out of question. We'll see.

Anyways, spring is in the air!

25
WHERE IS EVELYN?!…

Saturday, March 7th, 1992. Greg surprises me with a beautiful bouquet of roses and a card. The bottle of champagne I bought is ready to open.

Fifteen years. Where did the time go by? Tumultuous times, lots of challenges, too many arguments, but also great memories, and above all, two beautiful and smart daughters. Fifteen years ago, at the beginning of March a big earthquake shook a considerable part of Romania. A magnitude of 7.2, the earthquake caused a lot of damage. The epicenter had been situated in the most seismic part of Romania, the Vrancea Mountains. Over 1,500 people had died and 11,000 more had been injured. Almost 33,000 buildings had been damaged or completely destroyed, and right after the earthquake 35,000 families had been left without a shelter. Ceausescu declared a state of emergency. Luckily, we were not affected in the city where we were living, but our civil ceremony was only a few days away, in a different city, at about 100 km distance. The first thing I did the morning after the earthquake was to call the City Hall of that city. I was relieved to know that it was still standing, and our marriage had not been cancelled. It was all that mattered!

Greg and I met by chance, at a cinema theatre, five months before we got married. It took us just five months to realize we were meant for each other. Or were we…? It was not love at first sight, but we definitely clicked with each other. We seemed to have similar interests, we were talking about art and history, classical music and opera, theatre plays and movies, we were going hiking, cycling, skiing, and we were having long conversations about the books we were reading. I could easily admit that Greg swept me off my feet. A week after we met, we got tickets to see one of Verdi's operas. To my delight, he brought a bouquet of red roses which he presented to me in a very romantic fashion. He was gentle and kind, and quite soon I found out that he was also a good dancer. On New Year's Eve ball held at the Military Centre the Viennese waltz was our way to ring in the New Year, dancing around the large hall on the musical waves of the Strauss's Blue Danube, spinning around the elegant ballroom.

Fifteen years later. Here we are in Italy, at a crossroad, sometimes pulling apart, but most often overcoming our daily challenges.

* * *

We are tired today. Although it is Saturday, we both worked, the girls had school, so we will continue our fifteenth anniversary tomorrow. We will go to Rome, all the four of us, and enjoy the special celebration.

* * *

March went away in a blink of an eye. Our anniversary. Holy week. Easter Sunday—our second Easter in Italy to enjoy as a family. A few days of spring break for the children as well. Time to wind down a little. Rome is beautiful in spring. It is beautiful all the time, but in spring it is magic. Last year we went to see the Pope carrying the cross up on Via Crucis. We will try something else this year.

Rome has always been associated with flowers. Wisteria—purple and white, bright red and pink azaleas, orange blossoms with their inviting fragrance, roses everywhere, lilac, oleanders—Rome is a symphony of flowers. We start our day with a visit to the Vatican City. It's the place to be on such an occasion. The Pope giving his benediction above the crowds, from the top of Saint Peter's Basilica is of monumental importance. Before the ceremony reaches its end, we try to make our way out of the crowds on a fast pace. Then we spend the whole afternoon wandering about, without a precise destination in mind.

This week is truly special. Easter Sunday today, Easter Monday tomorrow (Pasquetta) and then on Tuesday it is April 21st which is the official birthday of Rome. According to an ancient tradition, Rome was founded on this date in 753 BC by Romulus, so there will be another special celebration. There will be fireworks and light shows, historic events and re-enactments held in Circus Maximus. We will have to decide where we want to go and what we would like to see.

And of course, just like on Christmas we eat panettone, the Easter version of it is in shape of a cross and is the *colomba*. Not to be missed!

* * *

Schooldays. Workdays. Commuting. Once a week a visit to Caritas. Sundays the only time to rest. The same schedule every day. And, as usual, picking up the girls from school and going to have our lunch at the kitchen soup in Via delle Sette Sale, adjacent to Colle Oppio Park. It is a total blessing. Our bodies need some refuelling, but the feeling of gratitude enveloping me surpasses my hunger. Evelyn always finishes her lunch faster than we do. It has become almost a regularity. She continues to eat "with her eyes," so she never finishes her plate which, subsequently, becomes my duty—no waste of food! Most of the times she sits quietly until Amanda and I finish our plates, but today she wants to go outside. It is a beautiful May day, the sun is so bright, so why not? She knows the place, there are so many people around, all of them refugees like us, most of them from African countries, and, as the chatterbox she is, she likes to engage in conversations with other people. Besides, almost everybody knows her. She is incredibly outgoing and convivial!

We finish our lunch 20 minutes later and we are on our way out to join Evelyn and get on our long commute to Santa Marinella. But wait! Where is Evelyn? I look around to spot her, but I can't find her. I ask some people if they have seen her, yes, they did, but nobody knows where she may be. Why would they, after all?! She is still a child, well, actually four months away from becoming an "official" teenager. People have other preoccupations than watching a restless girl. We start to frantically look around. I am totally scared. She's nowhere to be seen. What if she has been kidnapped? But no, that could not have happened in full daylight, with so many people around. Someone would have noticed. Both Amanda and I are in a state of panic. Where could she be? What if she went to the metro station? I'm trying to reason, but my anxiety is in the way. I cannot even make a phone call to dial the emergency line, we do not have a mobile phone. I'm sure I can go into some store and ask someone to call 113 so that someone can rescue us, but rescue from what?

By the time we find a way to make the phone call, give the details of our location and describe Evelyn, and by the time they come to join us where we may be at that point, Evelyn would be far away. I'm trying to read her mind, pretend I am Evelyn. Where would I be? What would I do?

"Let's go to the metro station, Amanda!" My voice is too stern to be confronted with any opposition. Still Amanda has a questioning look on her face. She seems to be waiting for an explanation.

"We have no time to waste! It doesn't help to call any emergency squad. There is nothing they can do that we cannot do ourselves. There would be rather a delay in this whole "operation" that would not help us, but rather encumber us."

There is no time for conversation. We pick up our pace and we head out to the Termini metro station, right next to the main railway station, Stazione Termini. It's about one-kilometer walk. I hope that maybe, just maybe, we can spot her on our way. Perhaps she has stopped to take a peek at some of those deliciously looking desserts in the pastry shops that we go by every day, but we never have enough money to buy any…

We know the metro station is a zoo. Hundreds of people going in all directions. Finding Evelyn in this crowd is next to impossible. It's literally like looking for a needle in a haystack. I'm still keeping my hopes up. Nowhere to spot her. No sign or trace of Evelyn. I am desperate, but I have to keep cool. It helps that Amanda is with me. If anything, she is always my moral support, but she is scared, too.

"Mom, maybe she took the metro to the Lepanto bus station."

Maybe.

My heart is pounding. My breath quickens as I am using every muscle in my body to stifle any whimpering. Fear is creeping over me like a hungry beast, holding me captive. My lungs are out of oxygen. I hear the pulse beating in my ears, blocking the thundering sound of the crowds, my neck muscles are jittery. Sweat is pouring down on my back, giving me unnecessary extra chills. My hands are trembling and my entire body is shaking. We are on the metro, and my hand holding on to the rail is betraying me. Parts of my body feel numb. Adrenaline is rushing through my blood vessels. The beast holding me almost took control of my entire body. There is a bitter taste in my mouth that I cannot seem to get rid of. My mind is still in the alert mode. Too alerted. My life flashes before my eyes. Where is Evelyn? Where could she be? My mind refuses to think that anything bad may have happened to her. The five metro stops make the 10 minutes-metro ride feel like an eternity.

We arrive at Lepanto metro station and rush through the crowds, pushing people out of the way. It's a frantic course for survival. It's a race. No time for courtesy. Making our way up the stairs, in the daylight, looking for the blue commuter buses, so many. No sign of my youngest daughter anywhere. My eyes are sweeping over the people. Where is she? A blue bus is moving out of the station. All of a sudden my eyes detect the shade of a motion behind a window. I freeze.

"Mom, Evelyn is on the bus! She is waving at us!" Amanda spotted her at light speed. Yes, Evelyn is waving at us. She is smiling, too. I can't believe it! I don't know whether to be relieved or mad. If we had come out of the metro station two seconds later, just two seconds, we would have missed seeing her on that bus. We wouldn't have known where she was or what could have happened to her. I can't fathom what the outcome could have been.

As the bus is slowly moving out of the bus hub into the traffic, I put my hands together and look up to the skies. Somebody-up-there is truly looking after us, looking over and taking care of us. I feel the heavenly love. Thank you.

My whole body is decompressing. My mind, too. Evelyn will go home before we do, but she has no key to the apartment, so she will still have to wait for us. I still don't understand. Why did she do it? What prompted her to take off like that? I know she has a strong personality, she likes to be free, but what was in her mind?

Next commuter bus is in 30 minutes. We arrive in Santa Marinella around 4:30 pm. Evelyn is in front of the building, waiting for us…What a day!!

26
ON THE MOVE AGAIN…

We are approaching the end of another school year. Nothing special for Evelyn. She is finishing the sixth grade. Amanda, though, is supposed to pass the final state examination of the first cycle of education. The lower secondary school level consists of three years, grades six to eight. This three-year period ends with a required state exam which will allow students to obtain the final diploma of the first cycle of education necessary for enrollment in the upper secondary school, or high school.

The exam is divided into written tests and an oral exam. An Italian language written test, a math and a foreign language test are the three compulsory parts of the written exams. The exam is passed if the average is at least 60%.

Amanda is preparing for her exams with an amazing determination and dedication. Her ambition is one of her major traits of personality. Studying on the bus, in spite of being tired, at home, on weekends—we know how keen she is to get a good mark.

"Mom, I think I might need glasses. Sometimes my vision feels blurred."

This is news to me. I don't wear glasses, but Greg does.

"Is it when you read, for up close, or is it more of an issue related to distance?" I don't have training in optometry, but I know the difference between myopia and farsightedness, but other than how the eyes adjust to see at certain distances, I don't know anything. "Do you have any symptoms?"

"Sometimes, mild headaches, but one of my teachers today noticed that I was squinting when I was looking at the board."

"Ah, so it must be related to seeing at the distance. We'll have to find a specialist."

Luckily, healthcare in Italy is affordable for anyone. Healthcare is provided to all citizens and residents by a mixed public-private system. The public part is the National Health Service, Servizio Sanitario Nazionale (SSN), which is organized under the Ministry of Health and is administered on a regional basis. Also, from what I read, Italy's healthcare system is ranked among the highest in the world. It spends a very high percentage of its GDP on healthcare and, as a result, it ranks well for performance according to the World Health Organization.

I am not sure if I need to request a visit to an ophthalmologist, or I can take Amanda directly to an optometrist. I opt out for the second alternative. Even if an optometrist is not a medical doctor, he will be able to detect any defect or abnormality, should that be the case. However, I am not quite sure how to go about this, where to find such a specialist. Giancarlo is my salvation. He will talk to Anna Rita and they will get back to me.

By the end of the week the problem is solved. We did find an optometrist in Civitavecchia, then an optician, and now Amanda has glasses. The visits to see the specialists were free. We only needed to pay for the glasses, but health comes first.

*　*　*

My visits to Caritas have become regular. Every week I make time to drop by. The employees know me too well by now, but no, still no answer from the Canadian Consulate. I don't know what to make of this issue. I feel powerless, defeated even, although I have no control over this. Every day brings a ray of hope, and it dies just like that with the sun going down in the twilight and with the nightfall. There are days when I almost dread going back to our apartment in Santa Marinella. The tension is high. Greg has had enough, and our discussions turn easily into arguments, followed by threatening suggestions to return to our home country. His mother's letters are not helping either. She suffers from depression and she is constantly encouraging him to go back to Romania.

"No, for God's sake! No and no and no!! I am not going back! The children will not either! If you want to go back, go for it! I am tired of all this shit! You want a divorce, we'll do that, too, but I am sorry. For me there is no return." I am completely enraged.

"Can't you see we are not getting anywhere?"

Indeed, arguing is not getting us anywhere, but no matter how optimistic I am trying to stay, his negativity is killing me.

* * *

Last week of school. Amanda's exams are going well. Next week we will have to move back to Fara Sabina. In summer the Ranieri family and all their relatives come to this summer resort (which is their property) to spend some time at the seaside. For us this has been our "resort" for the entire school year, September through June. Fara Sabina is the "countryside resort." We are truly blessed to have been granted this privilege of living rent-free in two amazing, picturesque places in Italy.

My mother's letters arrive with precise regularity. She keeps us updated on the political events unravelling in Romania. Apparently, this month both Houses of Parliament voted to hold presidential and parliamentary elections on the 27th of September. Initially they were planning on holding the elections on June 26th, but the government proposal was rejected. It's time I call her today.

"Hi, Mom. What's up?"

She picks up right away. It's almost as if the phone is at armlength at all times. Maybe it is.

"So nice to hear you." Her voice sounds so uplifting, no matter when I call or what we talk about.

"How are you doing? How is your business going?"

"Not bad. We are dealing with a new 'item.'"

"What do you mean by 'item'? Is it related to accounting, to taxes or what?"

"The government introduced the Value Added Tax (VAT). We have to learn a little about how to apply it in the tax returns of our clients."

"Did you not have a tax before?"

"Yes, it was a tax on the movement of goods, but this one is different."

"In which way?" Frankly, I don't know much about taxes, if any at all. I know that on our bills whenever we buy something in Italy there is an

"IVA" tax. That must be it. Before we left Romania, I think I remember about that tax of movement of goods, but we didn't get to live for too long in Romania after the Revolution, so I was not quite informed about how taxes were working. After we arrived in Italy, we never had an "official" job, our pay was, and still is, "under the table", so no tax forms, nothing to report, no income. We also have no credit cards, no banking accounts, not even debit cards, nothing. Our earnings are in cash, and all the money is always, literally, on my body, in a waist pouch, under my garments. There is way too much pickpocketing around, and we can never trust anyone, not even leaving our money in a "safe" place at out continuously changing locations. In fact, what is a "safe" place? Under the mattress? No.

"The value of this tax is set at 18%. The consumer prices went up, but this is stimulating for investments and exports." My mother sounds like she really adapted to the new tax rules. I'm glad that they keep busy. This business keeps their minds actively engaged.

"What else is new? I read somewhere that Stephen the Great has been canonized." Stephen the Great had been the ruler of Moldova, the eastern/north-eastern part of Romania for almost 50 years, from 1457 to 1504.

"Yes, he was indeed canonized, and also Constantin Brancoveanu."

Brancoveanu had been a prince of Wallachia between 1688 and 1714. If my memory was not failing me and if I could still remember something from a beautiful part of the Romanian history of the 18th century—which I liked, Constantin Brancoveanu had an important role in negotiating anti-Ottoman alliances with the Habsburg Monarchy and later on with Russia during the rule of Peter the Great. Despite his political moves, he was deposed from the throne by Sultan Ahmed III and brought under arrest to Istanbul, where he was imprisoned, tortured by the Ottomans, and eventually beheaded along with his four sons. Soon after, their heads were carried on poles through the streets of Istanbul, an episode which led to a great unrest in the city. Eventually, the five bodies were thrown into Bosphorus in order to prevent a rebellion of the Muslim population who were outraged by the injustice done to the Prince Brancoveanu. Later on, some Christian fishermen managed to recover the bodies from the water and sent them to the island of Halki in the Sea of Marmara where they have eventually been buried at a monastery. This was a part of history that I loved to learn as a student.

What a beautiful country Romania is! However, its geographical position on the continent has been quite disadvantageous. Throughout the centuries, Romania was continuously invaded by numerous migrating peoples including the Goths, Huns, Gepids, Avars, Slavs, Bulgars, Magyars, Cumans and Mongols who overran the territory of modern Romania. It was not until the 13th century when three small Romanian states emerged and evolved into the medieval principalities of Moldavia, Wallachia and Transylvania. It is unfortunate that today's Romania is following a political trajectory that may have a continuous negative impact on its proper development.

I'm trying to divert a little in my phone conversation with my mother, but she is bringing me back to reality, almost reminding me that our phone conversations are costly.

"Here is another interesting event: Michael Jackson had a concert in Romania a week ago."

"Really? Did you go?"

"Are you kidding me? You don't think we have better ways to spend our money on…We are still thinking about coming to visit you in Italy."

"Mom, hold on. Wait until we hear from the Canadian Consulate. We still have hopes, and then we will see what we can do next." Mom is relentless in her attempts of coming to see us. I'm sure they miss our girls tremendously.

The girls take turns to talk with my parents. It is really funny to hear them mixing Italian and Romanian words. It's true that the two languages, Latin as they are, are so similar to each other, so confusing the words between the two languages is easy. On top of the word mix, Evelyn's accent is so obvious, so easy to discern.

Since school days are numbered and the summer vacation is around the corner, the girls don't have any more homework, so a little walk to the downtown of Santa Marinella in the beautiful evening of mid-June would fill our hearts with happiness. This weekend Alberto Ranieri will come to pick us up and drive us to Fara Sabina again. We will have to pack our belongings, once more… Moving again…

27

BAD NEWS

Fara Sabina is as welcoming now as it was the first time when we came to stay here. We are on familiar territory, so we know how to go about everything. Once Alberto Ranieri is on his way back to Rome, it doesn't take long until the next-door neighbours come to visit us. They never come empty-handed. Whether it is home-made bread or some sweets, fresh fruits or veggies, they always bring us something. The two teenagers—a son and a daughter—make a good company to our girls.

Well, summer is here. At least the girls don't need to travel to Rome every day for three months now. Time to relax.

Greg is happy today. Or should I say "happier"? Since Santa Marinella is no longer a possibility for his work, he has resumed the job, still in constructions, in Rome, in the vicinity of the Spanish Steps, where he worked for a while last year. This is good news. We can both take the same bus in the morning when we go to work. Our return times will be different, but this is a good change.

Our teenage neighbours, Mario and Carla, keep our girls entertained while we are away, working in Rome. They are two or three years older than our daughters, and they all seem to get along wonderfully. Carla has a scooter, and she brings it over almost every day. They surely have fun driving it all over the yard. It doesn't take long until Evelyn ends up against a tree, but at least she hasn't damaged the scooter! Just her leg, so she will have a good-size scar above her left knee for the rest of her life. Well, there are all sorts of memories to treasure for ever… (I have mine, too! From a time when I was exactly Evelyn's age and when—being rarely allowed to venture out on my own—I went for a swim in a very unkept swimming pool in the vicinity of our home. A piece of broken glass on the bottom of the pool ruined my whole day. Actually, the whole month. The glass shard cut through my whole sole, the plantar area, penetrating halfway through my left foot. In the process of removing the piece of glass, I could see the white-pinkish flesh, one-centimetre-deep wound, all full of gushing blood. Nobody to ask for help. All alone, and at about a 30 minute-walking distance to our home. Blood all over. Walking slowly, almost impossible to put my foot down, hopping at times, leaving behind me a reddish track. As I slowly got closer to home, the blood was getting stickier, making my sandal feeling almost glued to my foot. I was hoping that maybe that would stop the bleeding. The pressing issue, however, was dealing with my grandmother. I could not tell her, but I couldn't hide it either. All I could do was pretending it was just a…superficial scratch. Right… Still, wrapping my foot for a whole month until it started to heal, was more than a hint for my grandmother that my "scratch" was rather serious. Still, I had to suck it up! It was a miracle it didn't get infected. I was left with a scar to remember for the rest of my life!)

* * *

"Mom, let's dance!" Hurt or not, Evelyn has enough energy to dance or hop around, no matter what. (Isn't she her mother's daughter??!)

"Sure. What music would you like?" Since this house in Fara Sabina is located at decent distance from the neighbours, the blasting music at high volume is not disturbing anybody.

"Anything you'd like."

"How about Queen?"

"Sounds great!"

Queen is my favourite band. Freddie Mercury died last November. I always loved their songs, the music, the beat, the way Freddie was capturing the audience and engaging them all in singing along.

"Mom, how about Guns N' Roses?" Amanda has her preferred rock band. She likes the heavy metal—hard rock beat.

"We'll play yours, too." As far as I am concerned, it doesn't really matter what band or what kind of music we play. I'm not a fan of hard rock, but as long as the music is loud and it makes them jump around, it's fun. We are bouncing and hopping, and I take turns in holding their hands and spinning them around.

There is no shortage of fun activities. The Ranieri family brought Daisy with them last Sunday when they came to see us, and decided to leave the dog with us for a while. It's sheer joy. Daisy is following us all around the yard, and I can forgive her that she chewed up my sandals!

Letters keep coming from my parents—always supportive, from my mother-in-law—mostly complaining, and from Greg's aunt in Canada. She submitted to the Canadian government a letter of sponsorship for us. I don't know how this is going to work. Which branch of government did she send it to? Is the letter being sent to the Canadian Consulate in Rome or will she have to mail it directly to them? Besides, we applied as independent immigrants, based on our skills. So, do we need to be sponsored? If it helps, why not? I'll have to inquire at Caritas this week.

Sunday evening. Very relaxing. We are all enjoying the view of the olive groves and the orchards, the Mediterranean pine trees, villages all spread out over the hills of the Rieti Province. It has been a very hot day, so the evening breeze feels so balmy. Daisy is sitting in Amanda's lap. The days are still long and we don't want to go to bed early. However, it's Monday tomorrow. The first workday of the week always feels more tiring than the others.

The phone is ringing in the main hallway downstairs. What time is it? Oh, it's only midnight. This can only be my mother. Poor woman. I know how this works. She places the phone call through the operator at 7 pm and the connection becomes possible five hours later!! I'm sure she feels guilty, but she knows we are happy to talk with her whenever it is possible.

I rush out of our bedroom and take the corner down onto the spiralling staircase. It's dark, but I don't have time to turn any lights on. I'm trying to get to the phone before it wakes everybody up. Ouch!! The last few steps of the spiralling staircase are uneven at the edges. I miss a step and I'm rolling down the stairs tumbling, almost nosediving, while my hands are flailing out in a desperate attempt to grab to some rail or something. I do stop, but only at the bottom of the stairs! At least I manage to not wake anybody up.

Something happened to my left foot. The pain is excruciating, but I quickly grab the phone. Still, I cannot stand.

"Hi, Mom." My voice almost gives me away while I am stifling my pain.

"Are you alright?" Mother always knows when something is wrong with her children.

"I'm fine, Mom. I was sleeping…"

"I'm sorry. You know how these phone calls are working."

"I know, Mom. Don't worry." I have no idea what she is talking about. The pain is unbearable. I am trying to feel my left foot, but the simple touch takes my breath away. Our conversation is short. I cannot engage in any reasonable discussions, but I'm making my mother believe that I was sleepy. We say goodnight to each other.

How do I get back to the bedroom upstairs? I'm calling Greg. He finally hears me.

"What's wrong?"

"I fell down the stairs. I'm afraid I broke my left foot…"

"Oh, my goodness…" He helps me get back to our bedroom, but the pain is intolerable. I have never had any broken bone in my life, so I have no idea if it's a fracture or not, but my foot is getting more and more bluish and it keeps swelling up. I cannot touch the ground. Some ice, a couple of painkillers later, and a light sleep make me superficially ignore the pain. I need to go to a hospital tomorrow. I don't know how and where… I need to close my eyes for a few hours.

* * *

"Good morning, Giovanna."

"My goodness, what's going on? Are you alright?"

Not only is my voice almost unrecognizable with the pain I am trying to suppress, but calling her at home in Rome on a Monday morning is a state of emergency by itself.

"I fell down…"

"How did you fall?"

"Down the stairs…I won't be able to come to work today. I need to go to a hospital."

"By all means. Work is out of question. I am afraid we won't be able to take you to a hospital." She sounds guilty. That's not why I am calling. I will make it somehow, but I need to know which hospital she is suggesting. "You need to go to Rome, obviously. I am suggesting the Emergency Room at Policlinico Umberto. From the bus station in Via Tiburtina there must be a means of public transportation. I am so sorry we cannot give you a ride."

"No worries. Greg is going to help me. I'll call you later after I come back from the hospital."

"Take care."

This is going to be extremely challenging. The house we stay in is at the top of a hill. I need to walk down on an unpaved alley to make it to the main road where the bus would pick me up. The girls are awake now. One more scared than the other. They have never seen me in such a state of despair. The effect of the painkillers is fading away. Holding on to Greg on one side and to Amanda on the other side, I make it down to the bus stop. I cannot put my foot down. All I can do is to hop on my right foot and take one jump at a time. My foot is so swollen that I cannot wear any shoe or slipper or anything. I tried a sock, but it didn't fit either, so I am half bare foot.

The bus is here. Greg is helping me get on the bus and off we go. An hour later we are in Rome. He helps me get on a tramway and another half hour later we arrive at Policlinico Umberto. I can manage from this point on, so Greg can go to work. Thank goodness health care is free.

I have never been in an emergency ward. It is a hectic place. Medical personnel running in all directions, stretchers coming in with new patients, all in different stages of emergency. The rooms are full, doctors and nurses are coming in and out, medical equipment being carried across the hallway. It is a scary place. My pain is not subsiding, and the foot is getting more and more swollen as I am sitting on a chair in the main hallway. It is 10 am.

Hours go by. It is 11 am. No chance. Nobody is looking at me. I am trying to catch someone's attention, but no luck.

Twelve o'clock. It's been twelve hours since I fell last night. At least in bed I could extend my leg, but sitting on the bus, sitting on this chair, I can feel the blood pumping hard through my veins. Even my skin feels stretched out. I am in severe pain. My tears run down my face, uncontrollably.

One o'clock. I am getting more and more desperate. I'm crying with pain, with helplessness, I am shivering and the agony is getting more and more intense. In a last attempt I stand up and I start hopping across the hallway, making my way to the first room with an open door. My eyes are swollen with tears and I cannot control the sobbing.

"Please, please somebody see me…" I am leaning against the wall, standing on one leg, and I feel my face getting cold. I know I am going to pass out. Before I fall a nurse catches me and I am carried away to a bed. At least I'm in the room. Soon after I am taken on a gurney to the x-ray department, and five minutes later I am told that my last metatarsal bone on my left foot is broken. A metatarsal? The smallest one even. Such a tiny bone causing so much pain…I'm taken away on the gurney to the main room. Half an hour later I'm in a cast. They give me a pain killer and they discharge me. I think my left foot is cursed…!

On my way home to Fara Sabina, in the countryside. I know how to go back, but this time I am alone. I will probably be able to put my foot down once in a while, I'll hop too if I need to, but the cast is heavy, so hopping will be challenging. Back to the tramway stop, back to the bus hub, back on the bus, and around 3 pm I am back home. I have to go up the hill one small step at a time. The girls cannot see me, so I have nobody to help me. At least, I am here.

Giovanna came later that evening to see me. She brought me a couple of crutches. She is so caring. I wonder if she ever thought that I could sue them. Even a thought like that was unconceivable! For all the help we received from them, for all their kindness and care, this was absolutely unthinkable.

Greg came back from work around 6 pm. He was happy to see me home and in a better mood. The evening ended on a relaxed tone. When I left the hospital, I've been told to go back in three weeks so they remove the cast. Well, for the next three weeks I'll pretend I am on a summer vacation!!

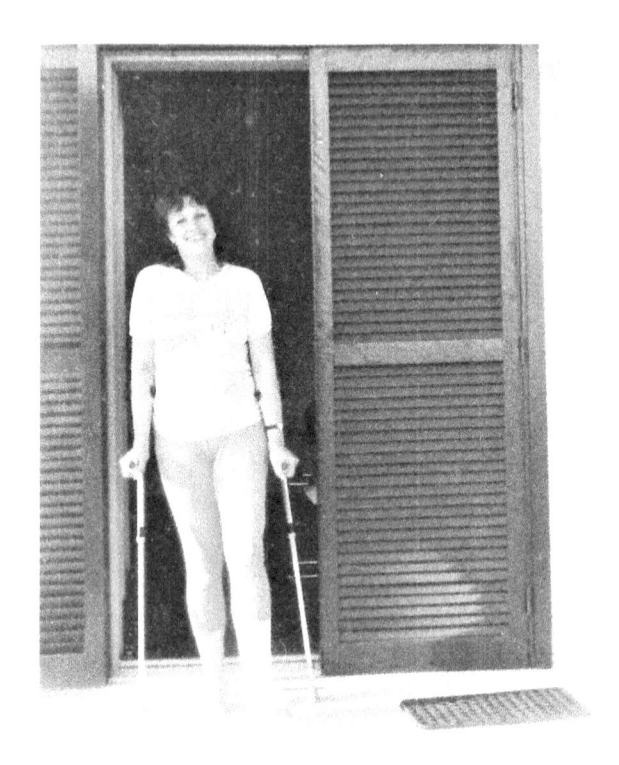

July 1992—hopping around on crutches.

July 1992—Daisy is chewing my sandals.

I SHALL NOT FAIL

August 1992—reading letters coming from our parents in the balmy breeze of a relaxing summer evening in Fara Sabina.

28

GOOD NEWS

"I have an idea." While enjoying a coffee on the outside patio, on a beautiful Sunday morning, new ideas are always welcome, and I am wondering what Greg has in mind.

"What is your idea?"

"We haven't seen Giancarlo and Anna Rita since we moved here. I was thinking that maybe we can invite them over."

"Great thought, Greg. Why don't you give them a call today?" After all, with my left foot in a cast, some entertainment would be more than welcome. I am sure they would be delighted to pay us a visit. It's been two weeks since I broke my foot. The pain is gone, the swelling is down considering that the cast feels a little loose, and some thoughts are crossing my mind.

"You know what I am thinking?"

"What?" Greg knows that when I am "thinking" about something, even if he may not agree, I am still going through with my plans. Most of the times.

"For the past couple of weeks I haven't been in touch with the Caritas people because I've been stuck with this cast on, so we don't know if there are any developments. I'm planning on going to pay them a visit this week, and walk in their office on crutches, just like this. It's not about impressing them because they don't have control over our file, but who knows? I'll have to try my luck."

"Are you sure? Are you comfortable enough to walk on crutches?"

"Well, it's not that I am going on a stroll across Rome. I'll be on the bus, on the metro, and there is just a little walking."

"If you really want to…?"

"I do." I see a ray of hope on Greg's face. At least he knows I do all I can to push forward with our applications. Maybe Tuesday.

* * *

"Buon giorno."

"Buon giorno, signora. What happened to you?"

"I just fell down on a staircase a couple of weeks ago. I'm getting better, but I can't quite walk yet…"

"Actually, it's good timing you came to see us. We were expecting to see you last week because we have good news for you. The Canadian Consulate has reviewed your application and you are scheduled to go for an interview in August."

"Really? Do we need anything?" I am overwhelmed. This is the greatest news we received in a long time. The news we were expecting. Coming to Caritas on crutches seemed to be the most auspicious moment.

"No, you just go to this appointment on August 10th at 11 am. They will ask you questions, so this will be an interview."

"Do we have to take the children with us, or…?"

"You don't need to take your children with you. The questions will be directed at you, so as parents you are in charge with your children anyways."

"What happens next?"

"Usually, this is good news. If your application had been rejected, you would have received a letter explaining the reasons, but since they want to see you, that means that you have a good chance to be successful."

"Grazie. Ciao!"

I wish I could fly back home to Fara Sabina. Still, I'll make it home before Greg does, so the good news will make his day, or the many days to come.

One more reason to invite Giancarlo's family. We can celebrate the great news.

Breaking the news to the girls made them extremely ecstatic. Dancing and jumping and bouncing around were their manifestation of happiness.

At least Evelyn's. That's exactly how they greeted their father when he came from work. Of course, the guess for such a euphoric manifestation was easy, so a glass of wine to turn a happy day into a happy evening was the most appropriate choice. My broken foot seemed to be a good omen, cursed or not!!

Tomorrow is my mother's birthday. She is turning 60. Sixty years old! All my mother dreamed of all her life as an employee working in the accounting department of a government-run company was to make it to the retirement age. All she wanted was to retire and then enjoy life. Retirement age was 55 for women back during the Romanian communist regime. She lived to see her dream come true, and today? No enjoyment. Their pensions are not enough, and the love of their life, their granddaughters, have left the country. I called her last night and we wished her happy birthday. She was sad. She never imagined that on a special occasion like this she would not have her dear family with her. However, when we shared the news of our upcoming interview at the Canadian Embassy her sadness made room to some excitement in her voice, at least for a few moments. Then she realized that she may not see us soon at all if we move to Canada…

"Mom, I am sure we will get to see you this summer. I don't know how and I don't know when, but we will find a way. We will not go to Canada without seeing you first. And after all, Canada may be far away, but it is not unreachable. It's still in the northern hemisphere! Enjoy your birthday, Mom! We love you."

The girls sang Happy Birthday to her in Italian. She thanked them and the conversation ended on a positive note. Mom seemed to partake in our moments of happiness.

***

Getting rid of the cast was not difficult. There was no point in going to Rome just for that. I was feeling well, there was no pain, just a little discomfort, but with a pair of good scissors in hand and a sharp knife, I managed to cut it off. I was still uneasy, though. Yes, a metatarsal was not a big deal, but since I had never had a broken bone ever in my life, I did not know what to expect, how fragile my foot still was, how tender the repaired fracture, how much pressure I was supposed—or allowed—to put on. It took me about a day to regain my confidence. Of course, I was still careful—no dancing, jumping, hopping around, just plain walking. It worked well.

Anna Rita, Giancarlo and Michele came to visit us last Sunday. We were so happy to share the good news with them, and that was a reason for extra celebration and more joyful moments.

A good meal, a couple of glasses of wine, a big watermelon—oh, so yummy—and the beautiful summer day!

29

FERRAGOSTO

August 15th is officially the Italian *ferragosto*. It's our second one in Italy, so we know now that almost the entire month of August is a "holiday period," so pretty much everything is closed for a week or two at some point. Offices suspend work, professionals shutter their studios, even doctors leave their practice to pack themselves onto the beaches! Luckily, our appointment at the Canadian Consulate is on the 10th, probably the last Monday before the officials go on their vacation, as well.

"Good morning." Greg has adopted his usual professional demeanour today. We need to look "polished", today more than any other days. He is the main applicant and, we need to leave a positive impression.

"Good morning. What can I do for you?" For a change, our conversation takes place in English, which is to be expected, obviously. After all, speaking English is a requirement.

"We have an appointment at 11."

"Let me check. Have a seat, please."

A short phone conversation and five minutes later, we are following this young lady to an office on the main floor.

"Please be seated. Somebody will be with you shortly."

"Thank you."

Indeed, "shortly" in Canadian terms has a different meaning than the Italian equivalent. Just two minutes later we are invited in an elegant office, all draped with the Canadian flag and other Canadian symbolic objects that we are not fully aware of, but we can superficially identify, especially the coat of arms of the Canadian provinces and territories. A feeling of thankfulness, of gratitude envelops me.

A middle-aged gentleman walks almost solemnly into the room. He stops in front of us and extends his hand:

"Good morning. My name is David Jackson and I am the vice-consul with the Consulate of Canada in Rome."

Greg shakes his hand and introduces himself. I do the same. As I clasp his hand in a brief, firm, up-and-down shake, I sense a degree of confidence, of trust. Something that makes me believe in a positive outcome of this entire encounter.

We are invited to sit on the two chairs located in front of a stately desk. Mr. Jackson is engaging us in a conversation, but his questions are addressed specifically to each of us, one at a time. No talking over each other, or interrupting or interfering!

"So, Mr. Bandol, you are the main applicant, correct?'

"Yes…" Greg is trying to overcome his visible emotion. He seems to be still affected by the interviews he had with the Canadian officials about two years ago while he was on his short visit to Canada.

"Tell me about yourself—mainly about your career, please."

Greg is gathering his inner powers in an attempt to look more confident. For the next 10 minutes he manages to sum up his duties as an engineer in the military back in Romania, continuing with the following years after he was "disciplinarily" dismissed from the army because of his political beliefs.

I cannot read anything on Mr. Jackson's face. His facial expression is neutral, although his eyes show a certain light.

My turn comes up. I am asked the same thing, so I am talking about my career as a teacher. I'm trying to keep it short and make it succinct. Teaching is teaching, so there are no embellishments.

"So, Mr. Bandol, you have been in Canada for a few months in 1990 - 1991. Can you please expand on that period of time, and the circumstances of your arrival, please?"

It's incredible how the word "please" is constantly inserted in every question he is asking us, as if we have choices. Must be a Canadian way of talking…?

Greg seems to be embarrassed to acknowledge that he tried indeed to take a shortcut and apply for refugee status directly from Canada. He knows by now that one mistake he made was to not apply for political asylum as soon as he touched ground in Toronto, but given those circumstances, that was impossible. Well, we are here today. Mr. Jackson knows very well what the whole story is, but this is probably the protocol.

Greg's recount of his arrival and the four months he spent in Canada not long ago seems to have met the standards, if there are any.

"You have chosen to immigrate to Saskatchewan, correct?"

"Yes." My husband appears to know the rules and not volunteer answers unless the questions expect an ample reply.

"Would you mind explaining why Saskatchewan is your province of choice?"

"I thought that since I already had some remote relatives in that part of Canada, Saskatchewan would be the right location for our new beginnings."

Short, concise, to the point. I don't know much about this province, other than what Greg told me when he came back. Since he spent a few winter months in the prairies, all that seemed to be worth remembering was the cold winter, the frigid temperatures, and the snow…Well, Canada is still Canada, cold or not. We chose to immigrate to this country, and so be it! Assuming that we get accepted.

The interview lasted about 45 minutes, at the end of which we have been told that our file would be reviewed, and then we would be scheduled for a second interview soon, within a few weeks. I don't know what to make of this final part of our interview. Is it good, is it not? Greg has mixed feelings, as well. I have never had the chance to meet any Canadians before, and definitely not officials, so I don't know what to make of their body language. Mr. Jackson's appearance, his affable yet cold manner of engaging us in a conversation didn't leave much room to any guessing. Since we are in Rome, we might as well drop by Caritas and see if we can get some feedback from them.

"Buon giorno."

"Ciao!" The Italians are such extrovert people. You will know right away if you got them on the wrong foot or the right one. The Caritas employees, all young, are always in a good mood. I'm introducing my husband whom they have never met.

"What's new?"

"We've just had our first interview at the Consulate of Canada, and we have been told that another one would follow soon, but we have no idea what to make of this first meeting… Are there any chances, or did we just screw it up?"

"What makes you think that way?"

"I don't know… It's just a feeling…"

"From all we know and we have been noticing with our clients, once you have been invited for a second interview, everything should be fine. You are on the right track."

Our conversation is short. I just needed a bit of acknowledgment. We say good-bye and we are on our way to Fara Sabina.

We have to call our parents today. If the stars are aligning and our immigration papers will be issued soon, that means that I have to find a way to see my parents. This is going to be tough for Greg.

"I'm thinking that we should see our parents this summer…"

"Who is "we"…?" Greg knows what his options are when it comes to travelling under the present circumstances, more precisely, none. First of all, our passports are with the Canadian Consulate in Rome, but although the girls and I would be able to obtain temporary travel passes that would allow us to leave Italy, and also come back, that possibility is non-existent for him. He has no status here.

"Well, you know…The girls and I…" I almost feel guilty for thinking about travelling without him. It would not be the first time. Yes, we are married, but it doesn't mean that I lost my independence. Back in Romania, during my summer breaks, I used to work as a travel guide for a government agency which was allowing people to travel abroad, where the word "abroad" was being applied to socialist and communist countries. I went to Poland, Eastern Germany, Czechoslovakia (which was one united country at the time), Soviet Union, Bulgaria—several times, taking Romanian tourists with me, mostly by train or by bus. Of course, I was sure there was always at least one "passenger" who was a "Securitate" agent and who was travelling for free, while keeping an eye on us to not go off the boundaries imposed by the communist regime and its abusive secret service. As a matter of fact, we, as regular citizens, were not allowed to keep our passports with us, at home. Yes, they were our passports, but the communist regime was in full control of our lives and our…freedom! What freedom??! 48 hours before going on any such excursion abroad we were supposed to go to the police and request our passports. Upon our return to our homeland, we were supposed to return them to the police department the very next day.

We did manage to travel a little, Greg as well, each of us independently of each other. The only time we went together was in 1981 on a cruise on the Black Sea, from Odessa to Batumi (which is today a city port in Georgia, on the east coast of the Black Sea). That was our first cruise. It was the only cruise we could go on during those times, yet it felt like a privilege, and it surely was. I was the guide leading a group of quite wealthy Romanian families (how was it possible that some Romanians were wealthy in those times?? I could never figure that out). Anyways, Greg was just accompanying me. The cruise was magnificent. It was a small-scale version of the Winter Palace of St. Petersburg's (Leningrad at the time), but a palace on the waves of the Black Sea.

So, leaving Greg behind this time is different. I may be able to see my parents, and his mother, as well, while he will not. However, even I have restrictions, as well. I can leave Italy, but I cannot go to Romania. Otherwise, why did I apply for a refugee status if I am considering going back to the country I fled from?

Too many details to discuss and lots of questions arising from each detail. However, it's almost mid-August, and shortly the month of August will start to slightly blend into September. For now we are just happy that today we scored a few good points! Happy *Ferragosto!*

30

HALT!

"Hi Mom! How are you?"

"We are watching the Summer Olympics in Barcelona. Romania received a lot of medals, and today it's just a recap of the last day festivities and closing ceremonies!" My mother's voice sounds happy. I'm glad I am calling at such a moment.

"I have news, Mom. We just had an interview at the Canadian Consulate and I think we have a good chance to get our immigration papers. We would like to come and see you, but coming to Romania is not a choice. Can you think of somewhere else?"

"I'm glad to hear the news. I'm thinking there might be a possibility. Can you travel to Hungary?"

"I don't see why not. What do you have in mind?"

"I'm thinking that maybe we can drive to Budapest."

"Are you serious? It's over 700 km. It will take you a whole day, at least. You also have to cross the border into Hungary, and border crossing always comes up with unexpected situations. Besides, John cannot drive a whole day without getting extremely tired."

My mother must be crazy! She doesn't drive and my stepfather is 65, not very old according to current standards, but that is too much for him. Too long the distance to cover in one day.

"Let me think. We will find a solution." Of course. My mother is the solution-finder. The problem-solver. How can I forget that?!

"What do you want me to do?" I cannot read her mind.

"Can you call back in a couple of days? I would like to call you back, but you know what it is like with our phone lines and the late connections…"

"Sure. I'll call you in two days. Will that give you enough time?"

"Yes. Sounds great!"

I'm sure my mother is now on a calling spree, trying to find out who among their friends, relatives or acquaintances would be able to help. On my side, I have some issues I have to deal with, as well.

* * *

The decision has been made. The three of us—the girls and I—will meet our parents in Budapest on August 19th. They will have a friend who will take turns with helping my stepfather behind the wheel. It will be a long journey for them, and it's up to them to decide on the details. All I know is that on August 19th they would be in Budapest. We have to tell them what time our train arrives and they will meet us at the main railway station.

Apparently, they are almost set, while I still have a lot of details to deal with. Obtaining travel documents for me and the girls. Buying train tickets. All we have is maps. (Fresh reminder: no internet, no Wi-Fi, no mobile phones).

The big day has arrived. Very early on the first commuter bus to Rome, go to the railway station in Via Tiburtina, board the train and off we go!

"Mom, this trip feels like the one we were on almost two years ago when we came to Italy."

"I wouldn't push it that far, Evelyn. That trip was more challenging than I ever imagined. I don't want to repeat any piece of it. It feels traumatic even today."

"Except for our stop in Venice…" Amanda seems to have fond memories of Venice. I do, too, but I have to keep in mind that at that time I had to detach myself from the role of a mother with two children in tow, almost living in a fantasy world with one destination in mind: Rome, but pretending we were tourists.

"Yes, it was magnificent, although a little short time-wise, but we did get to see what was the most important."

It is 7 am. The trip should take about 15 hours. Around 10 pm tonight we should be in Budapest. We have seats, we have food and water, this is not stressful at all, or at least not yet. We made arrangements to meet our party in front of Esprit Hotel, on one of the main streets of Budapest, Rakoczi Avenue, about 1 km walking distance from the railway station. We had been in Budapest a couple of times and I had an idea about going around the city. We are used to walking…

* * *

Italy's political geography has been conditioned by its rugged landscape. With few direct roads between some cities, and with the passage from one point to another traditionally difficult, Italy's towns and cities have a history of self-sufficiency, independence, and mutual mistrust. Travelling by train, without a worry in mind, we can see the beauty of the landscape, cities and towns so diverse, so different from one another. The terrain is roughly evenly divided between hilly and mountainous land.

The train crosses through Tuscany all the way along and through the Apennines which are among the world's rockiest mountains and which form the spine of the entire peninsula. It's a fast train, so the first stop is Florence followed by Bologna, and then Verona. We go east from this point and the Alps radiate in their full splendour.

The girls are dozing off or just looking out the window, enjoying the scenery. (We actually have seats this time!) Some passengers who boarded the train in Rome got off already. It's not crowded at all. As we approach the border with Austria, nobody else is in our compartment. This time we truly feel like tourists. We have been on the train for over seven hours now.

Tarvisio. The train slows down until it comes to a complete stop.

"Buon giorno. Passports, please." Two border patrol officers have opened the door and are checking our documents.

"We don't have passports. Only travel passes." I hand out our documents. No photo, just our personal information and our legal status in Italy.

"Signora, you are entering Austria and you do not have a visa for Austria."

"I don't understand. We are not getting off the train. We are in transit going to Hungary. I was not aware that we needed a visa. Nobody mentioned it to me…"

It's useless. I have nobody to argue with. They are not here to make conversation. We obey and get off the train voluntarily or they'll use other means. They are not moving, so we grab our luggage and get off the train.

What now? As we stand on the platform, looking helplessly at one another, the train starts moving slowly, disappearing into the white-capped Alps. I am stunned. Completely frozen. My parents are waiting for us in Budapest tonight. In about eight hours we would have been in Hungary, and now? No phone, no way to communicate with them.

Which way from here? Going back to Rome? That would be a total disappointment for my parents. Their hearts would be shattered. There must be a solution, but my mind is a blur. We start schlepping our luggage to the direction of an office. Maybe someone has an idea, but I don't know what to ask, where to start from. I'm sure anybody can read bewilderment and worry on my face. I'm a complete mess, but I need to stay composed, at least for the girls.

"Buon giorno, signora. What happened?" A very kind looking gentleman who seems to be working here is approaching us. I'm telling him the whole story.

"Would you like to make a phone call?"

I would like to, but whom am I supposed to call?

"Mom, why don't you call Dad?" Amanda's suggestion is not bad. Yes, I can call Greg, but then what? How is he going to contact my parents? They are on their way to Budapest, or maybe just arrived. Still, this is not going anywhere.

Two more people are joining our small group. They all want to know what happened, so I keep telling the story several times.

"So, Signora, I understand you need a visa to cross through Austria, right?"

"Yes, but we were not getting off the train. We were just in transit going to Hungary."

"It doesn't matter. While the train is on Austrian territory, even if you are only on the train and not on land, you still need a visa."

"This is absurd!"

"Yes, but these are the rules."

"So, is there any choice?"

I SHALL NOT FAIL

"You can go to Trieste tomorrow, there is an Austrian Consulate in Trieste and try getting a transit visa for Austria."

"In Trieste? How far is Trieste? And how do I get there?"

"Tomorrow morning at 6 am there is a train going to Trieste. It's not a fast train, but you would get there in about two hours."

"And then?"

"You go to the Consulate, and maybe if you are lucky, you get your visa and then you can board the next train to come back here and continue your journey."

All this sounds like a big puzzle, almost like a tortuous conundrum. More complicated than I could have ever imagined. I'm trying to put two and two together, and add another two or three or four…There seems to be no end in sight. I hear all these people talk, but they speak a different Italian dialect. It sounds like a mix of Italian and German. I need some quiet time to think. I need a break.

"Girls, let's have a bite and see if I can relax my mind a little."

I am asking for permission to leave the suitcase in the main hallway. No problem. It's all safe.

We take a backpack with some food and water and we cross the road. We can see the Alps in all their glory, the sun shining over the snowy peaks, sending the reflected light back in millions of beams. It is majestic.

"What do we do now? Does any of you have any idea?"

"Mom, Tony, your friend who has offered to drive with our grandparents, has a cellphone. Remember?"

"Yes, but I don't have his phone number…"

"We can call Dad and maybe he can call him?"

I believe Amanda is right. That is the only known element in this entire puzzle. Tony. And then what? Greg can talk with him, but what do we know what tomorrow is going to bring? Will I get a transit visa to go through Austria? No matter which solution I am trying to find, it's either a dead end, or bifurcation. Nothing is straight forward. The only thing to do is to give it a try. Our lunch is over. Or was it a dinner? Maybe just a snack.

"Signore, you said we can make a phone call?"

"Yes."

"It's a long-distance call. We need to call someone in Rome. Actually, not in Rome, but in the Province of Rieti."

"No problem. Feel free to make any phone call."

"Grazie."

"Hi, Greg. We ran into a huge problem." I'm trying to make the story as concise and precise as I can. He is listening calmly, as we are both reasoning seeking a viable solution. He agrees to call Tony and let him and our parents know that we will be late. Late or not making it at all…? Still a dilemma.

"How are the girls?"

"They are fine. Always helpful. Great support."

We say good-bye to each other and hope that our plan will work. If I make it to the Austrian Consulate, no matter what the outcome may be, I will call him again, and then we will go from there.

The evening is going by fast. Making plans, thinking of possibilities or impossibilities…It's night already. Where can we sleep? There is no bench. Some chairs, and a couple of tables. Maybe on the floor? I'm wondering if this floor has seen a broom or a brush lately…We are so tired. There is no hotel in sight, besides, the first train will be here at 6 am. I'm pulling out a couple of sweaters and some clothes that I had prepared for my parents and make our "beds" on these tables. I'm hugging Evelyn and pulling her close to me to keep her warm, but also my body is warming up to her body. It's cool in the Alps on an August evening.

Good night! How good it is going to be, we'll see. Rather a tough one, both factually and figuratively…

31

WE HATE YOU, MOM!!

I'm waking up stiff as hell. Not sure if I slept much anyways. This day is a race against the clock. If the plan we concocted is not going to work, everything is going to collapse and above all, my parents' disappointment would throw them in total distress. I hope my lucky star will guide me.

"Girls, it's time to wake up!" A hug and a kiss will give them some reassurance that all will go well. No coffee this morning. I'm tense enough and fully awake, so no coffee would make me more alert than I am already. Last instructions to the girls:

"You will both stay here! Stay put, be good, and wait for me. Evelyn, behave! There is some food in that backpack. We have to make it with what we have. If all goes well, I'll be back here around 2 pm. Here's the scoop! The return train I should be on stops here for only about two minutes, and there are only two possibilities: if I get the visa, that means that we can continue our journey, so in that case I won't have time to get off the train. You will wait for me outside, on the platform, suitcase and backpacks and all, you will see me waving at you and I'll help you get onboard and we will continue our trip.

If I am not successful—and, frankly, I am not even thinking that this might be an option or an outcome—so, in that case, I'll get off the train, join you and then we will wait for a train to go back to Rome."

The girls' expressions and attitude show nothing but compliance. No time for negotiations. No other options anyways. The train is here. Another hug and I'm on my way.

As I board the train and get myself a seat, I am trying to relax my mind. Easier said than done. My thoughts are partially with my girls, and partially with my parents. I left my daughters behind, alone, among strangers. God forbid that something might happen to them! Eight hours without supervision. It's not that they need adult supervision. After all, they will turn 13 and 15 years old this year, but still, this is a foreign country, we are among strangers. I trust them. They are mature enough to know how to defend themselves or how to act properly, should something happen. If anything, having sometimes lived in precarious conditions in our home country for the first part of their childhood—or even for the first few months of last year in the convent—prepared them well.

Memories from their childhood flood my mind. Back in Romania there was no second thought when it was coming to leaving the children alone at home for a couple of hours at a time. They were three and five years old, or four and six…If I needed to run to the grocery store and leave them unsupervised for an hour or so, I knew that they would be safe. Or so I was hoping. Yet, nothing ever happened, although our apartment was on the 5th floor, and the balconies were at little higher than an adult waistline. We must have trained them well. They never tried to stick anything in an electricity outlet (at 220 V!!!), never flooded the house, and—thank goodness—they never attempted to scale the balcony either. Good kids. Once in a while, during their hours-long playing outside with other kids, one of them was coming up, usually Evelyn, storming into the apartment and whining:

"Mom, I got into a fight with Flora and she hit me…Can you come downstairs with me…?"

"Sorry, kiddo, but I was not there with you on the ground and I don't know whose fault it is. How can I be the judge when I have no idea who started it and how you got in trouble?"

"But Mom…"

"Shush! You broke it, you fix it!" End of discussion. By the time she was back downstairs joining the other kids, the problem was gone anyways.

At other times, if Evelyn was getting in any conflict outside on the playground, she used to scream from the top of her lungs, loudly enough so I could hear from inside the apartment, five floors up.

"Mooooom!! Mom!!"

Yes, I could hear her, but the neighbours could hear her as well, and it was annoying. I was choosing to not help with their disputes. I had not been there, I had not been a witness, so how could I take sides, even if she was my daughter? What made me think she was right and the other kid was wrong?

"If you scream one more time, you'll come back in the house and you will not be allowed to play outside for two days!!" That was the closing argument. Problem fixed.

Were the girls in danger? Occasionally, but it wasn't until late that I found out about some of their "explorations." Evelyn was the most adventurous one between the two of them. One day she may have heard that cats, no matter from which height they were falling, they would always land on their four paws. She had to try it herself, obviously. I don't know where she found a cat, probably out in the streets. Apparently, Evelyn took the cat—just a kitten and maybe too…trustworthy—all the way to the top of the apartment building we were living in. On the roof top! The whole structure was divided into several buildings, each with its own entrance, all five floors high, and there was some space between one building and the next one, so anyone walking on the roof without a repair-related reason or permission or proper gear was prone to falling and, consequently, dying. Evelyn made it up to the roof top carrying the cat in her arms. The "experiment" had a fortunate outcome. The poor kitten survived, it may have landed on its four, and Evelyn came back down unscathed. Our lucky stars were watching from up above…

Yes, looking back to those times now makes me appear as an irresponsible mother. Not that I have excuses, but considering that throughout all my childhood years I had been totally deprived of freedom, all we wanted was to give our children the possibility to choose for themselves. Yes, sometimes those choices were not the right ones, but there were also consequences. Fortunately, none of them had been fatal. On the positive side, Greg was with me on this one, as well. We had both suffered from lack of freedom. We wanted our girls to be independent.

* * *

Trieste. The railway station is right on the Adriatic Sea. As the train is slowing down all I can see from the pier are the blue waters of the Gulf of Trieste. No time for daydreaming! I'm on a mission. A very decisive one.

Where is the Consulate of Austria though? Trieste is a big city. It's the capital of the Province of Friuli Venezia Giulia, but the city centre seems to be at walking distance from the railway station.

Asking questions left and right, 30 minutes of walking, and I am finally on the steps of the Consulate. It's almost 9 am. Apparently, they open at 9, but I am not alone. I feel my heart up in my throat. I count 12 more people ahead of me, in line, waiting for the doors to open. This cannot happen. I don't have time to wait. I need to be back at the railway station before noon. I have only one choice. Just one. The only train that would take me back to Tarvisio to join my kids and then keep going to Vienna leaves from Trieste at 11 am.

I'm desperate. All I can do is talk to the people and ask them politely to grant me the permission to go first. They all seem to be in dire situations, some look like refugees or immigrants, just like me, they all need a visa for Austria, for different reasons, of course. Mine is only a transit one. Still, I need to be the first in line.

Kindness. Compassion. Generosity. Pouring my heart out and explaining to these people, mainly women, some of colour, who definitely have kids of their own, they all understand my anxiety of having left my children behind, two unsupervised girls.

The door to the Consulate opens. Still, 10 more minutes go by until the officials are ready to see the first person in line. I am the one. Thank you, people!

I'm explaining to this gentleman what our situation is. I have a legal status in Italy and I am not trying to flee to Austria. I just need a transit visa so we can go to Hungary. Yes, I am Romanian, but I am not planning to break any laws. He looks at me with doubtful eyes, with incertitude. I know that the first news report that made its waves on the Austrian television network three years ago, after the Romanian Revolution, was a scandalous one. The government decided to open the borders, so the Romanian people were finally free. Right!! What was exactly freedom for some unruly individuals? They got on the first train and took off to some

European destinations. Vienna was one of them. Right on the Danube waters the beautiful white swans were gracefully gliding along the shores. Some idiots of a certain ethnic group caught a few swans and turned them into…food! It was appalling. Back in Romania at that time, while hearing that news, shame was not enough to express our true feelings. So, here I am today, I am a Romanian in need of a transit visa. I am not going to kill any swans…

Ten minutes later, which seemed like an eternity, a stamp is applied on my travel pass, I say "danke schön" and off I go. On my way out I thank the people waiting in line for their graciousness, and I wish them all good luck. I will catch the train and everything should be alright from this point on.

Three hours later the train stops in Tarvisio. Just for two minutes. The girls are waiting for me, just as I instructed them, luggage and all. They see me waving at them from the open door of the train as it slowly moves in until it stops at the platform. I get off, grab the luggage, help them hop on the train and, finally, we are on our way. We have about four hours to wind down. Next stop will not be Budapest, but Vienna. The only option. Still, there is so much unknown ahead of us. Where do we sleep tonight? I will have to find a hotel, but I have no Austrian money, no schillings. Besides, I have to call Greg back in Italy that we will not make it to Budapest tonight either. Ongoing puzzles…

* * *

Vienna. Final stop. For tonight, anyways. I need to exchange some Italian lira into schillings. I don't know how to operate an ATM machine, but coincidentally, some banks are still open. A few minutes later, schillings in hand, we are on our way to find a hotel. There are plenty of them, but we need one close to the station so we can get on the first train to Budapest tomorrow morning. Ibis Hotel will do it. It's a little more expensive than what I was planning, but we need a decent bed tonight. The girls are tired. I am too, but I also have some ideas…

"Girls, we are in Vienna…"

"So…?"

Right, so?

"Remember Venice two years ago?"

"What do you want, Mom?" Amanda is already objecting—for a good reason, and the tone of her voice makes me avoid her eyes.

"I am thinking about doing some sightseeing. It's not time to go to bed yet. Still early. I'll have to get you something to eat, too…" I know they are hungry, so I am hoping that I might lure them into going to have a bite and blend some tourist attractions in.

They know that there are no options. This is insane, but two years ago we pretended we were tourists in Venice, and we made it. We'll do the same thing today in Vienna! Who knows when, and if, we will ever visit the famous Vienna? So, off we go.

We are about three km away from the historic district, and there is so much to see around. The Opera house, one of the world's largest and most splendid theatres; the Hofburg Castle, the official residence of any Austrian ruler and maybe the most historically significant of all Vienna's palaces; the Parliament building, impressing with its Corinthian columns, boasting Greek influences; Stephen's Cathedral, Vienna's most important Gothic edifice; Karlskirche (Charles Church) which is Vienna's greatest baroque religious building. We don't go anywhere inside, but we keep taking photos. Memories for the rest of our lives.

I know this is totally crazy. The girls are dragging their feet, shuffling every single step on the way. Four hours later we make it back to the hotel.

"We hate you, Mom…" Too tired to argue. We fall asleep on a whim!

32

MY DANUBE IS BLUE!!

"Good morning, girls!"

Judging by their looks, they haven't forgiven me.

"What other crazy and stupid plans do you have in mind for today, Mom?"

Actually, I do. The train to Budapest is scheduled to leave at 2 pm from the main railway station, so we can still do some more sightseeing. Last night we stopped to call Greg from a payphone, so he could pass along the news. My parents should have been notified by now that we would arrive tonight, so they would meet us at the main railway station in Budapest. We can continue to pretend we are tourists.

No visit to Vienna would be complete without seeing the famous Prater Park. However, the girls are giving me an evil eye. I can take it!

Visiting the Prater is a little like stepping into another world. It is in fact one of Vienna's most popular recreation areas. It takes us an hour to make it to this enormous natural park between the Danube and the Danube Canal. It is stunning. There is something here for everyone, from thrills and spills in the Wurstel area, to the dinosaur-themed park for the kids.

The best-known attraction is the Wiener Riesenrad, a Ferris wheel, or the Giant Wheel. However, we don't have the time or the money to indulge in the extravagance of riding it. There are also bumper cars, carousels, roller coasters, shooting galleries, ghost trains, and so many more. Elsewhere in this vast park there's room for horseback riding, swimming in the stadium pool, football, cycling, tennis, and bowls—just by looking at a map.

The Prater is one km away from the Danube. What's another kilometre?!! We exit the park and we make our way to the closest bridge. Reichsbrücke. The Imperial Bridge. We don't need to be on the bridge. I just want to see the Danube. The fascination of my childhood.

The Danube as I can see it from this bridge is blue, dark blue. My childhood memories of the Blue Danube are etched in my mind and soul.

* * *

I was in the last month of the 8th grade. My elementary/middle school cycle was coming to an end, and so was my eight-year program at the School of Music and Fine Arts. The College of Education in our city was celebrating its centennial. Among the different events scheduled to celebrate this commemoration our local sinfonietta orchestra was also invited to perform. The orchestra was formed of 30 to 40 musicians, most of them music teachers but also "afficionados", all playing on different instruments. Since the Danube is not only the most important and largest river of my home country, but it is also the southern border, any classical pieces related to the Danube were by default part of the program. Johann Strauss's *Blue Danube* waltz was one of them, but even more traditional was the *Waves of the Danube* waltz [so-called "Anniversary Waltz"], composed by the Romanian composer Iosif Jovanovich in 1880. When the sinfonietta decided on its repertoire and started to practice, my violin teacher invited me to join this adult-only orchestra and he suggested I played the solo overture to the *Waves of the Danube* waltz. I was only 14 years old, and here I was, a young student, the only one, performing the solo prelude, not only in front of the orchestra, in front of my teachers, but also in front of the large audience. It was an emotional moment imprinting unwavering feelings of love, grace and gratitude in my heart.

* * *

I suddenly wake up from my daydreaming. I realize that the Danube is in my heart. It will always be. The waves of my childhood river are chanting and waltzing under my eyes, wrapping the earth and enfolding my soul. The river of my childhood is telling me that no matter what, we will succeed. We will make it. Yes, the **DANUBE IS BLUE**, indeed.

I am pleased. A few photos later to immortalize the moment and we are back on our way to the railway station of Vienna—the Wien Hauptbahnhof.

* * *

Finally in Budapest. The train is slowly moving to the platform. It stops. Our heads are sticking out the window. I see my parents waving at us. We wave back at them. It's such an exciting moment. I am grabbing my suitcase; the girls pick up their backpacks and we rush to get off the train. Hugging and kissing. Tears of joy, tears of solitude, tears of sadness and grief mixed with happiness. It's been almost two years since we left Romania. Two years since our train was leaving the main railway station in Bucharest, getting farther and farther away, leaving our parents heartbroken in the wake of the departing train; the silhouettes of my parents becoming smaller and smaller to the point of invisibility. I didn't make much of that moment then. We had our worries in mind about a future that was so uncertain. That was not a time to think of leaving my parents behind. However, today I realize that the suffering we left in our tracks has been imprinted on my parents' faces. They seem to be about 10 years older, although it's only two years that went by. However, the happiness I read in their eyes brings back beautiful and happy memories of the time we spent in our home country.

The hotel is not far away. Maybe 20 minutes walk from the station. I am glad that Tony had a cell phone. At least we had a way of communicating with them, also thanks to Greg who was able to play the intermediary role. Obviously, the two days they spent in Budapest while waiting for us, not even knowing whether or not we would make it, have thrown them in a tumult of indescribable proportions. Still, this is not the time to reminisce over the past two days. They belong to the past. It's time to enjoy the moment.

The girls are ecstatic. So are my parents and my mother-in-law. Obviously, my mother-in-law is somewhat sad because Greg was not able to come and see her, but we have more reasons to be happy than unhappy. Understandably, they also know that the possibility of not seeing us at all was quite significant only 48 hours ago. Anyways, we made it. Time to wind down. We drop the luggage at the hotel. My parents and my mother-in-law share the same room. They booked a room for me and the girls, as well. Tony has his own room.

We are all hungry, so a restaurant in the neighbourhood is the right place to sit and enjoy a conversation and a good meal. It feels like a true family reunion. Celebratory and joyous. Intense emotions are being triggered, and I realize how frail my parents are, living far away from us, feeling forgotten or even abandoned. We talk over one another, so high is the excitement.

"So, tell us about your life in Italy!"

"What do you want to know?"

"Everything!"

Everything… Everything? No, they don't need to know everything. Still, the mood is so upbeat that all the stories that come to our minds are positive. The girls talk about their school, about homework and our commuting, about our—short—weekends, about moving in and moving out, on the go all the time. Of course, my parents know all these stories already, but to hear the girls speak with an Italian accent, mixing and intermingling words from the two languages in one single sentence, all of this is a show on its own.

"How was Vienna?"

"Oh, grandma, don't ask! Mom is nuts! She dragged us all around the city as if this was the last day of our lives and we needed to enjoy every minute and second of it." Amanda is right. Carpe diem!

"You know your mother…" True. My mother knows me well, too, of course. I'm partially the "product" of my mother's and, especially, my grandmother's upbringing: wasting time is not an option. You have some time in your hands? Use it productively. Rightly so.

Suddenly I begin to see my parents' vulnerabilities, weakness, and humanness. This insight is bringing about a temporary wave of sadness, as I fully acknowledge their limitations but also their impact on me. However, this time, the sadness has a poignant but serene quality. We are all humans.

"So, when are you leaving for Canada?" I'm sure my parents would like to see that we get on with our lives and immigrate to Canada, but they are partially in denial.

"If all goes well, maybe this year."

"When is your next interview at the Consulate?"

"We don't know. Probably in September."

"Are you keeping in touch with Greg's relatives in Canada?"

"Oh, yes. All the time. They offered to sponsor us if our application as independent immigrants is not working out."

We are all tired tonight. Mostly emotionally tired. We will continue tomorrow.

* * *

Two more days go by. Too fast. We go on walks—sometimes shorter, sometimes longer, and we talk. My girls are enjoying tremendously seeing their grandparents again, reminiscing about childhood stories, about their kindergarten and school years, about our trips to the seaside in summer, playing on the sandy beaches on the Black Sea; about their great-grandparents who were living on the outskirts of the city, and the occasionally visits to their countryside house and farm, helping with picking some fruit from their orchards or trying to milk a cow, or just having fun.

"Did you go to any beaches in Italy?" Mom wants to know more about our life in Italy.

"Yes. We went to Ostia a few times, and also to Santa Marinella where we live from September through June. But in summer we have the house in the countryside all to ourselves, so we don't have time to miss any beach."

"So, if you are still in Italy in September, I assume you are going to a high school, Amanda, right?"

"Yes, we found a high school which is not far away from the middle school I just graduated from, but it will still be in Rome."

"Do you have books, notebooks, and all?" My mother assumes that she is in charge to provide supplies for the girls.

"Yes, plenty of everything. As for schoolbooks, we get them all for free from the school."

Last day to spend in Budapest. The weather has been beautiful and we have all enjoyed our time together, although extremely short. My parents are visibly getting more and more sad, as the evening melancholic darkness is obnubilating our minds and spirits. I can't but realize that being physically away from my mother for two years made me more aware of the impact she had on me, although not always very tangible, and the influence she exerted on me despite the many sombre moments of my childhood and teen years when I was being punished more often that I deserved or needed. Wounds? Yes. However, having learned to take care of my inner scars, I am now able to relate to my mother as she is now almost impuissant, almost helpless. I feel the shift happening which led me to feeling as if a heavy weight has been lifted off my shoulders. I've always been aware that we cannot change the past, and I now feel free from that unexplainable compulsion to alter the past or, sometimes, even the present reality. Missing my parents, especially my mother, makes me realize that there is nothing like family. The people we are related to by blood are expected to be our closest allies, our greatest sources of love and support. My mother has been, and still is, just that. All those times of misunderstanding and resentment, of bickering and badgering, are now gone. I feel attuned to myself, but it seems to be too late. I wish I had learned how to express my emotions while my mother was around and how to show her my love. They will go back home tomorrow and we will part our ways, again. Who knows for how long?

* * *

A last stroll along the Danube is bringing the day to an end. The Danube…This long river, the longest in Europe, running through 10 countries, continues to be my fascination, a true enchantment carrying along memories from my childhood. Its waters may not be always blue, but the beautiful Budapest evening sky reflecting on its waters makes the Danube look blue. It brings a sense of serenity and stability, a dose of inspiration and wisdom. It feels calming and it's my symbol of reliability. Yes, my Danube will always be blue…

I SHALL NOT FAIL

August 1992—Vienna, our unexpected stop on our way to Budapest, Hungary. A short break.

August 1992—Vienna. Counting the Austrian schillings I had just exchanged in a bank.

*Romania, as a grade 8 student and part of the local sinfonietta.
Playing the prelude to the "Waves of Danube" Waltz.*

Budapest, Hungary. A tender moment with my mother.

Budapest, Hungary. My mother and my stepfather—the day before our return to Italy. Their facial expressions of sadness and desolation speak for themselves.

33
CANADA, HERE WE COME!

I detest separations. Last night my mother stopped talking. She became reserved, her confidence seemed to have disappeared. The shine in her eyes was gone, and she looked so distant. I realized that a feeling of hopelessness was engulfing her.

Today her voice is soft and fragile. It's as if her heart is going to break any minute now. I am on the verge of tears myself although I am desperately trying to hide my emotions and keep my face and my words straight and stern. However, the train is here. We don't know when, or if, we are going to see them again. The girls are visibly shaken. My stepfather, my mother-in-law, our friend, as well. It's a feeling of death in the air.

The train is moving. Slowly distancing itself from the railway station, picking up speed, leaving my parents lonely again, desolate, hapless and hopeless. Guilt? Yes, but we have two children whose future lives are in our hands.

* * *

The 14-hour train trip back to Rome was mostly silent. It is the end of August. For a couple of weeks we continue to stay at Fara Sabina. Our daily routine is the same: going to work in the morning, coming back home in the afternoon, or evening for Greg. Our reunion after returning from Budapest has felt like homecoming. Greg was definitely happy and mostly relieved to see us back home, to continue our life together, to go ahead with our plans, to see our hopes turning into reality. My weekly stops at Caritas continue as usual. They still haven't heard anything from the Consulate. Restlessness, anxiety at times; all our emotions are on high alert.

Sunday, August 30th, 1992. On the last Sunday of each month the Vatican Museums are free of charge. We did visit them last year, but assuming that we will be leaving Italy soon, we decide to have a second visit. It doesn't matter how many times one goes to visit the Vatican, the mesmerizing atmosphere is still there. We also learn new things every time.

I knew that the Vatican Museums collection "officially" began in 1506, when Pope Julius II purchased the "Laocoön," an ancient Greek sculpture depicting a Trojan priest and his sons being strangled by sea serpents, which was their punishment for trying to warn Troy about the Trojan Horse. However, I didn't know when the sculpture was put on public display. Over the years, the Vatican collections grew to more than 70,000 works of art. It is one of the oldest and most-visited museums in the world and is also considered the world's largest museum.

The crowds are still abhorrent. Continuously walking as if on a cruise control, at a slow speed, but there is still no time to really stop and admire the most important pieces. It is a way of killing our increasing nervousness.

We also visit the Vatican Gardens this time. For this one we needed to take advantage of a guided tour. It was worth the effort and the little money we spent, as access to the gardens is quite limited, so we had the chance of strolling the huge area of the gardens in relative peacefulness. Besides, the extremely well-maintained gardens offer astounding views of St. Peter's dome in all of Rome.

On our way out, the last visit is at the Vatican Post Office, which is not part of the Museums. Throughout our time spent in Italy, we often sent letters from Vatican, just for the sake of having Vatican stamps on our letters. Not only this, but because it has its own stamps, along with an undeniable reputation, it seems to be extremely reliable. Given the Vatican City's unique status as its own tiny country, apparently it sends more mail around the world than any other post office in any country.

Our Sunday in Rome ends with a traditional "gelato." Of course, we are avoiding the place where over a year ago we had been charged an arm and a leg! In the meantime, if the price was not clearly in sight for anything, we learned to ask.

* * *

The new schoolyear is starting in a couple of weeks. We have to collect our belongings again so we can move back to Santa Marinella. As usual, Alberto Ranieri or maybe Giovanna will give us a ride back. Hopefully for the last time. We also found a high school for Amanda, always in Rome, while Evelyn will continue to go to the same middle school.

Today I will have to stop at Caritas on my way back from work.

"Ciao, Maria! So good to see you! We have great news for you!"

Of course, I know—or I assume—what he is going to tell me, but I need the details.

"You are scheduled for another interview at the Consulate!" He sounds excited. I guess I have become a "regular" with my weekly visits for over a year now.

"When?"

"Next Monday, at 11 am."

"Anything else we need to know or to do?"

"No, just go for your appointment and everything will go from there."

"Can I assume that this will have a happy ending? The long-anticipated response?"

"Of course. This is the best news. It means that you are on your way to Canada already!"

I am exhilarated. Too bad we don't have cell phones. The time on the commuter bus to Fara Sabina and the wait until Greg will be home would have been shortened. We can really pack up now. Our move back to Santa Marinella will be a breeze.

* * *

The big day is here. We know our way, to the Canadian Consulate and the procedures to follow. The same gentleman is interviewing us, Mr. David Jackson. After a short courtesy conversation and some preliminary discussions, a few more anticipated questions followed by the expected concise answers, we are given our passports with the long-awaited and much desired visas.

I SHALL NOT FAIL

We have been accepted as independent immigrants, based on a point system. Our education, knowledge of English and independence have scored very high. Besides, we earned a few extra points since Greg's aunt offered to assist us in Canada upon our arrival, as well as with our subsequent adjustments. We are told that we would have no problems finding jobs according to our qualifications. For me, apparently, it will be somewhat easier to find a job in teaching. Really? They need teachers in Canada who have been trained in other countries? I find hard to believe, but it doesn't matter. I am so happy. So is Greg. However, Mr. Jackson has a genuine smile which converts into a question.

"For curiosity, why did you select the city of Regina to move to?"

I don't understand the question. What difference does it make? Canada is Canada. Greg is hesitating to answer. I there any impediment? Are there any problems? Clearly, Greg doesn't know what to make of this question either. Mr. Jackson is realizing that we are a little confused.

"Why?" Greg's cautious reply came in form of a question.

"Because there are so many mosquitoes in Saskatchewan, as well as all over the prairies!"

"Well, the mosquitoes will not impede us from achieving our dreams, we hope…" Greg's timid but confident reply seems to satisfy Mr. Jackson. We shake our hands, he wishes us good luck and we are on our way out. Victory!

Mosquitoes? Who cares?! We are on our way to Canada, or almost!! Mosquitoes or not!

On our way back to Santa Marinella we stop at a pay phone to call everywhere. Our parents in Romania, Giovanna, Anna Rita, too, although we will see Giancarlo on the commuter bus. We cannot call Greg's aunt in Canada because it's too early in the morning in the province of…mosquitoes!!

We share the good news with our friends on the bus, Signor' Romano and Giancarlo. Obviously, all the people on the bus hear our excitement and they share our joy. Amanda will start her high school, although she won't have much time to adjust. So, for a week or so, we will continue to commute to Rome and back.

We will also need to buy plane tickets. What would be a good day to leave? Any day! Still, we need to organize our belongings, to get rid of what we don't need, to send a few parcels to Romania, and above all, to send to Canada the many books we acquired during the last couple of years, especially the girls' school textbooks that they used for the past two years. It is very unlikely they will ever need them in Canada, but they are precious memories. Canada, here we come!

34

CARABINIERI…

Our departure for Canada has been decided. October 7th. It's a Wednesday. Our flight will be on Air Canada, Rome to Toronto, Toronto to Regina. We are all extremely excited. Greg's aunt has been notified of our time of arrival. Our luggage is being organized already, but the suitcases are still waiting to be filled up. This is the time to enjoy our last walks along the Tyrrhenian Sea, down to Santa Marinella to the centre of the town, last visits to see Anna Rita and her family, but we are still going to school and to work every day.

A last visit of the owners of this apartment, the Ranieri family, turns our departure into a moment of celebration. The two girls and their parents come to see us. Photos and hugs, joy and excitement. Even Daisy is with them!

In the evening they are taking us out to a nice restaurant in Santa Severa. It is the first time we are going to a restaurant in Italy. It may not be expensive for locals, but for us it has always been prohibitive. A nice meal and a glass of wine for the adults, and the evening ends on a festive note. However, Giovanna has a surprise for me. She pulls out of her purse a delicate, elongated jewelry box with a note attached to it and she hands it to me. I am flabbergasted with emotion. A beautiful pearl necklace. Grey pearls and a pendant in the shape of a heart right in the middle, made out of small faux diamonds. It is so beautiful. Greg is helping me to put it around my neck. I feel so special. They thank me for the time I worked for them, for my dedication and my daily assistance with the little chores I was helping with around their home in Rome. I am amazed. They thank me? We have all the reasons in the world to thank them. Without them we would not have been where we are today. We would not have been able to save about $15,000 over a span of almost two years. As I am mentioning this detail, I'm discreetly feeling my money pouch around my waist, just as a reassurance that it is still there.

After the nice celebratory meal they are taking us home.

* * *

We expected the next few days until our departure to be uneventful. Or so we hoped…I continued to go to work and take the kids with me in the morning. Greg was going to his construction site, as well. We needed to stay busy above all. In the late afternoon we were usually on our way home to the apartment on the Tyrrhenian Sea, in Santa Marinella.

It's the first week of October. Only a few more days until our great departure. Beautiful weather. Summer-like almost. We get off the bus and take the corner on Via Botticelli towards our condo building. Weird. The little gate opening into the back yard is unlatched. Well, maybe we forgot to close it before we left this morning. We go up the four stairs and take a few steps towards the main entrance. Stupefaction and panic! The main door into the condo building is slightly open, too. Nobody has the keys to this door but Greg and I. We continue to take a few timid steps forward, tiptoeing carefully. What if someone is coming out of the building? Someone with a gun? Do they have guns in Italy?

As we are fearfully approaching the main entrance into the building, we are trying to take a peek inside, without getting too close. It's dark inside the staircase, the apartment is on a high ground floor, but we can see that the entrance door is open, as well. It's obvious someone broke into our apartment. Instinctively, I touch my money pouch again. It's there. As usual. The pearl necklace, too. I take a deep breath. We turn around and we rush out in the street to the first payphone. We know the emergency numbers. The national gendarmerie, the Carabinieri, is what we need to call. 112. An officer on duty picks up the phone. Running out of breath I am telling him what we think happened and where we are located. We are waiting outside.

Two minutes later a Carabinieri car, a beautiful navy-blue Alfa Romeo, with lights flashing and sirens on, takes the corner onto our street. It is a scene from the movies! Three police officers, two in the back and one on the passenger side are holding machine guns, hanging over the open windows, left and right. Only the driver doesn't have his machine gun out! They stop the car, leaving the lights and the engine on, and they storm into the apartment building, up the stairs, weapons in the position of attack, and they walk in the room, one at a time. We are waiting outside in awe.

Five minutes go by. No shots. Nobody killed. They checked the apartment. There is no danger, so we are allowed to go inside, but we are warned.

"Signora, your apartment is a mess. Somebody broke in. You may want to check if there is anything missing, but stay calm. If you want to write a report, come to the office so you can submit your claims."

"Grazie."

One of the Carabinieri is coming with us back into the apartment, maybe to reassure that we are safe once we get back inside. Then he leaves.

Safe? Yes, we are. Instead, the apartment is upside down, literally. Bookshelves on the floor, books all over the place, our belongings everywhere (luckily, we got rid of many unwanted items because we will leave soon). A few objects had been stolen: two pairs of gold earrings belonging to the girls, and a pocket watch with an attached chain which Greg had received from his father before he died. If anything else was missing, it was not too important. Greg's watch and the girls' earrings had sentimental value rather, although only 14K gold. After almost two years of having lived in Italy wearing our earnings on me, in my waist pouch, every single day, made sense. Added to that treasure the necklace I had just received from Giovanna, the plane tickets and our passports, and my body "bank" came to its right justification.

Greg came home later in the evening. In the meantime we had cleaned up, so the mess was gone by the time he came back from work. We discussed whether or not to report to the police. What for? We were going to leave in three days. It would not have led anywhere and, on top of everything else, we would have been gone, should any burglar had been found, which was unlikely. So, let's consider everything water under the bridge.

However, the excitement of the day—which Greg has missed, was the Carabinieri scene. When we came to Italy two years ago I was afraid that we would be killed by…Carabinieri!! That's what we had seen in the movies during our years of living in Romania. There was, obviously, no reason for that. It was funny though that during our last days in Italy the Carabinieri, whom we were fascinated by, played a role in our lives. A small one, a totally different one, but still just like in the movies!

35

WELCOME TO CANADA!

The big day has arrived. However during the last three days while checking everything to see if the luggage was ready, if everything was packed up, if the plane tickets were in order, we decided to have a last look at our passports. What we noticed was scary. Our passports were expired! How could this be possible? We got our passports back from the Canadian Consulate about two weeks ago and the passports were already expired? How was it possible that we got visas on expired passports? That was something that had no explanation. What do we do now? What are the options? If we apply for new passports, who knows when we get them and by then our visas to immigrate to Canada will expire. We seem to be at a crossroads again, from no fault of our own making. We are totally baffled. Terrified, too. What do we do? We have to take our fate in our hands, just as we did several times in the past, and pray that it will work out somehow. We have to keep going. We have plane tickets, too. We don't know what is going to happen next, but we can only take one step at a time and advance little by little.

The day of our departure has arrived. Giancarlo has arrived to give us a ride to the airport. Fiumicino airport is close enough to Santa Marinella, so it is a pleasure to see him again and say goodbye one more time.

Our flight is in three hours. We check in, send the suitcases away, and we are told that we will have to pick them up at the final destination. So far so good. Nobody has made any mention or remark with regards to our expired passports. Finally we are just about to go to the gate. As we go through customs, the Italian official looks at our passports and points to the date saying:

"Do you know that your passports have expired?" We pretend we do not understand what he's talking about. We look baffled, but what choice do we have at the last minute? We shrug and choose to keep going. After all, the visa giving us the permission to immigrate to Canada is in each of our passports. We are still afraid. Totally overcome with emotions.

Waiting for the time to board the plane takes my breath away occasionally. However, we are still happy. We are finally boarding. Put the backpacks in the overhead. Sit. Buckle up. All the four seats are in the middle row. I have never been on a plane before. Greg has, when he flew from Romania to Canada and then, from Canada to Italy, but I and the girls have never been on a plane. Air Canada is awesome!

Throughout the past years, back in our home country, we had travelled considerably. Every summer we were going somewhere around the country, taking the kids with us by car, showing them the beauties of our country. Also, in summer we were always going for our two-week vacation on the Black Sea. In winter we used to go skiing, so travelling by car was the norm. As of us, as adults, during our travels abroad, we had only travelled by train or by bus, but I have never been on a plane.

The hours go by, one by one, slowly, too slowly. Nine hours later we are in Toronto. My heart is in my throat. What is going to happen next?

Obviously, we go through customs. As it is to be expected, the custom officer notices that our passports are expired, and he starts questioning us. We are both trying to answer at the same time, talking almost one over the other, but the stern look on the officer's face makes me shut up. He disappears in the office behind his desk, and then comes back. We're pulled aside and told to wait. What now? Are we going to be sent back to Italy? They invite Greg inside. Apparently, there will be an interview. We have no idea how long it is going to take. Our layover is two-hours long. Hopefully, he will not be detained.

Fifteen minutes later they let Greg free. They invite me inside. Interrogation follows. I am befuddled. Frightened. I can hardly find my words. Another half an hour goes by. Our fate is in their hands now. We are losing control. The girls are holding my hands, each of them on one side. Their support gives me a little strength.

I am terrified, crying inconsolably with utmost fear. Fatigue takes over me, as well. Because of the stressful situation, I could not close my eyes during this entire flight. My hands are shaking. My whole body is collapsing.

Thirty minutes later an officer comes out with two pieces of paper. Our names and our daughters' names are on these documents. This is a Minister's permit that allows us to immigrate to Canada. With one condition. We have to apply for new Romanian passports and, as soon as we receive them, we have to "technically" apply again for immigration and then we will receive our papers as residents. No problem. We can breathe now. This means that we can continue our trip all the way to Regina, Saskatchewan.

Almost four hours later we finally arrive in Regina. We collect our luggage, and we are out. We are extremely tired, but in the airport there is a whole group of people waiting for us, with welcome placards and with our names on the signs. It's truly emotional. We are in Canada. We finally made it!

Greg's aunt is taking us in their car to our already rented apartment. They've paid the rent for us for the whole year, and they also furnished it. The cars stop in front of a four-story building. We are led towards the entrance into a two-bedroom apartment. They unlock the door for us, and they invite us in. It is warm and it is so hospitable.

We are exhausted. I'm trying to keep my eyes open, and it's only the excitement that prevents me from falling asleep while talking. Our guests are treating us with cakes and flowers and drinks. Luckily, they leave after about an hour. We say goodbye to the last couple.

We are in Canada. We lock the door and go to bed. We are home! Finally. A dream come true. Our true home. **CANADA. Oh, Canada…**

Canada 1996—our citizenship ceremony.

Canada 1996—the symbolic cake sent to my classroom by my colleagues after the citizenship ceremony.

AFTERWORD

I swear
That I will be faithful
And bear true allegiance
To Her Majesty Queen Elizabeth the Second
Queen of Canada
Her Heirs and Successors
And that I will faithfully observe
The laws of Canada
And fulfil my duties
As a Canadian citizen.

Three and a half years, mostly prosperous, have gone by since we set foot on Canadian soil. These last three years, abounding with (mostly) positive and successful experiences and a continuous array of accomplishments, went by fast. We have all been on a steep learning curve, continuously adjusting and adapting to our new way of life—from housing, to schooling, to social integration and culture, to obtaining decent jobs, overcoming obstacles that seemed insurmountable at times, while constantly experiencing an immense personal growth, both emotionally and mentally.

Moving to Canada was another new beginning that we were facing as a family, but this "new beginning" was materializing, was filling up our hearts with stability, with a growing confidence that we were capable of withstanding new difficult situations, handling new adversities, but remaining productive throughout.

Events continued to roll out in our life with no end in sight, but the outcome of everything we were doing has been constantly positive. And today is the big day. Yes, it is a momentous event that we have been waiting for and dreaming about for quite a while, a unique celebration with an extremely meaningful significance.

As we recite in chorus the Oath of Citizenship, I can hardly contain my emotions of serenity and relief, of contentment and optimism, but mainly of gratitude and pride. Since our arrival to Canada, our daughters enrolled in school, Greg found work in his professional field and I had my degrees validated. I completed a Master's Degree in Education, I obtained the qualified teacher status and, consequently, I received my teaching certificate (after all, Mr. Jackson, the vice-consul who had interviewed us in Italy about four years ago proved to be right! Yes, I was teaching again!). Last year I landed a job as a French immersion teacher teaching French Language and Literature in a prestigious high school in our city.

Our citizenship ceremony was approaching, so while breaking the great news to the administration, the principal suggested that our school host the ceremony, thus bringing awareness to our students (who had never seen a live ceremony of this kind) and enhancing their understanding and appreciation of the values inherent to Canadian society. All the school staff was on board with this ceremonial proposal. So, here we are today, all gathered in the large gymnasium of our high school, about 1,500 students sitting on the telescopic bleachers that had been pulled out to accommodate the entire teenage population of our school, solemnly witnessing this jubilant celebration.

The school gymnasium has become today a display of Canadian symbolism, beautifully decorated with emblems representing honour and pride. The Canadian flag, displayed behind the judge is in the place of honour, with the maple leaf in full view to the young audience, and the portrait of the Queen in the centre of the stage as if Her Majesty is overseeing the ceremony. Finally, the Coat of Arms is also exhibited in its full magnificence: the Crown (a rendition of St. Edward's Crown, representing Canada as a constitutional monarchy), the crest with its addition of the maple leaves, the escutcheon with its symbolic three lions as well as the French fleur-de-lys, and above all, the ribbon marked "desiderantes meliorem patriam", meaning "desiring a better country", and last but not least, the motto also in Latin: "a mari usque ad mare" ("from sea to sea").

I am ecstatic. We will finally, and officially, call Canada our home, but I honestly felt like being part of the big Canadian family as soon as we landed in Toronto, over three years ago. However, I have been waiting for this solemn moment to become a Canadian citizen for the past three years. My ceremonial outfit cannot be more Canadian! I'm wearing a red dress and white shoes. Greg is wearing a navy-blue suit, a white shirt and a red tie. The girls have their own attire.

The entire "team" of officials are entering the gymnasium: a Royal Canadian Mounted Police officer in his full red serge uniform, the citizenship judge wearing the solemn regalia (a black judicial gown with burgundy accent and a white decorative collar), followed by the clerk wearing a barrister's robe and a white barrister tab, as well as by the principal and assistant principals of our school, all marching to a solemn tune played by a bagpipe player, also dressed up in a traditional kilt, plaid and feather bonnet included, and accessorized with belt buckles, a sporran cantle, a feather bonnet badge and the plaid brooch.

The Royal Canadian Mounted Police officer opens the ceremony in the name of the Queen, and he is then followed by the clerk's introducing the applicants for citizenship: "Your Honour, in accordance with the provisions of the Citizenship Act, it is my privilege to present to you the applicants for citizenship who have complied with the requirements of the Citizenship Act and are now ready to take the Oath of Citizenship and become Canadian citizens."

The judge addresses the crowd with a short speech outlining the duties and responsibilities of being a Canadian citizen, and then she instructs us all to stand, to raise our right hand while she is leading us in the recitation of the Oath of Citizenship in both English and French. A monumental silence envelops the gymnasium. Judging by the behaviour of the students witnessing the ceremony, I sense a feeling of magnificence presiding over the crowd. I am truly impressed by the conduct of our students. As rambunctious as teenagers normally are, the aura of solemnity has brought them all to a moment of reverence, of a patriotic celebration, unifying them all in this celebratory occasion. The entire audience, all the students stand, raise their right hands and repeat the Oath of Citizenship. It is extremely emotional. Powerful. Glorious.

We are then invited to sign the oath document and the judge presents each of us with our Certificate of Citizenship. After some closing remarks from the judge, the ceremony is concluded with the singing of the national anthem in English and in French. Conversations ensue, and a lively ambiance is replacing the previous formal atmosphere. My excitement culminates with a "very Canadian" surprise cake that my colleagues sent to my classroom. Here, on my desk, I find a beautifully decorated cake, with a red-and-white topping symbolizing the Canadian flag, along with a card: "Congratulations, Maria!"

Yes, indeed. Congratulations to us all! We are Canadian citizens. The country we dreamed of, extending from sea to sea, the country that has accepted us, included us, offered us best opportunities, embraced us, and made us feel welcome.

Thank you, Canada!

THE END

Lightning Source UK Ltd.
Milton Keynes UK
UKHW010739110621
385337UK00001B/28